Home Gardens *and* Agrobiodiversity

Home
Gardens

and

Agrobiodiversity

EDITED BY

Pablo B. Eyzaguirre and Olga F. Linares

Smithsonian Books
Washington

Copy editor: Jean Eckenfels
Production editor: Robert A. Poarch
Designer: Brian Barth

Library of Congress Cataloging-in-Publication Data
Home gardens and agrobiodiversity / edited by
Pablo B. Eyzaguirre and Olga F. Linares.
    p. cm.
  Includes bibliographical references and index.
  ISBN 1-58834-112-7 (cloth)
    1. Kitchen gardens—Tropics. 2. Agrobiodiversity—
Tropics. 3. Agrobiodiversity conservation—Tropics.
I. Eyzaguirre, Pablo B. II. Linares, Olga F.
  SB320.8.T7H66 2004   2003058983
  635'.0913—dc22

A paperback reissue (ISBN 978-1-58834-288-1) of the original
cloth edition.

British Library Cataloguing-in-Publication Data available.

Manufactured in the United States of America.
  14 13 12 11 10   5 4 3 2

Contents

Part 3. Managing and Conserving Genetic Diversity in Key Crops

Acknowledgments

We should like to thank the numerous persons and institutions that have contributed to the making of this book. First and foremost, we are grateful to the International Plant Genetic Resources Institute (IPGRI), and its former director general, Geoffrey Hawtin, and to the Smithsonian Tropical Research Institute (STRI), and its director, Ira Rubinoff, for their unwavering moral and financial support. Next are the two outside readers whose enlightened comments greatly improved the content and argument of this work. Then there are the numerous persons who typed, corrected, and revised many parts of the manuscript: foremost among these are Anne Huie and Nicole Demers of IPGRI and Beate Christy of STRI. The maps were redrawn by Patrizia Tazza at IPGRI, and the photographs were edited and printed by Lina Gonzalez of STRI. We also thank the German Federal Ministry for Economic Cooperation and Development and the German Agency for Technical Cooperation (GTZ) for funding many of the studies in this book.

It is always worth emphasizing that the ultimate authors of a book such as this one are the numerous farmers who have invested their time, energy, and thought in improving the home gardens that they so carefully manage. May their efforts result in the enhanced agrobiodiversity that is neeeded to feed the rural peoples of the world.

Introduction

Pablo B. Eyzaguirre and Olga F. Linares

Home Gardens as Reservoirs and Hotspots for Agrobiodiversity

This book is concerned with the diverse ways that home gardens are created and managed by peoples throughout the tropical world and how they contribute to the conservation and sustainable use of agricultural biodiversity. Home gardens are microenvironments within a larger farming system that contain high levels of species diversity and may contain crop species or varieties of species different from those found in surrounding agroecosystems. It is this concern with how home gardens contribute to maintaining and enhancing biodiversity within agricultural systems that underpins the research contained in this book.

Much excellent work has already been published on the structure and function as well as the economic and nutritional contributions of home gardens around the world. It thus forms a solid basis for the new research focus of this book, namely, how home gardens can serve as reservoirs and breeding grounds for agrobiodiversity. The chapters in this book take a comparative approach to home gardens, using methods that were discussed and agreed upon by multidisciplinary research teams across seven countries: Cuba, Guatemala, Venezuela, Ghana, Nepal, Vietnam, and Ethiopia. The country case studies provide empirical examples of the way agrobiodiversity is managed within home-garden systems and their sustainability across distinctive ecologies and social situations. The chapters also focus on new and dynamic processes that are affecting the sustainability and diversity within home gardens, such as the example of urbanization and migration in Senegal or market forces and policies that may lead to genetic erosion in home-garden species. Several chapters address the methodological issues raised by including home gardens within agrobiodiversity conservation perspectives and strategies. Principal among these are the small population sizes of key species and the rapid changes in the composition and uses of home gardens. Taken together, these studies contribute to our understanding of the interactions that exist between ecological, socioeconomic, and cultural processes. These interactions and factors determine the crop and tree diversity within home gardens; they can also serve to identify home-garden systems that maintain and add biodiversity to the farming systems at large and promote the health and sustainability of both agro-ecosystems and households.

Definitions of Home Gardens and Their Ecology

The contribution of home gardens to agrobiodiversity is linked to the complex multifunctionality and structure of these microenvironments. It is not surprising, therefore, that home gardens have been discussed and defined from several perspectives. From an ecological and land-use perspective, home gardens involve the management of multipurpose trees, shrubs, annual and perennial agricultural crops, herbs, spices, medicinal plants, fish ponds, and animals on the same land unit, in a spatial arrangement or on a temporal sequence. Home gardens can be considered a multifunctional agroforestry system with distinct canopy structure from root crops to tall trees (Lundgren and Raintree 1983; Nair 1985; Fernandes and Nair 1986). Among the characteristics of agroforestry systems are their ecological and functional complexity, as well as an intimate mix of annual and perennial agricultural crops with shrubs and trees.

From a social perspective, the common and distinguishing feature of home gardens is that they are culturally constructed spaces managed by household members, albeit in very different ways. "Household gardens supply and supplement subsistence requirements and generate secondary direct or indirect income. They tend to be located close to permanent or semi-permanent dwellings for convenience and security" (Niñez 1984). It is common for plants in home gardens to be used in multiple ways. Most woody plants kept in home gardens (e.g., coconut, *Pluchea indica, Artocarpus* sp.) produce outputs such as fuelwood, timber, fodder for animals, various types of food crops, or ornamentals (Aiyelaagbe 1992; Aiyelaagbe 1994). Multiuse plants may make various contributions to income; for example, in Indonesia, the fruit of banana trees contribute 74 percent and the leaves 26 percent of the total income made from bananas (Soemarwoto and Soemarwoto 1981; Soemarwoto and Conway 1991). Furthermore, the value of tree species is assessed not only in terms of a product but also in light of their contribution to the sustainability of the ecosystem. Trees are important in adding soil nutrients, reducing soil erosion, reducing soil and ambient temperature, and regulating sunlight. They may define boundaries and create space and inviting contexts for social gatherings. Fish ponds are an integral part of home gardens in Vietnam and in some parts of Indonesia. Many crops that need a sizeable water supply, such as *Ipomoea aquatica, Eichhornia crassipes,* and *Sagittaria sagittifolia,* are planted in or close to fish ponds or irrigation channels (Hodel et al. 1999).

Several terms have been used to describe these garden production systems, such as "house-compound land," "garden culture," "mixed garden," "homestead area," and "backyard garden." The term "home garden" is preferred because it stresses the close relationship between the garden and the social group residing at home. Since home gardens are defined by their proximity to dwellings, they can be separated from other gardens or patches with similar structure and species diversity found in forest swiddens, along roadways, railways, or irrigation ditches, away from house sites.

Home gardens can be static or "moving." In such tropical regions as Southeast Asia, the Pacific, and the Amazon in South America, where shifting cultivation is still practiced in some areas, home gardens or cultivars are "moved" from settlement to settlement. They represent an intermediate phase that interrupts the usual succession from young swidden to old swidden. Home gardens that have been abandoned often find their way back to a natural forest type of existence. (Balée and Gély 1989).

Home gardens share some aspects of swidden and agroforestry systems, but are still distinctive, due in large part to the greater degree of complex management that is applied. Also, home gardens are continuously cultivated and receive significant additional inputs that distinguish home gardens from swiddens. Thus, an increase in agricultural production may be achieved, not by enlarging the amount of land that is cultivated, but by applying intermittent amounts of low-cost and part-time labor (often by women) to improve small parcels that are permanently cropped with a wide variety of cultivars. Fertility in these plots is maintained by "optimum use of household refuse, animal manure, plant or crop residues, and nutrient cycling" (Okigbo 1990: 334). Weed control is reduced by shade and pioneer plant species. In sum, home gardens have to be considered in the context of the broader land-use systems in the surrounding environment. When located near diversity-rich natural environments such as tropical forests, they may contain fewer species. In areas where natural ecosystems are affected by severe resource degradation and population pressure, home gardens may tend to concentrate more species.

Variation in Home-Garden Structure and Composition

Home gardens vary in size and structure according to their ecological, socioeconomic, and cultural environments. They can, however, be differentiated into temperate or tropical gardens, and subsistence or cash crop gardens (Niñez 1986; Esquivel and Hammer 1992a). In tropical regions with year-round rainfall, a continuous range of vegetables and fruits is available. In regions having marked wet and dry seasons the harvest of many crops is seasonal (Sommers 1985). In general, tropical home gardens are characterized by high species diversity in a layered-canopy configuration similar to natural forests, with each component having a specific place and function (Soemarwoto and Soemarwoto 1982; Michon 1983; Karyono 1990; Michon, Mary, and Bompard 1986; Okafor and Fernandes 1987; Padoch and de Jong 1991; McConnell 1992; Anderson 1993a; Rugalema, O'Kting'ati, and Johnson 1994).

The layers or canopies consist of (a) a root crop and herbaceous layer on the ground; (b) next, the level of annuals or small perennials; (c) an intermediate bush and tree level; and (d) a large tree layer at upper levels. However, layers are not static and the boundaries are not always exclusive and distinct. In tropical home gardens, the root crop and herbaceous level is dominated by vegetables, medicinal plants, sweet potatoes, and yam, followed by annuals and small perennials such as taro, cassava, sugarcane, tobacco, bananas, coffee, and papayas. The intermediate level is often occupied with various fruit trees, such as *Annona* sp., guava, cashew nut, rambutan, mango, jackfruit, breadfruit. The upper tree layer consists of fully grown fruit trees (e.g., coconut, durian) and various other food-producing and/or timber trees (e.g., *Moringa* sp., *Sesbania grandiflora*, *Pterocarpus* sp., kapok).

The diversity in physical conditions (light, space, microclimates) promotes a wide variety of species with different needs. Differentiated root structures take up nutrients from various soil levels, and aerial plant architecture requires plants to adapt for spatial and biological interactions. Although the plants may seem to be randomly placed, the space is fully used in order to maximize yields from the garden. Plants that require greater than usual quantities of water, such as bananas and taro, are commonly found close to the well or fish ponds. Plants that are used for daily food, such as vegetables and spices, are planted close to the kitchen. Ornamental plants and plants of high value that need special protection are found in front of the house (Bompard et al. 1980; Christanty et al. 1986). The ability of certain species, such as *Artocarpus heterophyllus* and *Cocos nucifera,* to adapt to a limited land space, to ensure food security during the dry season, and to provide traditionally used products throughout the year accounts for their wide distribution throughout the tropics.

There is no fixed size for a home garden. Studies of home-garden systems in different ecozones and geographical regions showed that the average size of the home-garden unit is around 0.1–0.5 ha (Brierley 1985; Danoesastro 1985; Tennakoon 1985; Fernandes and Nair 1986; Kumar, George, and Chinnamani 1994). Home gardens near forests are often not clearly demarcated from their neighboring, less managed areas of secondary growth owned by the same household (Padoch and de Jong 1991). However, home gardens may be bound by fences in order to keep the livestock or wild animals away. Home gardens occur in high human population densities (urban situation) as well as in areas of low densities, depending on the needs, opportunities, market situation, ecological settings, and the amount of labor available within the household (Niñez 1986; Alvarez-Buylla Roces, Lazos Chavero, and García-Barrios 1989; Padoch and de Jong 1991). In remote villages, subsistence production usually predominates, whereas in villages close to cities commercial production and ornamental uses become more important (Soemarwoto and Soemarwoto 1981; Christanty and Iskandar 1985).

Home-Gardens Biodiversity and Ecosystem Functions

The study of biodiversity—that is, the study of the variability of all living things and the systems of which they are a part—is increasingly focused on the crucial role performed by a mixture of organisms and communities in maintaining ecosystem resilience (Perrings et al. 1995a; Loreau et al. 2001). High biodiversity is indeed crucial for structuring diverse ecosystems, such as tropical forests. A constant preoccupation within agricultural development schemes is that "modern" agriculture often leads to a loss of intraspecific genetic diversity (Iwanaga, Eyzaguirre, and Thompson 2000). Other large-scale factors leading to genetic erosion include the disappearance of species through habitat conversion and the drastic reduction in ecosystem diversity as a result of land clearing (Holling et al. 1995). Complex changes affecting the species composition of communities—particularly those plants, pests, mammal populations that are important in structuring "natural" ecosystems—often lead to reduced diversity and loss of resilience. Because they are managed in such a way as to be continually productive, home gardens often escape these degenerative processes. The chapters in this volume demonstrate the important ways in which people concentrate diversity in a small area through the creation and management of home gardens.

Although home gardens may be extremely variable in size and design, depending upon variations in soil type, drainage patterns, and cultural preferences (Gliessman 1990a), they are all characterized by a high degree of biodiversity. "In a study of home gardens in both upland and lowland sites in Mexico, it was found that in quite small areas (between 0.3 to 0.7 ha) high diversity permitted the maintenance of gardens that in some aspects were similar to the local natural ecosystems" (Gliessman 1990a: 162). These Tlaxcala and Cupilco home gardens had diversity indices (according to the Shannon-Wiener species diversity index) of 3.84 and 2.43, respectively, which are relatively high for an agricultural system. Home gardens in the outskirts of Guanacaste Province in Costa Rica were also diverse. The seventy-one plant species grown in 1985 in a 1,240 square meter area gave the garden a diversity index of 3.55 (Gliessman 1990b: 382). A species diversity index measures two related components: species richness and relative abundance. By way of comparison, it has been calculated that the index diversity of "modern" agriculture in Ohio was 0.60 in 1982; the index is very low because most of the land was planted in five major crops (Barrett, Rodenhouse, and Bohlen et al. 1990). On the other hand, the aseasonal (or nonseasonal) Pasoh forest in the Western Ghats of India has a diversity index of 2.44, which is quite comparable, despite methodological discrepancies, to the home gardens of Mexico and Costa Rica.

On the basis of the sheer number of species—that is, using species lists—a survey of home gardens in the Maya town of Xuilib listed 404 species of plants, whereas only 1,120 species are known for the entire state (National Research Council 1993: 106–7). In the Atlantic lowlands of Costa Rica, a mapping project revealed 26 tree species, 16 perennial ornamentals, 8 annual/biennial crops, and 6 herbaceous species in a garden measuring 3,250 m². Gliessman (1990b: 384) points out that the plants were distributed in five functional areas: (a) a low-diversity planting of crops of potential commercial value, (b) a high-diversity irregular planting of trees, shrubs, herbs, and vines, (c) a low-diversity widely spaced planting of trees for recreational purposes, (d) a high diversity intercropped planting of ornamental herbs and shrubs, and (e) a moderate-diversity fencer row surrounding the garden and made up of fruit and firewood tree species. It is this structural complexity that is the basis for the flexibility, dynamism, and adaptability to change—in short the resilience—of the home-garden agroecosystem.

People structure agricultural systems and introduce the genetic materials into them by selecting and manipulating the genetic variability of crop plants and domesticated animals (Heywood and Baste 1995: 10). It is this constant "tinkering"—this continuous bricolage—with the kinds, numbers, and mix of species that gives home gardens flexibility, dynamism, and, above all, resilience. In other words, in this garden system "nutrients are efficiently recycled through both ecological diversity and human manipulation" (Gliessman 1988: 446). Home gardens are doubly insured that the mix of communities and species is viable by the forces of both natural selection and human selection. Constant experimentation makes home gardens important reservoirs of germplasm. It is their function as nurseries—for seedlings to transplant to agricultural plots, for native species with which to reforest—that links home gardens with the surrounding natural forest. Here it is important to note that if home gardens are abandoned they tend to revert to the natural, surrounding vegetation. That is, no loss of ecosystem resilience is implied by the conversion of home gardens to forest, unlike, for example, the conversion of forest to pasture. It is important, therefore, to think of home gardens as components of a broader environment made up of managed agroecosystems as well as less managed, more "natural" ecosystems.

Additionally home gardens have other advantages characteristic of sustainable agroecosystems (Barret, Rodenhouse, and Bohlen 1990: 631) such as reduced need for chemical fertilizers and pesticides; they also have the mechanisms for retaining and recycling nutrients and the capacity to control erosion.

The fundamental goal of conserving biodiversity, however, is not species protection for its own sake "but the protection of the productive potential of those ecosystems on which human activity depends" (Perrings et al. 1995b: 301). In other words, the dynamics of economic systems are dependent on the dynamics of ecological systems. The ability of ecosystems to maintain productivity under a wide gamut of environmental conditions is directly dependent upon biodiversity conservation—a biodiversity that takes into account the biological properties of the mixture of component species. The fact that biodiversity loss is ecosystem specific, and not simply global in some undetermined way, is encouraging. It means that viable systems, where effective ecosystem functions are conserved, can evolve or be developed. This applies as much to so-called natural systems as to the agroecosystems developed by people.

Species Variation in and across Home Gardens

Home gardens have complex histories; they continuously evolve in response to actions of the garden manager and the effects of various stochastic occurrences. Trade and the informal exchange of plant material has led to the accidental and deliberate introduction of a number of species (Ranjit Daniels and Vencatesan 1995). Not all plants found in a garden were originally planted with a definite purpose in mind. Some remain from previous agricultural uses of the same area, others belong to spontaneously occurring useful forest plants, and still others originate from accidentally discarded seeds (Christanty and Iskandar 1985). Wickramasinghe (1995) estimates that 40–60 percent of the vegetation growing in home gardens are established unintentionally.

The protection, selection, or weeding of spontaneously occurring species or varieties is an important feature in the management of species diversity within home gardens. Enrichment results when individual members of a household choose to cultivate the varieties of special interest to them. Variability in plant composition often reflects divergent preferences among household members and the different emphasis they place on using plants for particular purposes. A study conducted in the Peruvian Upper Amazon found that households with the highest diversity of crops in their home gardens depended on the gardens for their subsistence needs, since their outfields had low crop diversity (Salick and Lundberg 1990). Low on-farm returns necessitate the diversification of income sources, encouraging the use of wild or home-garden products.

A study of home gardens in Santa Rosa, in the Peruvian Amazon, revealed significant variation in the composition of plant species diversity across gardens (Padoch and de Jong 1991). Of a total of 168 plant species identified in the study sample, 65 species appeared only in one garden and only 22 species were represented in more than half of the gardens. Among the most widely distributed species were *Inga edulis,* orange (*Citrus sinensis*), cocona (*Solanum sessiliflorum*), yute (*Urena lobata*), and banana (*Musa spec.*). In 41 home gardens of a small hamlet in West Java (Soemarwoto 1987), 219 different species (11,264 individuals) were found in the dry season, and 272 different plant species (19,259 individuals) in the wet season.

A number of possible factors may underpin species and intraspecies variation within and across home gardens. Tropical home gardens are often described as sustainable land-use systems, but there are no detailed analyses of home gardens to support this assertion, nor is there consensus on what sustainability means in the context of home gardens. Torquebiau (1992) identified a series of sustainability descriptors for home gardens, providing examples of indicators from different home-garden studies. Sustainability is described at the level of ecological, economic, and social systems. However, does a sustainable system also imply that specific plant genetic resources are conserved over time? For example, ecological, economic, political, or sociocultural factors may cause variation and change in the composition of home-garden species and varieties. Land-tenure rights can influence conservation practices, as well as the amount of diversity represented in perennial crops. Farmers who do not own the land they work are unwilling to make long-term improvements, or grow crops that can be harvested only after one or two years; they see no sense in putting much effort into land that can be taken away from them at any time by the landowner (Arnold 1987; Asare, Oppong, and Twum-Ampofo 1990; Michon, Mary, and Bompard 1986; Salick and Lundberg 1990).

Population pressures and land scarcity, as well as concentration of land ownership, may lead, at least initially, to a rise in the productivity of the land through diversification (risk management) and intensification (increasing biomass output) (Nair and Krishnankutty 1985; Arnold 1987; Rajagukguk 1989). In villages with few off-farm jobs the diversity and numbers of species grown in home gardens is generally high. When labor is in short supply people grow more perennials and less annuals since perennials require less intensive care (Stoler 1975).

Home-garden managers are flexible; they are capable of seizing new opportunities. They consciously manipulate the ecological succession of the gardens. Home gardens established by migrants in Vietnam and Indonesia often contain higher diversity of plant species than gardens cultivated by long-time residents. When people move from their place of origin to a new area, they often take with them seeds from their favorite crops, thus enriching the local array of crops.

Home gardens may also contain species introduced from the wild. Collection of wild foods from noncultivated lands may add significantly to the food security of poor rural households (Guijt, Hinchcliffe and Melnyk 1995). Women are primarily engaged in wild-food management and harvesting, particularly of vegetables and fruits, whereas children are particularly involved with the collection of fruits (Maundu 1987). Some of these gathered wild species become commonplace in home gardens after an initial step of experimentation. As drought and desertification reduce the availability of wild foods in Sahelian Africa, women plant and protect wild fruit trees such as *Lannea microcarpa, Butyrospermum parkii, Saba senegalensis,* and *Zizyphus mauritania* their home gardens (Kassogue, Dolo, and Ponsioen 1990). As many of the gathered products are scattered across a wide area, home gardens ease their collection and use by concentrating several species on one site. A home gardens study in Northeastern Thailand revealed that nondomesticated plants were found in 88 percent of the gardens managed by women.

The rate of introduction of wild species into home gardens has increased during the last decades as access to noncultivated land decreased (Moreno-Black, Prapimporn, and Sompong 1994). Possibilities for domestication and incorporation of specifically endangered wild species should be explored further (Juma 1989; Wachiira 1987). Home gardens are often a refuge for wild species that are threatened by deforestation, environmental changes, and urbanization. Whereas weedy plant species that can quickly regenerate and survive in marginal environments on field edges or degraded land are less susceptible to changes in agricultural land use, fruit trees are less resilient to agroecological changes because they are slow to mature.

Home gardens not only contain a broad spectrum of species but they also contain different kinds of cultivars. Up to ten different cassava varieties can be found within the same small garden in Java. They are cultivated for their different tuber taste, edible leaf qualities, and cooking characteristics. Similarly, different banana cultivars serve different purposes: as dessert, steamed for snacks, as a staple food, for brewing drinks, or for their leaves, as wrappings and table settings (Soemarwoto and Conway 1991; Rugalema, O'Kting'ati, and Johnson 1994). In addition to their immediate production benefits, home gardens are also important sites in that they ensure the survival and conservation of many indigenous plant species otherwise threatened with genetic erosion or even extinction (Okafor and Fernandes 1987; Juma 1989).

Besides local crops collected from the wild, many exotic species have also been introduced into home gardens. Some of these have adapted themselves to the local surroundings and may even contain new genetic traits unique to the local plant varieties of that area. For example, chayote (*Sechium edule*), a vine producing a tropical fruit used as a vegetable, was introduced and is widely grown in home gardens of Nepal and Southwest China, where it is also used as a root crop and leafy vegetable. Home gardens may provide good contexts to study evolutionary processes of plant selection as people adapt plants to new and changing environments. Cuban home gardens are notable for the combination and adaptation of plants from Africa, Europe, and Asia into a "conuco" system derived from the root and tree crop systems of the indigenous peoples (Esquivel and Hammer 1992a and 1992b; Castiñeiras and others 2000).

The Social Functions That Home Gardens Perform

A primary function of many home gardens is subsistence food production that buffers fluctuations in the cash economy (Price 1983; Wickramasinghe 1992; Torres

1988; Penny and Ginting 1984). Since crops often have different production cycles, home gardens ensure an almost continuous supply of food products. For many poor people, the year-round availability of food, firewood, and construction materials is crucial to economic stability. Home gardens provide employment for the farm family during the off-season by producing cash crops and materials to be used to make handicrafts or household tools that are also a source of income. As villagers become increasingly engaged in wage labor, they spend less time gathering part of their food from the forest or other common property resources, making the home garden a crucial source of essential nutrients in their diet. In the rice-based farming systems of Vietnam and Indonesia the production of vegetables and fruits in home gardens often increases during periods between the rice harvests. In the Philippines, a survey by the Food and Nutrition Research Institute showed that three out of four Filipino households had a home garden, and that 20 percent of food consumed by families is home-grown (Torres 1988). In urban areas such as Lusaka, Zambia, it is estimated that 60 percent of all households in low-income areas cultivate an urban garden to supplement their diet with vegetables and fruits they cannot afford to buy in urban markets (Sanyal 1985).

Some of the plants in home gardens are also found in the agricultural fields managed by the household. In such cases, home gardens often serve as a genetic reservoir in case of field crop failure resulting from diseases or pests (Niñez 1984). They are maintained as convenient places to raise plants that are frequently used or need special care and protection, to experiment with crop cultures, or to provide services such as shade, shelter, aesthetic satisfaction, or useful things for the household (Price 1983; Alvarez-Buylla Roces, Lazos Chavero, and García-Barrios 1989; Padoch and de Jong 1991; Anderson 1993b).

Other plants are maintained for use in practices that sustain local culture, for example, ceremonial yam in the Pacific, divine gifts and offerings in tribal communities, golden bamboo in Indonesia, said to ward off bad luck. Another purpose of home gardens is to maximize the range of species and interspecies diversity in order to augment culinary value and food diversity (Mula and Gayao 1991). Plants that are not valued as food or for cultural reasons are cultivated for their role in improving habitat quality, such as soil enrichment or conservation of water and soil resources (Jose and Shanmugaratnam 1993).

Home gardens have a high impact on the health and nutrition of the family. Households that collect fruits and vegetables from the garden or from the wild tend to suffer less from protein malnutrition and vitamin deficiency than those that do not (Immink, Sanjur, and Colon 1981; Soemarwoto et al. 1985; Abdoellah and Marten 1986; Campbell 1987; Immink 1990; Pingle 1991). Stoler (1981) observed that vitamin A deficiencies were less common in agriculturally poor areas in Java because staple foods were supplemented by low-cost leafy green vegetables and pulses.

Home Gardens and Household Income

Whereas most home-garden production is for household consumption, any marketable surplus, and most commodity crops such as coffee, tobacco, tea, peanuts, cashew and various spices can provide a valuable cash income for families (Price 1983; Corlin et al. 1989; Padoch and de Jong 1991; Shalaby 1991). The cost of production in home gardens is relatively low compared with the contribution that home gardens make to subsistence and income. Studies of the household economy in Java concluded that, compared with other available employment opportunities, home gardening provides one of the highest returns to labor (Stoler 1981). In Vietnam, the income derived from home-garden products is often three times more than the income from the rice fields (Linh and Binh 1995).

Transmigrants' gardens in Indonesia provide 28–60 percent of all agricultural produce by smallholders; of this 46–80 percent was consumed by the household (Colfer et al. 1985). Michon, Mary, and Bompard (1986) estimate that a hectare of garden in West Sumatra produces US$365–$500 a year and that the garden's cash value is equal to 60 percent of annual rice production. Alvarez-Buylla Roces, Lazos Chavero, and García-Barrios (1989) mention figures of up to US$625 per household in a community they studied in Mexico. In Kandy home gardens in Sri Lanka, cash crops such as cloves, pepper, tea, coconut, banana, coffee, nutmeg, and areca contribute to a high farm income. On average, cloves contribute up to 42 percent and pepper up to 15 percent of the income.

Analyses of resource use and consumption patterns of smallholder households in the Solomon Islands singled out the age of the female household head and the degree of cash crop income as factors influencing the size of the food gardens planted by the households (Fleming 1989). A strong shift toward greater reliance on purchased staples where cash cropping has been expanded are described by Jones, Fleming, and Hardaker (1988) and Marten and Abdoellah (1988). When market demand and the price paid for a certain plant product increases, the cultivation of this plant will spread, most probably replacing those species and varieties with little or no immediate economic return.

Commercialization often causes a decline in plant diversity. A study in Quintana Roo, Mexico, that investigated the correlation between diversity of plants found in gardens and related environmental and cultural features showed that garden diversity was lower near large produce markets (Fey 1989). Home gardens close to big cities in West Java showed a serious decline in varieties of fruit trees present, including mango, banana, or rambutan. Areas that contained seventy-five mango cultivars in the 1920s now have only forty-eight left (Soemarwoto 1987). Commercial home gardens are dominated by a few plant species such as fruit trees, vegetables, or ornamental plants and usually lose their multistorey structure. In addition, the introduction of modern varieties of coconut, clove, or coffee may displace local cultivars, causing genetic erosion of important species. The loss of the traditional structure leads to a decrease in genetic diversity and may also have serious ecological consequences such as increased soil erosion and the outright loss of traditional varieties.

Home gardens are found in practically every household where local plants not only augment cash income but also serve the household as food, fuel, medicine, fodder, construction material, and ritual paraphernalia. Home gardens are found in rural areas as well as in urban settlements. The urban food production garden is often an innovative addition by poor households to the informal sector of the urban economy (Niñez 1985; Sanyal 1985; Linares 1976).

Home-Garden Management Practices, Gender Roles, and Decision-Making

The allocation of labor and responsibilities between men and women in crop production is affected by different factors such as land-use patterns, diversity of crops, division of labor in the household, size of the farm, socioeconomic status of the family, ethnic group, and so on (Fortmann 1990). The important role that women play as agricultural producers and users of genetic diversity is increasingly being recognized. In some places, economic and population changes have forced women to take a leading part in field agriculture. Women have extensive knowledge of multiple plant uses since they rely on diverse biological resources to provide food and income and to satisfy the multiple needs of the household.

There are limited statistics that describe in detail the time allocation and decision-making patterns for specific crops (Bajracharya 1994). However, it is widely observed that women are often responsible for processing and storing food grains for home consumption and seeds for planting the following season. In tribal villages in India women have traditionally been the seed selectors and custodians of germplasm for the next season's planting (Ravishankar et al. 1994). In vegetable production, 90 percent of decisions are taken by women, whereas in fruit production men make most decisions (Acharya and Bennett 1981; Bajracharya 1994).

It is widely assumed that women are responsible for home gardens. But does this responsibility include all activities and decision making in the home garden? Are there differences from culture to culture? Although women's labor input is important, the view that gardening is solely a female activity might be a stereotype. In Nepal, women alone make 30 percent of the decisions on what crop to plant on agricultural fields while 18 percent are made by men alone. Women also exchange seeds with neighbors and friends and introduce new crop varieties into the husband's family at marriage. Decisions on what seed to select for the following season are taken at a rate of 60 percent by women alone, 21 percent by men, and 11 percent by both. Wickramasinghe (1991) describes one or the other gender taking responsibilities for different kinds of plants found in home gardens of Sri Lanka. Both genders also take part in the management of home gardens in urban regions of Papua New Guinea. However, if men work in other land-use systems or are engaged in wage labor, women do most of the labor in the gardens (Vasey 1985; Vasey 1990).

Land tenure affects the role that women play in homestead plantations in Bangladesh, where the extent to which women participate depends on the size of farms (Hossain, Abedin, and Hussain 1990). In landless households, women made decisions to the same extent as or even more than their husbands; in larger farms planted with trees and vegetables women were much less involved. The selling of fruits and vegetables on the market was clearly the domain of the husbands in all farm size categories. Women held almost full responsibility for seed production. Each gender may place a different value on genetic resources and their environmental functions. The gender division of resources, knowledge, work, and products may reflect conflict, complementarity, or coincidence of men's and women's interest in land-use systems (Rocheleau 1989). In Sierra Leone, for example, women are responsible for the harvest and sale of minor forest products such as fruits and seeds, whereas men are responsible for the sale of honey, timber, and bamboo wine. Men often decide what trees are to be harvested; this can sometimes cause a loss of income to women who collect fruits for sale on the market (Leach 1990). More detailed studies are needed to investigate conflicting values, perceptions, and decisions taken within households that manage home gardens.

Factors Undermining the Maintenance of Biodiversity in Home Gardens

Projects focusing on home-garden systems during the past twenty-five years have had two principal research objectives in mind: the setting up of comprehensive ethnobotanical lists of species grown and used in home gardens and the nutritional improvement of low-income populations in developing countries. Many projects have been guided by western models of kitchen gardening. These horticultural models based on temperate vegetables are difficult to adapt to the social and environmental conditions of the tropics. Not enough scientific attention has been paid to traditional subsistence gardening systems within the tropics. Few attempts have been made to investigate local food species in terms of their traditional value and nutritional characteristics, and fewer efforts still have been made to build on the potential of traditional food supply systems and to integrate them into home-garden projects (Niñez 1985; Sommers 1990; Fernandes and Nair 1986; Cleveland and Soleri 1987). Home gardens can provide an ideal setting in which to understand and develop local gardening practices adapted to the environmental conditions and food cultures of local communities. Negative experiences and failures with past home-garden projects have contributed to their underestimation by policymakers who ignore the valuable role they can play in rural development efforts. The introduction of imported vegetables and varieties held in high esteem by extension services has at times also undermined the use of better-adapted indigenous and traditional vegetables.

Changes occurring under increasing demographic and economic pressures fuel concern for the future of traditional home gardens and the genetic reservoir they contain (Rico-Gray et al. 1990; Michon and Mary 1994). For some plant species, cultural pressures, low yields, and gender bias are leading to their neglect and declining use. Degradation may also occur through ill-devised government development plans. In some countries such as Thailand, Malaysia, and Mexico, traditional home-gardening practices are seen as old-fashioned, and the sophisticated knowledge that complex species management in home gardens entails is declining (Rerkasem and Rerkasem 1985; Anderson 1993a). Growing trends in off-farm employment for Indian women means that they have less time for work at home, including tending home gardens (Ranjit Daniels and Vencatesan 1995). Younger women were found to have little knowledge of, and negative attitudes toward, home-garden work. A study that analyzed intrahousehold dynamics in the Eastern Caribbean revealed that female-headed households face particular labor and input constraints that limit their output, choice of crops, and amount of land cultivated (Chase 1988). In many parts of Africa, migration of young people to urban areas leads to labor shortages as older people are left to manage the home gardens. The knowledge and experience of how to manage home-garden species is not being transmitted to the younger generation and may eventually be lost (Fernandes, O'Kting'ati, and Maghembe J. 1984; Juma 1989).

In many regions traditional home-garden systems are in a transitional stage; they are being replaced by more lucrative cash crop plantations and monocultures (Poyyamoli and Mathew 1991; Michon and Mary 1994). In Kerala, India, a study of homestead tree cropping showed that in spite of their ecological stability home gardens are on the decline (Nair and Krishnankutty 1985). They are being replaced by commercial farms that, in the long run, are neither ecologically and economically sustainable, nor socially desirable. Garden conversion often implies drastic modification of the traditional vegetation composition leading to serious problems, such as pests and soil erosion and degradation. However, more and better quantitative data is still needed to understand the interactions that exist between home-garden plants and the households that manage them. Only then will we be able to assess the sustainability of home-garden systems with some measure of accuracy (Millat-e-Mustafa 1998).

Home Gardens and Biodiversity: A New Approach

Current research has identified three features of home gardens that are important for in situ (on farm) conservation of agricultural biodiversity. First, home gardens are refuges for crops and crop varieties that were once more widespread in the larger agroecosystem. Second, they are sites for experimenting with the introduction of new cultivars resulting from exchange and interaction between cultures and communities. Third, home gardens are important systems for the study of crop evolution and plant genetic resources because of the complex species diversity and interactions that characterize them.

The authors of the essays in this book are actively engaged in conducting research on the dynamics and distribution of species diversity and genetic diversity within home gardens and across home-garden systems. The dynamic nature and multiple uses of home gardens raise important questions concerning the stability of this microecosystem and its potential role as a viable conservation unit. The chapters that follow address the problem of how to identify the sorts of strategies that help to incorporate these microsystems into a complementary in situ program. Our ongoing research provides the kinds of quantitative and qualitative data on the interactions between plant species and varieties, and between people and the plants they manage, that are necessary in order to justify the vital contribution that home gardens can make to food security and biodiversity conservation.

There are various ways in which the approach used in this book makes a novel contribution to home-garden studies. The studies are comparative across the tropical world, embracing Africa, Asia, Latin America, and the Caribbean, where home gardens are important repositories and sources of agricultural biodiversity. The studies are strategic. They aim to produce practical information on how home gardens can contribute to the conservation of diversity in agroecosystems that may be neglected and subject to genetic erosion. The studies contribute to our understanding of the link between conservation and use. Such an understanding could enable us to identify ways of including home gardens as a farmer-managed component of in situ programs for conserving agrobiodiversity. Research on the biodiversity contributions of home gardens may be in an early stage, but the studies reported on here doubtless increase our understanding of how and what portion of crop genetic diversity exists within home gardens, and how such diversity can be maintained.

The chapters in this book describe studies that are, above all, dynamic. They trace the effects that changes in cultural value and household uses of species have on the diversity found within home gardens. Inevitably, constraints that limit the production, value, and use of plant species always exist. The authors explore ways to overcome these biological and socioeconomic barriers in order to insure continued and expanded use of home gardens to enhance biodiversity. This is part of a dynamic "conservation through use" approach. The focus is on the links and exchanges that occur between home gardens so that the boundaries and key parameters that identify them as viable conservation units can be better defined.

Finally, the studies are multidisciplinary. This "conservation through use" approach looks at the genetic, agronomic, economic, and cultural factors that affect the structure, composition, and stability of home gardens. The authors pay particular attention to how changing ecological and cultural factors, as well as markets and terms of trade, affect the choice of species and varieties to be grown in home gardens. This background knowledge is essential if we are to plan effective systems for the support and inclusion of home gardens into national conservation strategies for the conservation of agrobiodiversity.

Organization of the Book

The book is divided into three parts. The first part is on theory and methods, the second consists of country case studies across various geographic regions, cultures, and ecozones, and the third part addresses the genetic diversity of some key home-garden species.

The first chapter under theory and methods, by Guarino and Hoogendijk, addresses fundamental issues in conservation biology at the ecosystem and genetic level. These issues have to do with partitioning of ecosystems into microenvironments and the effects on population size and genetic structure of the crop species maintained in home gardens. They are central to understanding both the genetic richness and stability of home gardens from a conservation perspective. The second chapter, by Jürg Schneider, introduces methods of cultural analysis that are central to the definition and management of home-garden systems. He looks at how ethnic identity is both expressed and reflected in home gardens as cultural definitions of space, environment, and food. Schneider uses examples from the rich set of home-garden studies in Indonesia to examine how their perseverance as reservoirs and sources of genetic diversity is linked to the maintenance of local knowledge systems and cultures. The third chapter in this section on methods, by Fundora, Shagarodsky, and Castiñeiras, addresses a fundamental problem in conservation biology: how to sample the genetic diversity within small populations of useful plant species in home gardens. Sampling and measuring the amount and distribution of genetic diversity maintained by farmers over time and across home gardens is central for determining if home gardens are indeed rich reservoirs, refuges, or localized hotspots of agrobiodiversity. In addition to sampling for small population sizes across home gardens, the issue of germplasm exchange is also central. A single home garden on its own is not a secure niche for conserving plant genetic resources. Quite often, a simple and logical decision by the household in response to economic, cultural, or demographic changes can alter the composition of plants and crop varieties in a garden. Only by identifying and linking a representative sample of similar home gardens within a cultural and ecological system can home gardens conserve genetic diversity for some species. The methods proposed by the Cuban scientists address these fundamental issues of distinctiveness, stability, and change in the genetic resources maintained in home gardens. Such methods can be applied to identify a working sample of home gardens and home-garden systems that can be monitored by national institutions such as crop gene banks, biosphere reserves, ecology institutes, or botanic gardens that are interested in conserving and using biodiversity and plant genetic resources.

The second section of the book provides a holistic perspective on the structure, management practices, and distribution of home gardens across ecological regions and cultures. The country case studies included are based on surveys that document the richness of plant diversity within home-garden systems and the wide variation in home-garden types across ecozones. The case studies identify key parameters for home-garden systems that are used to develop a typology of home gardens and the processes that affect their diversity. This typology is a first step for monitoring and supporting home-garden agrobiodiversity conservation in developing countries. At the same time, the comparative studies emphasize the structure and function of plant diversity in ways that explain the wide distribution, resilience, and longevity of home-garden systems in the tropics. These shared traits and processes include the ability of home-garden systems to adapt to environmental and socioeconomic changes.

In the chapter on Vietnamese home gardens, L. N. Trihn discusses the socioeconomic changes in Vietnam's agrarian sector that have resulted in the erosion of traditional crops and the introduction of new species and varieties. Home gardens have been both refuges for crop diversity that is no longer supported by agricultural policy and points of introduction for new diversity to meet the new demands of markets and local food cultures. The chapter documents the ethnic differences that account for crop choices and levels of diversity; subsistence farming was also associated with high levels of diversity in home gardens.

The chapter by Shresta, Gautam, Rana, and Sthapit on Nepalese home gardens looks at mountain agroecosystems where the species composition in gardens changes with altitude. Here changes in home-garden biodiversity are associated with migration, markets, and development projects. In general, these changes have not been favorable to the crop diversity maintained in gardens. A better understanding of the value and uses of crop diversity within home gardens could help development projects build upon this traditional reservoir of biodiversity.

The Ethiopian home gardens studied by Zemede Asfaw are oriented around a unique species, enset (*Ensete ventricosum*, sometimes known as "false banana") that surrounds Ethiopian rural homesteads in several local cultures. The chapter focuses on the management practices in enset home gardens thus illustrating how a key species can provide a focus for a diverse set of crop and tree associations and for the monitoring of home-garden biodiversity in Ethiopia.

The home gardens of Ghana cover a wide range of agroecological zones from the humid forest to the guinea savannah. In this context, the species composition of the home gardens varies greatly at the ends of the spectrum. However, certain key management practices with respect to gender roles, the importance of markets and germplasm exchange, and gene flow between home gardens are central to the stability and diversity of the three main types of home gardens documented by Bennett-Lartey and his colleagues.

Small-scale agriculture in Venezuela has been in decline for half a century, as oil revenues have funded food imports and large-scale mechanized farms. Recent economic crises have refocused attention on the potential of Venezuela to meet its own food needs; in addition, a growing environmental concern has led to increased interest in sustainable agriculture. The Venezuelan conucos documented in the chapter by Quiroz, Gutiérrez, and Pérez de Fernández provide an entry point for the revitalization of small-scale agriculture that maintains biodiversity. The conucos described in this chapter are isolated and scarce. The authors argue for policy measures to link and support these conucos as a step toward a renewal of sustainable small-scale agriculture in Venezuela, in particular to revive production of traditional legumes, root crops, and fruits.

The final case study on peri-urban home gardens in the Casamance region of Senegal by Linares highlights the dynamic nature of home gardens in time and space. Armed conflict in the rural areas of Casamance has accelerated the migration of people to urban areas. This potentially disruptive transition in livelihood and culture has been bridged to a significant degree by the establishment of traditional home gardens in urban areas. First and foremost, home gardens provide livelihood options to migrants who have yet to acquire the skills and resources that enable them to compete in the new urban environment. Home gardens also provide urban migrants with a link back to their rural villages where they obtain germplasm, skills, and additional labor. Peri-urban home gardens form a cultural and biological patchwork that favors the exchange of germplasm, management techniques, and knowledge across households and ethnic groups as well as between urban and rural areas.

The final section of the book consists of four chapters focusing on the genetic diversity of key crop and fruit tree species that are found in gardens across the tropics. The chapter by Gessler and Hodel examines the ways that farmers classify and manage intraspecific diversity within Vietnamese home gardens. Sthapit, Rana, Hue, and Rijal analyze the management of diversity of taro and sponge gourd cultivars in Vietnam and Nepal, where cultural practices and local tastes are major factors in the selection and management of genetic diversity in these species. The authors argue that home gardens are apt systems for both crop improvement and crop conservation for those species that have been neglected by formal research and development. In the Americas, peanuts and peppers are also key home-garden species; farmers keep distinctive varieties and germplasm that they can eventually multiply for more extensive use. In both cases crop varieties with valuable genetic traits are still maintained in home gardens although they may be rare in the fields. Many tropical fruit trees are long-lived species with recalcitrant seeds and thus are difficult to conserve, characterize, and evaluate ex situ. Home gardens provide a good setting to evaluate and conserve the diversity of large tropical fruit trees such as sapote (*Pouteria sapote*), a characteristic tree of the upper storey in home gardens. The fruits were characterized to assess the distribution of genetic traits of sapote in three ecozones. Those trees producing fruits with traits that were favored by consumers were identified as a source of germplasm for the selection and propagation of elite lines of this delicious tropical fruit.

In summary, the book provides a holistic perspective on biodiversity in home gardens. It covers the ecological structure and function of the species and crop varieties that are found in home gardens and plots their distribution. The research documents the distribution and uses of plant genetic diversity within home gardens. This is not a passive or residual diversity from larger ecosystems that have been converted. It is rich diversity that has been positively selected and managed in accordance with the cultures and livelihood needs of rural households. Households manage this home garden diversity in ways that enable them to cope with change and adapt their crops and crop combinations to new situations. It is crucial to understand the dynamic relationship that exists between plant communities and households. Such knowledge can help us identify the specific mechanisms and strategies to be used when including home gardens as part of biodiversity conservation efforts. We can then move beyond the well-known development functions of home gardens as sources of income and nutrition to envision their future role in genetic conservation and enrichment.

References

Abdoellah, O. S., and G. G. Marten. 1986. The complementary roles of homegardens, upland fields, and rice fields for meeting nutritional needs in West Java. In G. G. Marten, ed., *Traditional Agriculture in Southeast Asia: A Human Ecology Perspective*, pp. 293–325. Boulder, Colorado: Westview Press.

Acharya, M., and L. Bennett. 1981. The rural women of Nepal: An aggregate analysis of 8 village studies. The Status of Women in Nepal. Centre for Economic Development and Administration, Kathmandu.

Aiyelaagbe, I. O. O. 1992. Fruit crops: Are they relevant for agroforestry development? *Agroforestry Today* 4: 12–13.

Aiyelaagbe, I. O. O. 1994. Fruitcrops in the cashew-coconut system of Kenya: Their use, management, and agroforestry potential. *Agroforestry Systems* 27 (1): 1–16.

Alvarez-Buylla Roces, M. A., E. Lazos Chavero, and J. R. García-Barrios. 1989. Home gardens of a humid tropical region in Southeast Mexico: An example of an agroforestry cropping system in a recently established community. *Agroforestry Systems* 8: 133–56.

Anderson, E. N. 1993a. Gardens in tropical America and tropical Asia. *Biótica, Nueva Epoca* 1: 81–102.

Anderson, E. N. 1993b. Southeast Asian gardens: Nutrition, cash, and ethnicity. *Biótica, Nueva Época* 1: 1–11.

Arnold, J. E. M. 1987. Economic considerations in agroforestry. In H. A. Steppler and

P. K. R. Nair, eds., *Agroforestry: A Decade of Development*, pp. 173–90. Nairobi, Kenya: International Council for Research in Agroforestry (ICRAF).

Asare, E. O., S. K. Oppong, and K. Twum-Ampofo. 1990. Home gardens in the humid tropics of Ghana. In K. Landauer and M. Brazil, eds., *Tropical Home Gardens*, pp. 80–93. Tokyo: United Nations University Press.

Bajracharya, B. 1994. Gender issues in Nepali agriculture: A review. HMG Ministry of Agriculture/International Policy Analysis in Agriculture and Related Resource Management. Winrock International, Kathmandu, Nepal, Research Report, no. 25.

Balée, W., and A. Gély. 1989. Managed forest succession in Amazonia: The Ka'apor case. In D. A. Posey and W. Balée, eds., *Resource Management in Amazonia: Indigenous and Folk Strategies*. Advances in Economic Botany 7: 129–48. Bronx, New York: New York Botanical Garden.

Barrett, G. W., N. Rodenhouse, and P. J. Bohlen. 1990. Role of sustainable agriculture in rural landscapes. In C. Edwards, R. Lal, P. Madden, R. H. Miller, and G. House, eds., *Sustainable Agricultural Systems*, pp. 624–36. Ankey, Iowa: Soil and Water Conservation Society.

Bompard, J., C. Ducatillion, P. Hecketsweiler, and G. Michon. 1980. A Traditional Agricultural System: Village — Forest — Gardens in West Java. Université des Sciences et Techniques du Languedoc, Montpellier. Diplôme study report.

Brierley, J. S. 1985. West Indian kitchen gardens: A historical perspective with current insights from Grenada. *Food and Nutrition Bulletin* 7 (3): 52–60.

Campbell, B. M. 1987. The use of wild fruits in Zimbabwe. *Economic Botany* 41 (3): 375–85.

Castiñeiras, L., and others. 2000. La conservación in situ de la variabilidad de plantas de cultivo en dos localidades de Cuba. *Revista del Jardín Botánico Nacional* 21 (1): 25–45. Cuba: Universidad de la Habana.

Chase, V. 1988. Farming systems research in the Eastern Caribbean: An attempt at analyzing intra-household dynamics. In S. V. Poats, M. Schmink, and A. Spring, eds., *Gender Issues in Farming Systems Research and Extension*, pp. 171–82. Boulder, Colorado: Westview Press.

Christanty, L., and J. Iskandar. 1985. Development of decision-making and management skills in traditional agroforestry: Examples in West Java. In Y. S. Rao, N. T. Vergara, and G. W. Lovelace, eds., *Community Forestry: Socio-economic Aspects*, pp. 198–214. Food and Agricultural Organization of the United Nations (FAO), Regional Office for Asia and the Pacific; Environment and Policy Institute, East-West Center, Bangkok, Thailand; Honolulu, Hawaii, USA.

Christanty, L., O. S. Abdoellah, G. Marten, and J. Iskandar. 1986. Traditional agroforestry in West Java: The Pekarangan (home garden) and Kebun-talun (annual-perennial rotation) cropping systems. In G. G. Marten, ed., *Traditional Agriculture in Southeast Asia: A Human Ecology Perspective*, pp. 132–58. Boulder, Colorado: Westview Press.

Cleveland, D. A., and D. Soleri. 1987. Household gardens as a development strategy. *Human Organization* 46 (3): 259–70.

Colfer, C. J. P., C. Evensen, S. Evensen, F. Agus, D. Gill, A.Wade, and B. Chapman. 1985. Transmigrants' gardens: A neglected research opportunity. *Proceedings, Centre for Soil Research Annual Technical Meetings,* Bogor, Indonesia.

Corlin, C., A. de Kartzow, G. Nilsson, H. Olsson, and A. B. Interforest. 1989. FTP in Vietnam: Base-line and diagnosis study. Socioeconomic Part, Technical Part. Working paper 100, Foresters, Trees and People, Food and Agricultural Organization of the United Nations (FAO), SIDA, Swedish University of Agricultural Sciences, International Rural Development Centre, Uppsala.

Danoesastro, H. 1985. The Socio-economic aspect of tropical home gardens. The First International Workshop on Tropical Home Garden. Bandung, Indonesia: Institute of Ecology, Padjadjaran University and Tokyo: United Nations University.

Esquivel, M., and K. Hammer. 1992a. Contemporary traditional agriculture: Structure and diversity of the "conuco." In K. Hammer, M. Esquivel, and H. Knüpffer, eds., "... *Y Tienen Faxones y Fabas muy Diversos de los Nuestros* ...": *Origin, Evolution and Diversity of Cuban Plant Genetic Resources,* 1: 174–92. Gatersleben, Germany: Institut für Pflanzengenetik und Kulturpflanzenforschung.

Esquivel, M., and K. Hammer. 1992b. The Cuban home garden "conuco": A perspective environment for evolution and "in situ" conservation of plant genetic resources in Cuba. *Genetic Resources and Crop Evolution* 39: 9–22.

Fernandes, E. C. M., A. O'Kting'ati, and J. Maghembe J. 1984. The Chagga home gardens: A multistoried agroforestry cropping system on Mt. Kilimanjaro, Northern Tanzania. *Agroforestry Systems* 2: 73–86.

Fernandes, E. C. M., and P. K. R. Nair. 1986. An evaluation of the structure and function of tropical homegardens. *Agricultural Systems* 21: 279–310.

Fey, R. L. 1989. Diversity index usage in the geographic study of home gardens in Quintana Roo, Mexico. Ph.D. thesis, University of Colorado, Denver.

Fleming, E. M. 1989. Resource use and consumption in smallholder households in Solomon Islands: Analysis of some key relationships. South Pacific Smallholder Project 1989, University of New England, Occasional Paper no. 14, pp. 35.

Fortmann, L. 1990. Women's role in small farm agriculture. In M. A. Altieri and S. B. Hecht, eds., *Agroecology and Small Farm Development,* pp. 35–43. Boca Raton, Florida: CRC Press.

Gliessman, S. R. 1988. The home garden agroecosystem: A model for developing sustainable tropical agricultural systems. In P. Allen and D. Van Dusen, eds., *Global Perspectives on Agroecology and Sustainable Agricultural Systems.* Proceedings of the Sixth International Scientific Conference of the International Federation of Organic Agriculture Movements, 2: 445–49. University of California, Santa Cruz: Agroecology Program.

Gliessman, S. R. 1990a. Integrating trees into agriculture: The home garden agroecosystem as an example of agroforestry in the tropics. In S. R. Gliessmann, ed., *Agroecology: Researching the Ecological Basis for Sustainable Agriculture,* pp. 160–68. New York: Springer Verlag.

Gliessman, S. R. 1990b. Understanding the basis of sustainability for agriculture in the tropics: Experiences in Latin America. In C. A. Edwards, R. Lal, P. Madden, R. H. Miller, and G. House, eds., *Sustainable Agricultural Systems,* pp. 378–90. Delray Beach, Florida: St. Lucie Press.

Guijt, I., F. Hinchcliffe, and M. Melnyk. 1995. The hidden harvest: The value of wild resources in agricultural systems—A summary. International Institute for Environment and Development, London (UK): International Institute for Environment and Development (IIED)

Heywood, V. H., and I. Baste. 1995. Introduction. In V. H. Heywood and R. T. Watson, general eds., *Global Biodiversity Assessment,* pp. 1–20. Published for the United Nations Environment Program (UNEP) by Cambridge: Cambridge University Press.

Hodel, U., M. Gessler, H. H. Cai, V. V. Thoan, N. V. Ha, N. X. Thuu, and T. Ba. 1999. *In Situ Conservation of Plant Genetic Resources in Home Gardens of Southern Vietnam.* 1996. Rome, Italy: International Plant Genetic Resources Institute (IPGRI).

Holling, C. S., D. W. Schindler, B. W. Walker, and J. Roughgarden. 1995. Biodiversity and the functioning of ecosystems: An ecological analysis. In C. Perrings, K.-G. Mäler, C. Folke, C. S. Holling, and B.-O. Jansson, eds. *Biodiversity Loss: Economic and Ecological Issues,* pp. 44–83. Cambridge: Cambridge University Press.

Hossain, S. M., M. Z. Abedin, and M. S. Hussain. 1990. Women's role in homestead plantation. Homestead Plantation and Agroforestry in Bangladesh. Joydebpur, Bangladesh. Bangladesh Agricultural Research Institute, Food and Agricultural Organization of the United Nations (FAO) Regional Wood Energy Development Programme, Winrock International Institute for Agricultural Development, 82–89.

Immink, M. D. C., D. Sanjur, and M. Colon. 1981. Home gardens and the energy and nutrient intakes of women and preschoolers in rural Puerto Rico. *Ecology of Food and Nutrition* 2: 191–99.

Immink, M. D. C. 1990. Measuring food production and consumption and the nutritional effects of tropical home gardens. In K. Landauer and M. Brazil, eds., *Tropical Home Gardens,* pp. 126–37. Selected papers from an International Workshop held at the Institute of Ecology, Padjadjaran University, Badung, Indonesia, 2–9 December 1985. Tokyo, Japan: United Nations University.

Iwanaga, M., P. Eyzaguirre, and J. Thompson. 2000. Integrated plant genetic resources management for sustainable agriculture. In K. Watanabe and A. Komamine, eds., *Proceedings of the 12th Toyota Conference: Challenge of Plan and Agricultural Sciences to the Crisis on Earth in the 21st Century.* Georgetown, Texas: Landes Bioscience.

Jones, S., E. M. Fleming, and J. B. Hardaker. 1988. Smallholder Agriculture in Solomon Islands. Report of the South Pacific Smallholder Project in Solomon Islands, 1985–86. South Pacific Smallholder Project, University of New England, Armidale, New South Wales, Australia, Project Report, OQEH.

Jose, D., and N. Shanmugaratnam. 1993. Traditional home gardens of Kerala: A sustainable human ecosystem. *Agroforestry Systems* 24 (2): 203–13.

Juma, C. 1989. Biological Diversity and Innovation: Conserving and Utilizing Genetic Resources in Kenya. Nairobi, Kenya: African Centre for Technology Studies.

Karyono. 1990. Home gardens in Java: Their structure and function. In K. Landauer and M. Brazil, eds., *Tropical Home Gardens*, pp. 138–46. Tokyo, Japan: United Nations University Press.

Kassogue, A., J. Dolo, and T. Ponsioen. 1990. Traditional soil and water conservation in the Dogon plateau Mali. International Institute for Environment and Development (IIED), Dryland Networks Programme Issues, Paper 23.

Kumar, B. M., S. J. George, and S. Chinnamani. 1994. Diversity, structure and standing stock of wood in the home gardens of Kerala in peninsular India. *Agroforestry Systems* 25 (3): 243–62.

Leach, M. 1990. The Reciprocal Constitution of Gender and Resource use in the life of a Sierra Leonean Village. Ph.D. thesis. University of London .

Linares, O. F. 1976. Garden hunting in the American tropics. *Human Ecology* 44 (4): 331–49.

Linh, V. B., and N. N. Binh. 1995. *Agroforestry Systems in Vietnam*. Hanoi: Agriculture Publishing House.

Loreau, M., S. Naeem, P. Inchausti, J. Bengtsson, J. P. Grime, A. Hector, D. U. Hoop, M. A. Huston, D. Raffaelli, B. Schmid, D. Tilman, and D. A. Wardle. 2001. Biodiversity and ecosystem functioning: Current knowledge and future challenges. *Science* 294: 804–8.

Lundgren, B., and J. B. Raintree. 1983. Sustained agroforestry. In B. Nestel, ed., *Agricultural Research for Development: Potentials and Challenges in Asia*, pp. 37–49. The Hague, Netherlands: International Service for National Agricultural Research (ISNAR).

Marten, G. G., and O. S. Abdoellah. 1988. Crop diversity and nutrition in West Java. *Ecology-of-Food-and-Nutrition* 21 (1): 17–43.

Maundu, P. 1987. The importance of gathered fruits and medicinal plants in Kakuyuni and Kathama Areas of Machakos. In K. K. Wachiira, ed., *Women's Use of Off-Farm and Boundary Lands: Agroforestry Potentials*, pp. 56–60. Nairobi, Kenya: International Centre for Research in Agroforestry (ICRAF).

McConnell, D. J. 1992. *The Forest-Garden Farms of Kandy, Sri Lanka*. Rome: Food and Agricultural Organization of the United Nations (FAO).

Michon, G. 1983. Village-forest-gardens in West Java. In P. A. Huxley, ed., *Plant Research and Agroforestry*. International Council for Research in Agroforestry (ICRAF), Nairobi, 13–24.

Michon, G., and F. Mary. 1994. Conversion of traditional village gardens and new economic strategies of rural households in the area of Bogor, Indonesia. *Agroforestry Systems* 25: 31–58.

Michon, G., F. Mary, and J. Bompard. 1986. Multistoried agroforestry garden system in West Sumatra, Indonesia. *Agroforestry Systems* 4 (4): 315–38.

Millat-e-Mustafa, M. 1998. An approach towards analysis of home gardens. In A. Rastogi, A. Godbole, and S. Pei, eds., *Applied Ethnobotany in Natural Resource Management: Traditional Home Gardens*, pp. 39–47. Kathmandu, Nepal: International Center for Integrated Mountain Development.

Moreno-Black, G., S. Prapimporn, and T. Sompong. 1994. Women in northeastern Thailand: preservers of botanical diversity. *Indigenous Knowledge and Development Monitor* 2 (3 special issue).

Mula, R. P., and B. T. Gayao. 1991. Urban and rural homegarden in the highlands of the Northern Philippines: The case of Sweet Potato. Benguet State University, La Trinidad, Benguet, Philippines, Final Report.

National Research Council. 1993. *Sustainable Agriculture and the Environment in the Humid Tropics.* Washington D.C.: U.S. National Academy Press.

Nair, P. K. R. 1985. Classification of agroforestry systems. *Agroforestry Systems* 3 (2): 97–128.

Nair, C. T. S., and C. N. Krishnankutty. 1985. Socio-economic factors influencing farm forestry: A case study of tree cropping in the homesteads in Kerala, India. In Y. R. Rao, N. T. Vergara, and G. W. Lovelace, eds., *Community Forestry: Socioeconomic Aspects,* pp. 115–30. FACI Regional Office for Asia and the Pacific; Environment and Policy Institute, East-West Center, Bangkok, Thailand; Honolulu, Hawaii, USA.

Niñez, V. 1984. Household gardens: Theoretical considerations on an old survival strategy. International Potato Center, Lima, Research Series, Report no. 1.

Niñez, V. 1985 Working at half-potential: Constructive analysis of home garden programmes in the Lima slums with suggestions for an alternative approach. *Food and Nutrition Bulletin* 7 (3): 6–14.

Niñez, V. K. 1986. The household garden as a lifeboat. *Ceres* 19 (4): 31–36.

Okafor, J. C., and E. C. M. Fernandes. 1987. Compound farms of southeastern Nigeria: A predominant agroforestry homegarden system with crops and small livestock. *Agroforestry Systems* (Netherlands), 5 (2): 153–68.

Okigbo, B. N. 1990. Sustainable agricultural systems in tropical Africa. In Clive A. Edwards, R. Lal, P. Madden, R. H. Miller, and G. House, eds., *Sustainable Agricultural Systems,* pp. 323–34. Boca Raton, Florida: CRC Press.

Padoch, C., and W. de Jong. 1991 The house gardens of Santa Rosa: diversity and variability in an Amazonian agricultural system. *Economic Botany* 45 (2): 166–75.

Penny, D. H., and M. Ginting.1984. *Home Garden, Peasant and Poverty.* Yogyakarta, Indonesia: Gadjah Mada University Press..

Perrings, C., K.-G. Mäler, C. Folke, C. S. Holling, and B.-O. Jansson. 1995a. Introduction: Framing the problem of biodiversity loss. In C. Perrings, K.-G. Mäler, C. Folke, C. S. Holling, and B.-O. Jansson, eds., *Biodiversity Loss: Economic and Ecological Issues,* pp. 1–17. Cambridge: Cambridge University Press.

Perrings, C., K.-G. Mäler, C. Folke, C. S. Holling, and B.-O. Jansson. 1995b. Unanswered questions. In C. Perrings, K.-G. Mäler, C. Folke, C. S. Holling, and B.-O. Jansson, eds., *Biodiversity Loss: Economic and Ecological Issues,* pp. 301–8. Cambridge: Cambridge University Press.

Pingle, U. 1991. Greening of Central Indian Wastelands. International Symposium Food and Nutrition in the Tropical Forest: Biocultural Interactions and Applications to Development, 10–13 September 1991. Paris: United Nations Educational, Scientific, and Cultural Organization (UNESCO).

Poyyamoli, G., and A. G. Mathew. 1991. Home Gardens of Kerala—A case study of selected homesteads of Karulai Village, Malapuram District, Kerala. Working Paper. School of Ecology and Environmental Sciences, Pondicherry University, Pondicherry.

Price, N. 1983. The tropical mixed garden: An agroforestry component of the small farm. Short course on Agroforestry for the Humid Tropics, Centro Agronómico Tropical de Investigación y Enseñanza (CATIE), 15–23 March, 1982.

Rajagukguk, E. 1989. Agrarian law, land tenure and subsistence in Java: Case study of the villages of Sukoharjo and Medayu. *Dissertation Abstracts International, Humanities and Social-Sciences* 49 (8): 2372.

Ranjit Daniels, R. J., and J. Vencatesan. 1995. Role of women in the origin and maintenance of home gardens. Second Congress on Traditional Sciences and Technologies of India, Dec. 27–31, 1995. Anna University, Madras.

Ravishankar, T., L. Vedavalli, A. A. Namibi, and V. Selvam. 1994. Role of Tribal Communities in the Conservation of Plant Genetic Resources. MSSRF, Madras.

Rerkasem, B., and K. Rerkasem 1985 A discussion paper on the management of home gardens. The First International Workshop on Tropical Home garden. Bandung, Indonesia. Institute of Ecology Padjadjaran University (Bandung) and United Nations University (Tokyo).

Rico-Gray, V., J. G. García-Franco, A. Chemas, A. Puch, and P. Sima. 1990. Species composition, similarity and structure of Mayan homegardens in Tixpeual and Tixcacaltuyub, Yucatan, Mexico. *Economic Botany* 44 (4): 470–87.

Rocheleau, D. E. 1989. Gender division of work: Resources, and rewards in agroforestry systems. *Second Kenya National Seminar on Agroforestry*, pp. 228–45. Nairobi, Kenya: International Centre for Research on Agroforestry (ICRAF).

Rugalema, G. H., A. O'Kting'ati, and F. H. Johnson. 1994 The home garden agroforestry system of Bukoba district, North-Western Tanzania. 1. Farming system analysis. *Agroforestry Systems* 26 (1): 53–64.

Salick, J., and M. Lundberg. 1990. Variation and change in Amuesha agriculture, Peruvian Upper Amazon. *Advances in Economic Botany* 8: 199–223.

Sanyal, B. 1985. Urban agriculture: Who cultivates and why? A case study of Lusaka, Zambia. *Food and Nutrition Bulletin* 7 (3): 15–24.

Shalaby, M. T. 1991. Household productivity in new rural settlements in Egypt: Perspectives on kitchen garden. *Third World Planning Review* 13 (3): 237–59.

Soemarwoto, O. 1987. Home gardens: A traditional agroforestry system with a promising future. In H. A. Steppler and P. K. R. Nair, eds., *Agroforestry: A Decade of Development*, pp. 157–70. Nairobi, Kenya: International Council for Research and Agroforestry (ICRAF).

Soemarwoto, O., and G. R. Conway. 1991. The Javanese home garden. *Journal for Farming Systems Research-Extension* 2 (3): 96–117.

Soemarwoto, O., and I. Soemarwoto. 1981. Home gardens in Indonesia. Paper for the Fourth Pacific Science International Congress. Singapore, 1–5 Sept.

Soemarwoto, O., and I. Soemarwoto. 1982. Homegarden: Its nature, origin and future development. Workshop on ecological basis for rational resource utilization in the humid tropics of South East Asia, pp. 130–39. Malaysia: Universiti Pertanian.

Soemarwoto, O., I. Soemarwoto, Karyono, E. M. Soekartadiredja, and A. Ramlan. 1985.

The Javanese home garden as an integrated agroecosystem. *Food and Nutrition Bulletin* 7 (3): 44–47.

Sommers, P. 1985. The UNICEF Home Gardens Handbook for People Promoting Mixed Gardening in the Humid Tropics (Philippines). United Nation's Children Emergency Fund (UNICEF), New York.

Sommers, P. 1990. Advancing Pacific Island food gardening systems: Some observations and suggestions. In K. Landauer and M. Brazil, eds., *Tropical Home Gardens*, pp. 193–202. Tokyo: United Nations University Press.

Stoler, A. 1975. Garden use and household consumption pattern in a Javanese village. Ph.D. dissertation. Columbia University, New York.

Stoler, A. L. 1981. Garden use and household economy in Java. In G. E. Hansen, ed., *Agricultural and Rural Development in Indonesia*, pp. 242–54. Boulder, Colorado: Westview Press.

Tennakoon, A. S. 1985. The role of minor export crops in the integrated rural development project. *Sri-Lankan Journal of Agricultural Science* 22 (1): 49–51.

Torquebiau, E. 1992. Are tropical agroforestry home gardens sustainable? *Agriculture, Ecosystems and Environment* 41 (2): 189–207.

Torres, E. B. 1988. Socioeconomic aspects of backyard gardening in the Philippines. Philippine Council for Agriculture, Forestry and Natural Resources Research and Development, Los Baños, Laguna, Philippines. Seminar Consultation Meeting Report No. 69.

Vasey, D. E. 1985. Household gardens and their niche in Port Moresby, Papua New Guinea. *Food and Nutrition Bulletin* 7 (3): 37–43.

Vasey, D. E. 1990. On estimating the net social and economic value of urban home gardens. In K. Landauer and M. Brazil, eds., *Tropical Home Gardens*, pp. 203–13. Tokyo: United Nations University Press.

Wachiira, K. K. 1987. Women's Use of Off-Farm and Boundary Lands: Agroforestry Potentials. Final Report. Nairobi, Kenya: International Council for Research in Agroforestry (ICRAF).

Wickramasinghe, A. 1991. Gender issues in the management of home gardens: A case study of Kandyan home garden in Sri Lanka. International Symposium on Man-made Community Integrated Land Use and Biodiversity in the Tropics. Academia Sinica, Xishuanbanna, China.

Wickramasinghe, A. 1992. Village Agroforestry Systems and Tree use Practices: A Case Study in Sri Lanka. Forestry/Fuelwood Research and Development (F/FRED) Project. Bangkok, Multipurpose Tree Species Network Research Series, 17.

Wickramasinghe, A. 1995. Home gardens: Habitations rescuing biodiversity. *Mpts News* 4 (2): 1–4.

Part 1

Theory and Methods

one

Microenvironments

Luigi Guarino and Michiel Hoogendijk

A Patchy Landscape

The landscape that rural communities and households manage is far from homo-geneous. It is in fact composed of a variety of different environments, both natu-ral and artificial, that are used in different ways, perhaps at different times, perhaps by different sections of the community. Many of these environmental patches are small and dispersed, contrasting strongly with their surroundings. The term "microenvironments" has been used to describe them, and examples include river banks, springs, alluvial pans, silt traps, hedges, and animal wallows (Chambers 1990). In many tropical regions home gardens are an important type of artificial microhabitat.

Microenvironments in general—and home gardens in particular—have often been neglected by agricultural research, extension, and development workers be-cause of their small size, their specialized conditions (very different from agricul-tural experimental stations), and their often ephemeral nature. Moreover, they tend to be the preserve of marginalized members of society, such as women and children, and they contain "minor" crops. However, they undoubtedly play an important role in household nutrition, health, and income. They can act as reserves and fallbacks in times of need or shortage and are often the source of medicinal plants and other high-value products.

Home gardens are also recognized as sites for innovation and experimentation and are well known for their species diversity. It has therefore been suggested that they are potentially important loci for conservation of plant genetic resources. However, while there has been much work on the species-level diversity of home gardens, less is known about the genetic diversity within the species found in home gardens, which is the focus of this chapter. Taking as a starting point the fact that home gardens are indeed microenvironments in a patchy agricultural landscape—with all that this implies in terms of population sizes, gene flow, and selection pressures—we make suggestions on what their likely contributions are to the level, structure, and temporal trend of genetic diversity and, therefore, to its conservation. The aim of the paper is not to review actual results but, rather, to suggest possible avenues of investigation based on theoretical considerations.

Home Gardens as Microenvironments

There is significant variation among home gardens in function, diversity, and composition. For example, species composition may vary along altitudinal and aridity gradients even within the same geographic region. Home gardens in remote areas tend to be made for subsistence production, whereas home gardens in areas close to major cities tend to be oriented more toward commercial production and ornamental uses. Also, species composition and diversity may change with time, both seasonally and over longer periods. However, some features of home gardens are relatively constant, indeed characteristic, and may be expected to have consequences for the genetic diversity of the species they contain:

Size: Home gardens generally occupy patches around a dwelling that are relatively small compared with the fields and orchards the family cultivates. These patches are often pieces of land that are not suitable for any other use, or that would otherwise be lost. Although (or because) high numbers of species may be present in the small space available, often only a few individuals of a species are grown. In the case of large trees and other species, only one or two individuals may be present in the typical home garden.

Isolation: Home gardens may be immediately surrounded by farmers' fields, orchards, pastures, and perhaps more or less disturbed natural vegetation, but they tend to be sharply delimited from their surroundings and from each other. Walls, hedges, fences, and other barriers commonly delimit home gardens and isolate them. In addition, home gardens are characterized by being vertically structured and closely tended (see below). This creates specialized environmental conditions within the home gardens that are sharply different from those in surrounding areas, further adding to their isolation.

Proximity: The family usually lives near, if not within, the home garden. The area can thus be closely and continuously monitored and managed, especially by women and children, making it an ideal site for observation and experimentation. Organic litter from the household is often spread on the plot in a systematic way; the litter may contain crop seeds that are thus sown unintentionally. Close attention, and organic inputs, tend to create edaphic, microclimatic, and biotic conditions that will be markedly different from conditions existing in other patches within the landscape. Also, because of its proximity, the home garden tends to be a multipurpose area, addressing many of the different needs of the household; this contributes to patchiness within the home garden itself.

Heterogeneity: Pronounced vertical structure is a defining feature of home gardens. This has important consequences. It means that overall microclimatic conditions within the home gardens may be considerably different from those that obtain in the farmer's fields and orchards, which are likely to have quite different structures. However, it also contributes to heterogeneity within the home garden itself, as does the multiuse nature of home gardens. Another contributing factor is the fact that the home garden is often managed in a patchy manner; for example, deposition of organic litter may only occur in some areas. The end result, as it were, is microenvironments existing within the microenvironment; a horizontal structure as well as a vertical structure.

Genetic Diversity in Home Gardens

To summarize, considering home gardens as microenvironments within a patchy agricultural landscape focuses attention on their relatively small size, their isolation from the surroundings and from each other, their proximity to the house, and their internal heterogeneity. What do these home-garden features mean for the level and structure of genetic diversity within a given crop and for how these are likely to change with time?

Let us take the following scenario as a model for how plant adoption into home gardens may have proceeded. At some time in the distant past, a number of different farmers in an area started to grow a particular plant in their home gardens, all of them having obtained a small quantity of seed from a single source population, say another community or a wild stand. Thereafter, they used part of the first year's harvest for next year's planting material, with the result that in the course of time some farmers lose their seed and are forced to obtain more from their neighbors or from the original source population. The result is a metapopulation, or "a set of local populations connected through migration and recolonization" (Gliddon and Gaudet 1994). The consequences that a metapopulation structure has for genetic change and conservation have been discussed by, among others, Gliddon and Gaudet (1994) and Barton and Whitlock (1997). Although developed to model the population genetics of wild plant and animal populations, the metapopulation concept has also been applied to crops—for example, by Brush (1999), who uses it in his discussion of crop genetic erosion—and it may thus be useful in looking at the population genetics of home-garden crops. Briefly, in the large, randomly mating populations described in textbooks on genetics, selection is the principal evolutionary force at work. In assemblages of small populations, on the other hand, genetic drift and the counterbalancing force of migration come into their own (Giles and Gaudet 1997).

In the first place, then, crop populations in home gardens will tend to be small to very small. They are likely to be biased samples of the population from which the material, whatever it may have been, was initially sampled and may thus be liable to genetic drift over time (Barrett and Kohn 1991). Small subpopulations, even when derived from the same source population, will, when completely isolated from each other, tend to become differentiated genetically purely by chance despite undergoing similar selection pressures. Slatkin (1994: 5) states that "Gene flow is a major component of population structure because it determines the extent to which each local population of a species is an independent evolutionary unit." He further affirms that in small populations the effects of random genetic drift become the predominant force controlling reduction in genetic variation.

The movement of material among subpopulations can retard, halt, or even reverse the loss of genetic variation—even when only a few immigrants are involved per immigration—provided that the population size is over 100 individuals and there is no selection. In the above example, one would predict that the material currently grown by farmers in different home gardens should have allele frequencies quite different from each other and from the original parental population.

Furthermore, there may well be a variety of niches present in a home garden so that a range of different selection pressures may be at play within its confines. This means that different ecotypes or landraces could be maintained within the home garden, resulting in significant differentiation among some crop populations, again if gene flow among the niches is restricted. On the other hand, when confronted with intense fine-scale mosaics, small populations with limited potential to adapt to specific environmental niches could come under intense selection for a "multipurpose genotype," showing general adaptation.

In addition to divergence among home gardens, and possibly to some extent within them, there is likely to be considerable genetic divergence between landraces in home gardens and those in other types of patches within the agricultural landscape. This is because selection pressures will be considerably different in home gardens due to the quite distinct microclimatic, edaphic, biotic, and management conditions that obtain. The particular nature of home gardens will also mean that some specific landraces will be favored for inclusion over others; for example landraces that require more careful tending, or that are used in small quantities for ritual or specialized purposes, or that produce a particularly highly valued product, or that are preferred by women as opposed to men.

Although conspecific landraces may be growing in nearby fields, and wild relatives be present in the surrounding weedy or natural vegetation, the physical and ecological isolation of home gardens may well mean that the small populations found in them are effectively cut off genetically from their neighbors. Variation in maturation time could be a particularly strong isolating mechanism. However, although movement of pollen may well be limited for many species, seed movement by people between other landscape patches and the home garden may occur. Examples of human involvement might constitute material collected from the wild, new landraces sown for testing, or varieties rescued because they have low quantities of seeds or poor quality seeds.

Based on this discussion, we have summarized the forces that lead to an increase, or a decrease, in genetic variation at the different levels within and among home gardens and with other landscape patches and have predicted the results that obtain from the interplay of these forces (Table 1.1).

Home Gardens and Conservation

How can we use these predictions to develop conservation strategies for genetic resources taking place in home gardens? On balance, within-population variation is likely to be generally low in home-garden crops because of low population sizes. This is particularly significant in view of the fact that intrapopulation variation is usually mentioned as a defining feature of landraces. It may not in fact be the case for landraces grown in home gardens. The populations may also suffer from inbreeding depression. An effective population of 500 individuals has been

Table 1.1

Changes in genetic variation and predicted results

Level of variation	Increasing forces	Decreasing forces	Predicted result
Within population variation	Gene flow among populations	Genetic drift in small populations	Low
Among population variation within a home garden	Natural and artificial selection in different niches within home gardens	Gene flow among populations in close proximity; selection for multipurpose gene type	Probably low, may be higher for inbreeders and vegetatively propagated crops
Differentiation among home gardens	Drift and distinct artificial selection pressures	Natural selection for similar environmental conditions	May be high if no seed exchange
Differentiation between home gardens and other landscape patches	Natural and artificial selection	Seed movement	Probably high

suggested as a minimum size needed to maintain genetic variation in a finite population, balancing mutation and genetic drift, and a population of fifty individuals as a minumum size to reduce inbreeding depression (Frankel and Soulé 1981). Lawrence and Marshall (1997) multiply the first figure by ten to account for the difference between actual and effective population size caused by such factors as breeding system and distribution of progeny size. Brown (1999) agrees that 5,000 individuals is a "handy yardstick" for in situ conservation. Such population sizes for most species would be unusual in home gardens.

Hauser, Damgaard, and Loeschcke (1994) suggest two management strategies that can be applied in situations where a population suffers inbreeding depression (that is, a loss in fecundity). One is to increase the effective number of individuals, for example, by ensuring as high an outcrossing rate as possible. Harvesting could be done evenly from as large a number of individuals as possible, and agronomic practices adopted that reduce the impact of inbreeding effects at particularly sensitive stages of the life cycle. A second strategy would be to introduce variation to loci fixed for deleterious alleles by controlled back-cross pollinations from a distinct donor population.

Genetic differentiation among habitat niches within home gardens may well be limited to a small number of visual traits under particularly intense selection pressure by farmers, with the genetic background of the material being generally homogeneous. To encourage or maintain differentiation among niches, it would be necessary to strengthen or adopt management practices aimed at minimizing gene flow among the ecotypes or landraces maintained in the different microenvironments within the home garden and maximizing the ability of the populations to react to selection. For example, farmers could be encouraged to keep seed lots strictly separated and to place as much distance as possible between areas within the home garden devoted to different landraces or ecotypes of the same species, perhaps even setting up physical barriers to cross-pollination. Effective populations sizes should also be increased (see above), and selection pressures intensified. Clearly, the problem will not be so acute for inbreeding species or, indeed, for vegetatively propagated crops.

It follows from the prediction of significant genetic divergence among home gardens that a program to conserve genetic variation of the various species must include a number of home gardens. Albeit in the context of sampling for ex situ conservation, Brown and Marshall (1995) propose 50 sites per ecoregion as a benchmark. In contrast, Lawrence and Marshall (1977) suggest that an effective conservation program could be designed based on just one subpopulations because most variation in cross-pollinating crops occurs within, rather than among, subpopulations. Lawrence and Marshall add that the case for divergence is thus not as strong as it may at first seem. However, when dealing with the kind of small populations found in home gardens, this objection, which has in any case been strongly questioned by Brown (1999), does not seem to be relevant.

Normally, one would propose that multiple sites for conservation should be in as many different agroecological zones as possible (Brown and Marshall 1995). It is by no means clear, however, that this proposition is appropriate for home gardens. A case could be made that two home gardens in two distinct climatic areas might be considerably more similar to each other in terms of their microenvironment than two fields in the same two different climatic areas. This is because the structure of the home garden provides a buffering effect and because substantial levels of organic inputs are used. An important question for genetic-resource conservation is thus to what extent does material from home gardens in distinct agroecological zones exhibit divergence in climatic adaptation.

The key variable here is seed movement. Even a low migration rate—one or two seeds per generation—between home gardens is theoretically sufficient to reduce genetic divergence. Thus, the amount of seed exchange would need to be investigated when developing a conservation strategy based on home gardens. It may well be the case that more genetic divergence is present between two geographically adjacent home gardens whose owners do not participate in seed exchanges than between two home gardens located in distinct agroecological zones whose owners regularly exchange planting material because they are related or because they form part of the same cultural group or trading network. Social, economic, and cultural "nearness" may be more important than macroenvironmental similarity in determining genetic divergence of populations among home gardens and, therefore, in choosing home gardens to be included in conservation efforts.

Finally, the prediction that there should be significant genetic divergence between home gardens on the one hand, and other landscape patches on the other hand, implies that, for species found in both home gardens and other landscape patches, an effective conservation strategy cannot consider home gardens only or ignore them altogether. The extent to which home gardens will have an important role to play depends on the proportion of the total genetic diversity that is found *only* in them. This is likely to differ markedly among species. Native horticultural crops for which seed of improved varieties is readily available may provide a good example of cases where large fields of homogeneous improved varieties are grown for commercial purposes. Small patches of relatively diverse landraces grown in home gardens for household consumption may provide instances where home gardens would be critical for conservation of genetic diversity. A somewhat different situation is illustrated by native fruit trees or medicinal plants that are present in large populations in the surrounding natural vegetation, but in much smaller quantities in home gardens. Here, it is the genetic variation found in the home garden that is a subset of that found in another landscape patch. Nevertheless, home gardens could again be a significant component of an overall conservation strategy if the material they harbor is in some way "elite," that is, specifically selected for particular, especially prized characteristics.

For crops that are currently found only in home gardens, the extent to which genetic differentiation occurs between home gardens and other landscape patches obviously does not arise. What should be considered here, however, is whether their introduction to other landscape patches may be advantageous, or indeed necessary, if they are to be conserved. It may well be the case that genetic improvement and larger-scale commercial production of some landraces may offer a useful strategy for conserving at least a portion of the genetic diversity found in home gardens. Similarly, home gardens may have a role to play even for crops that are not currently grown there. The introduction of some species into home gardens may strengthen their conservation, for example, by facilitating participatory breeding under conditions of close scrutiny and continuous monitoring. Clearly, if a crop is to be introduced into the home garden, care should be taken to circumvent the problems associated with small population sizes discussed above and to guard against the possibility of displacement of home-garden species by the new introduction.

It should be emphasized in closing that the genetic diversity predictions outlined in this chapter are just that, predictions based on a particular model of crop metapopulations inhabiting home gardens as microenvironments in a patchy landscape. The conclusions regarding conservation strategies that have been drawn are therefore contingent on the predictions being accurate. The first step to be taken must therefore be test these predictions by carrying out genetic diversity studies using both neutral markers (whose distribution will be affected by random drift and migration) and adaptive traits (depending on migration and selection) (Barton and Whitlock 1997).

Acknowledgments

Many thanks to David Williams and Tony Brown for their comments and advice.

References

Barrett, S. C., and J. R. Kohn. 1991. Genetic and evolutionary consequences of small population size in plants: Implications for conservation. In D. A. Falk and K. E. Holsinger, eds., *Genetics and Conservation of Rare Plants*, pp. 3–30. New York: Oxford University Press.

Barton, N. H., and M. C. Whitlock. 1997. The evolution of metapopulations. In I. Hanski and M. E. Gilpin, eds., *Metapopulation Biology: Ecology, Genetics and Evolution*, pp. 183–210. San Diego: Academic Press.

Brown, A. H. D. 1999. The genetic structure of crop landraces and the challenge to conserve them *in situ* on farms. In S. B. Brush, ed., *Genes in the Field: On Farm Conservation of Crop Diversity*, pp. 29–48. Boca Raton, Florida: Lewis Publishers; Ottawa: International Development Research Centre (IDRC), and Rome: International Plant Genetic Resources Institute (IPGRI).

Brown, A. H. D., and D. R. Marshall. 1995. A basic sampling strategy: Theory and practice. In L. Guarino, V. Ramanatha Rao, and R. Reid, eds., *Collecting Plant Genetic Diversity: Technical Guidelines*, pp. 75–91. Wellesbourne: Commonwealth Agricultural Bureau.

Brush, S. B. 1999. Genetic erosion of crop populations in centres of diversity: A revision. In J. Serwinski and I. Faberova, eds., *Proceedings of the Technical Meeting on the Methodology of the FAO World Information and Early Warning System on Plant Genetic Resources*, pp. 34–44. 21–23 June 1999. Prague: Research Institute of Crop Production, and Rome: Food and Agricultural Organization of the United Nations (FAO).

Chambers, R. 1990. *Microenvironments Unobserved*. Gatekeeper Series No. 22. London: International Institute for Environment and Development (IIED).

Frankel, O. H., and M. E. Soulé. 1981. *Conservation and Evolution*. Cambridge and New York: Cambridge University Press.

Giles, B. E., and J. Gaudet. 1997. A case study of genetic structure in a plant metapopulation. In I. Hanski and M. E. Gilpin, eds., *Metapopulation Biology: Ecology, Genetics, and Evolution*, pp. 429–54. San Diego: Academic Press.

Gliddon, C., and J. Gaudet. 1994. The genetic structure of metapopulations and conservation biology. In V. Loeschcke, J. Tomiuk, and S. K. Jain, eds., *Conservation Genetics*, pp. 108–14. Basel: Birkhäuser Verlag.

Hauser, T. P., C. Damgaard, and V. Loeschcke. 1994. Effects of inbreeding in small plant populations: Expectations and implications for conservation. In V. Loeschcke, J. Tomiuk, and S. K. Jain, eds., *Conservation Genetics*, pp. 115–29. Basel: Birkhäuser Verlag.

Lawrence, M. J., and D. F. Marshall. 1997. Plant population genetics. In N. Maxted, B. V. Ford-Lloyd, and J. G. Hawkes, eds., *Plant Conservation: The In Situ Approach*, pp. 99–113. London and New York: Chapman and Hall.

Slatkin, M. 1994. Gene flow and population structure. In L. A. Real, ed., *Ecological Genetics*, pp. 3–17. Princeton: Princeton University Press.

two

Toward an Analysis of Home-Garden Cultures

On the Use of Sociocultural Variables in Home Garden Studies

Jürg Schneider

Culture and the Specificity of Plant Use

Knowledge is, to a substantial degree, culturally transmitted, and different cultures vary widely in their knowledge of plants and in the uses they make of plant species and varieties. Thus, culture is a basic determinant of plant use or, to put it differently, every use has a cultural component. Much as in ethnobiological research, today one has to take an approach in which cultural factors are considered crucial to the differentiated reproduction of knowledge.[1]

Culture can be seen as a system of preferences and prohibitions, priorities and neglect. The influence of such rules and institutions is evident in any inventory of plants used by a particular culture. It is a process affecting decisions of individual cultivators through—to name a few social factors—status concerns, categories of acceptable vs. unacceptable food, age concerns, aesthetic preferences, among many others. Thus the category "use" is a complex one having a number of cultural connotations.

Unfortunately, the cultural domain is often associated with a residual sphere of tradition and ritual that is seen as essentially stable. Such views strongly contrast with interpretive notions of "culture" as the complex symbolic dimension of human behavior in all spheres of social life, including the economic and technical (Barnard and Spencer 1996). Culture-as-meaning has to be seen as a pervasive aspect of society, yet as an inherently unstable one because in the very process of cultural learning, political contestation and interpretation continually change cultural meanings.

Which Notion of "Culture" Is Appropriate to Home-Garden Studies?

Students of tropical home gardens have long been aware that cultural factors play a determining role in the structure and function of these agroecosystems. Christanty (1990: 9), for example, affirms that "personal preferences and attitudes, socioeconomic status, and culture are the main determinant factors for home garden appearance, structure, and function." Among the factors mentioned by Christanty (1990), socioeconomic status seems best represented in the body of research done on home gardens, and culture least. Sociocultural aspects have not been in the forefront of home-garden studies because a structural and functional approach has dominated the majority of studies carried out in the 1980s, as aptly summarized in a book edited by Landauer and Brazil (1990).

In home-garden studies, the culture concept is used in conjunction, and often interchangeably with, ethnic affiliation. In West Java, for example (Abdoellah and Isnawan 1980; Ahmad, Martadihardj, and Suharto 1980), the ethnic categories "Sundanese" and "Javanese" are represented as coterminous with two distinct cultures. Particular species growing in home gardens are often considered as markers of ethnic or cultural identity. In the same village, the Sundanese grow sweet potato as a tuber crop, whereas the Javanese prefer cassava (Abdoellah and Isnawan 1980: 451). Evidence from the same study shows both structural similarities—for example, the dominance of food plants in the home-garden system—and differences, and yet the cultural dynamics that lie behind these phenomena have been largely ignored.

The historical studies conducted by the Dutch scholar G. J. A. Terra (1932, 1953; Ochse and Terra 1934) on the development of home gardens in Java represent an exception to this situation. Terra postulated a diffusion of home gardens (or Indonesian *pekarangan*) from Central to West Java—inhabited by a majority of ethnically distinct Sundanese—starting in the late eighteenth century. His work represents an early attempt to relate the development of tropical home gardens to some sort of social and cultural dynamics. Drawing from early colonial sources, Terra did an analysis of traditional settlement structures in order to demonstrate that home gardens in West Java are a relatively recent phenomenon. The traditional village layout in the Sundanese settlement area lacked space for home gardens. As West Java underwent a major transition toward a more intensive type of agriculture beginning in the mid-eighteenth century, the Sundanese began establishing home gardens by building a house on a plot of land planted with diverse trees and used as an orchard. Thus, the high diversity and the large size of Sundanese home gardens—compared with the Javanese home garden—can be explained on the basis of their recent genesis from managed agroforestry.

In his later articles, Terra tried to correlate the presence of home gardens with other characteristics of the agricultural and social systems of which they were part; for example, to matrilineal and patrilineal types of descent or to the practice of cattle-raising and herding (Terra 1952/53). Informed as they were by cultural-diffusionist concepts, his theories have become largely obsolete: cultures are treated as sets of cultural elements within distinct areas, rather than as cultural processes resulting from the management practices and representations of home-garden cultivators. For example, he considered the coastal Malays to be "jacks of all trades" without a specific cultural inheritance (Terra 1952/53: 314). Incidentally, they were also lacking a distinctive home-garden culture. Populations in ethnically mixed areas suffered a similar theoretical fate. In the fruit-growing areas south of Jakarta, where ethnically mixed populations live, Terra notes that farmers take up "any paying proposition" (1953: 181), leading to an early flourishing of fruit orchards for commercial production. He excluded such commercial developments from his analysis of home gardens because these people lacked a "resilient agricultural tradition"; thus, he missed the opportunity to study a dynamic blend of various cultural traditions.

However, Terra's writings still convey to the contemporary reader a sense of the richness and variation of home gardens in Southeast Asian cultures by regarding them as manifestations of cultural history and indicators of agricultural development. Terra can thus be considered the founding father of a prolific research tradition focused on the Javanese home-garden systems, a tradition that was continued by Soemarwoto and his colleagues (Soemarwoto 1985; Soemarwoto et al. 1975; Soemarwoto and Conway 1991) and by other ecologists based in Bandung (West Java). This group of researchers has made the home-garden system one of the best-documented complexes on a global scale.

Ethnicity and Variation in Home-Garden Studies

The concept of ethnically bounded home-garden systems is part of the work of the new group of researchers that followed in Terra's footsteps. Using a standard definition, we can define an ethnic community as a group of people whose members share a common name, a particular territory, and numerous elements of culture. They possess a myth of common origin and partake of the same historical memory, which bestows upon them a feeling of solidarity (Sokolovskii and Tishkov 1996).

A comparison of home gardens tended by Javanese peoples with those tended by Sundanese farmers has, as we have mentioned, been used to show that ethnic affiliation can be correlated with differences in home-garden crops (Abdoellah and Isnawan 1980; Christanty et al. 1986: 142). Thus, a village located in the transitional zone between West Java and Central Java revealed a number of differences between its Sundanese and Javanese inhabitants. Javanese home gardens had more food and medicinal plants; Sundanese had relatively more vegetables and ornamentals. Javanese cultivators selected cassava and ganyong (*Canna edulis*) as food plants, whereas Sundanese went for sweet potato (Abdoellah and Isnawan 1980: 448). Varying cultural preference may also explain the greater quantity of vegetables in Sundanese gardens. In addition, one of the associations identifying a home garden as Sundanese, as opposed to Javanese, is the combined occurrence of locus bean (*Parkia speciosa*), Rambutan (*Nephelium lappaceum*), guava, yam (*Dioscorea hispida*), and elephant yam (*Amorphophallus campanulatus;* Christanty et al. 1986: 149).

An empirical survey of Javanese and Sundanese home gardens demonstrated quite clearly, however, that the structure and composition of ethnic home-garden types are influenced by other types of home-garden systems. Among the two ethnic groups, the basic structure and function of their home garden was similar. No marked differences occurred, either in the number of species or in the number of plants by functional groups. Differences were usually found more at the species level than at the aggregate level. Should these differences between Javanese and Sundanese home gardens be explained globally, as a result of Javanese culture having "influenced" the structure of the Sundanese home garden, as Abdoellah and Isnawan (1980: 447) do? Here, a dynamic cultural process is invoked, but the cultural variable remains on a very abstract level. Why should the Javanese home-garden type affect the Sundanese one, but not vice versa? If these cultural models indeed affect each other, this should appear in the daily interactions of the village population. Management practices, exchange of planting material, and other activities would potentially demonstrate how and why such processes take place. The complex notion of "culture" could then be more easily disaggregated into processes of knowledge transfer, status considerations, networks for seed exchange, and so on.

Despite the association of particular home-garden types with specific ethnic groups, the ethnic factor should be used with caution to explain these configurations. Some points need to be emphasized, to avoid pitfalls in using the concept of ethnicity. First, ethnic affiliation is not a fixed entity but has to be seen from a constructivist perspective: it is relational, dependent on the self-identification of other ethnic groups, subject to reinterpretations, and negotiable. Therefore it is, as Barth (1969) has called it, an "inter-group boundary mechanism" with a situational logic. The assumption, often implicit, that an ethnic group has a fixed structure of home gardens can thus be highly misleading. Second, the strategies of cultivators change independently of the home-garden type prevalent in their ethnic community. In the case of home gardens in West Java, shifts in orientation by the cultivators transformed the structure into one with fewer trees and more commercially important species (Michon and Mary 1990). The reasons for this transformation were not cultural influences but economic opportunities. Finally, home gardens are ranked in accordance with the dominant or subordinate status of particular groups within a nation-state. Some features of a "proper" home garden following the Javanese model have been made part of a recommended and sometimes mandated national Indonesian culture.[2] State interference in the home-garden space is a problem that has not been studied so far. Anderson (1980: 444) brought up the hypothesis that the relative absence of interference or intervention from governments and landlords in home-garden activities is a reason for farmers to "develop a home garden with more vigour than they do other cropping systems." If the producer can keep the surplus resulting from intensified cultivation, he or she will put more effort into the home garden. In Indonesia, under Dutch colonial rule, home-garden cultivation (the Dutch term was *erfculteur*) was not free from state interference. Cultivation of coffee and tea as well as other subsistence crops was sometimes mandated in home gardens.

Home Gardens as Cultural Models

Addressing the issue of home gardens in the development processes, Cleveland and Soleri (1987: 260) state that: "Gardens in a given community . . . will also vary in regard to the influence of cultural models. It is even possible to find two quite different gardens within the same household, one traditional, and one based on an imported model." Thus, different models may exist side by side, influencing or replacing each other. Even so, one can observe a certain resilience or persistence of models actualized in particular home-garden systems. This is because home gardens represent an idealized structure, valued and perpetuated through time by people, often in the face of adverse economic and political conditions.

Cultural models are reflected in the specific layout of home gardens and in the kinds of plants and plant associations they contain. With respect to the spatial arrangement of home gardens in West Java, for example, we find that a home garden is divided into several named parts having their respective, culturally ac-knowledged functions (Ahmad, Martadihardj, and Suharto 1980: 455–56). There is a place in front of the house (Sundanese: *buruan*) that is not planted; it is kept clean and used as a space for social encounters and for agricultural tasks such as a drying paddy. The backyard (*pungkur*) is divided into a corner for garbage disposal and an orchard (*kebon*) that conforms best to the description of the home garden provided by Soemarwoto (Ahmad, Martadihardj, and Suharto 1980: 455–56). It displays a layered structure and contains a rich diversity of species that fulfill mul-tiple functions for its users. Finally, a part at the right side of the house (*pipir*) is used for storing firewood and agricultural tools.

Home Gardens and Social Status

"Wherever the dominant form of land tenure is tenancy, the flimsy shack of the tenant has no mixed fruit and vegetable garden around it, for his status is much too uncertain" (Pelzer 1945: 45). Two aspects of social status figure prominently in the literature on home gardens in Java and other parts of Southeast Asia. First, the ownership of a home garden marks the contrast between landowner vs. ten-ant, as expressed in Pelzer's quote. Second, and more recent, the introduction of an increasing number of ornamentals is an indication of growing prosperity. In the traditional rural context, cultivating a home garden indicates that the owner has the status of independent farmer or landowner. It sets him apart from the very poor, the tenants who, because of their insecure status, grow a few annual crops at most. Those who do not even have a pekarangan are still lower in social status; they lack food security and depend for their very survival on permission from landlords to use a small parcel of land. Logically, tenants are often allowed to grow annuals, but no tree crops (Ahmad, Martadihardj, and Suharto 1980: 455).

Within the home garden–owning group, plant composition may be indicative of wealth differences. The overall size of cultivated land at the disposition of a household may influence the plant composition of the home garden. For a central

Javanese village, Stoler (1981) found that a comparatively small amount of root and tuber crops—food for the poor in times of crisis—indicated that the household had enough land for cultivation of the more prestigious staple, namely, rice.

The distinctive feature of home gardens bearing on the status of individuals or families is the presence of ornamentals. This is the case both in rural and urban areas. Abdoellah and Isnawan (1980: 448) found that the number of ornamental plants in Bantar Kalong, West Java, was correlated with the ownership of better houses;[3] the wealthier strata of this village had significantly more ornamental plants. In the big cities, the middle class uses the home garden mainly as a recreational space; some fruit trees may be planted but ornamentals dominate. A market for ornamental plants is well developed and offers a wide range of products, including expensive palm species and orchids.

The transformation of the home garden from a messy but productive subsistence plot to a tidy but largely unproductive one appeals to a set of aesthetic concerns; it is part of the distinctions made between lower and middle classes. Where ornamentals are becoming a focus of home-garden management, they make a statement: one does not need to grow crops for home consumption, for one can afford to buy all necessary food in the market. Planting a modern urban home garden not only requires an investment, but also space, not often available in the dense settlements of the lower classes.

Households, Gender, and Home Gardens

Raffles (1988 [1817]: 81–82), in his famous *History of Java*, already articulated the generic link that exists between household, village, and home garden: "In the first establishment . . . of . . . new ground, the intended settlers take care to provide themselves with sufficient garden ground round their huts for stock and to supply the ordinary wants of their families. . . . The spot surrounding his simple habitation the cottager considers his patrimony and cultivates with peculiar care. He labors to plant and rear in it those vegetables that may be most useful for his family and those shrubs and trees which at once yield him their fruit and shade." Farming households establish their home garden as a place of first and last resort, and they do this in dense clusters of farmhouses—forming those green, tree-rich islands amidst open fields that are so typical of the traditional agricultural landscape of Java.

The concept of household has been the focal point in home-garden research ever since the beginning of research on *pekarangan* in Indonesia in the 1930s. However, many gaps remain with regard to the sociocultural analysis of household dynamics. What are the strategies based on household internal differentiation in terms of composition, kin and age structure, division of tasks, and wealth? There is great variability between households. The age of household head, for example, is often correlated with species diversity: the younger the household, the lower diversity in its home garden. This is probably best explained by the domestic cycle, whereby home gardens are established by young couples and grow in diversity throughout the cycle of the domestic unit. A parallel phenomenon is migration: in communities made up of recent migrants, home gardens also tend to have less species diversity (Gessler and Hodel 1997: 81).

Gender is another aspect of household differentiation bearing on home-garden operations and deserving further study. There has been a perception in the earlier literature that home gardens were mostly the domain of women. Most of this literature considers home gardens generally; it does not attempt to disaggregate tasks by crops and steps in the cultivation cycle. Not surprisingly, a review of pertinent case studies reveals a more complex pattern, and shows the need for more detailed research (Gessler, Hodel, and Eyzaguirre 1996: 7–9).

In all home-garden systems, the selection of species, their use, and crop management tactics are structured by gender differences, thus contributing to the production of differentiated knowledge. In Vietnamese home gardens, for example, women are not the only caretakers of home gardens. Rather, home gardens are managed jointly by households. Men invest even more labor in home-garden cultivation than women do, and they make most of the decisions about what to plant. This seems to be the dominant pattern, except for communities with a matrilineal kinship structure, where women manage home gardens (Gessler and Hodel 1997: 82). In general, root and tuber crops are the only plant groups that fall under women's supervision; other plant groups are not associated with a specific gender. For West Java, certain groups of plants (commercial crops, fruit trees, coconuts) are managed by men, while other groups (tubers, spices, vegetables, ornamentals) are managed by women (Ahmad, Martadihardj, and Suharto 1980: 456, based on the analysis of a data set of forty-one households in one village). However, this is a tendency, not an exclusive right. Growing specific home-garden species—from seed provision till harvesting—is not the prerogative of either gender.[4]

Gender-related differences are also manifest in the differentiation of management tasks, such as women doing seed production of most crops and men bringing the produce to market for sale. Such divisions of tasks can translate into specialized knowledge and different folk names for one and the same species. In one household in a Vietnamese village (Gessler and Hodel 1997: 55), for example, women were responsible for planting and harvesting sweet potato in the home garden. Having first-hand experience with plant parts buried in the soil, women used variety names based on root characteristics. Men mostly used variety names based on the shape of the leaves.

As these examples show, it is difficult to make any a priori generalizations on gender roles in home-garden management. "The gender division of resources, knowledge, work and products may reflect conflict, complementarity or coincidence of men's and women's interest in land use systems" (Gessler, Hodel, and Eyzaguirre 1996: 9). In general, most analyses should be based on direct observations and records of day-to-day operations rather than on normative statements by informants on which gender does what.

Knowledge and Home Garden Development

Knowledge about plant species and their cultivation in a home garden are unevenly distributed because the systems are diversified and tasks among the members of a group or society are differentiated. Among a group of individuals involved in home-garden cultivation, both gaps and continuities in knowledge are likely to occur. Shared knowledge is built up permanently within and between social groups—household, family, kin—and networks. Nevertheless, the character of these groups, and their role in the transmission of knowledge, has to be determined by empirical research. Discontinuities in the sharing of knowledge are likely to emerge at critical social interfaces" (for a theoretical foundation for the concept of "social interface," see Long 1992).

Ethnic or institutional boundaries, for example, constitute social interfaces and represent potentially important loci where the process of evaluation and transmission of knowledge can be studied. In the commune of Dran in Vietnam, for instance, shifting cultivators from various ethnic groups are initiating home gardens, adopting established practices from the ethnic Kinh living in the same community (Gessler and Hodel 1997: 15). The knowledge manifest in home-garden cultures can certainly spread or be applied in new social and economic contexts.

But how is the knowledge itself transformed in these processes of change? Various hypotheses have been proposed in the literature as preliminary answers to this question. The first one could be called the hypothesis of vanishing knowledge. Commenting on the recent development of the Sundanese home gardens, Soemarwoto expresses skepticism with regard to the resilience of this knowledge, which to him represents ecological wisdom[5] gained through generations of experience. He asks, how conscious are people who have acquired it? "Do they cherish it, so that they can defend it in times of change or stress?" (Soemarwoto 1985: 211). His fear is that people are not fully conscious of the knowledge represented in their home-garden practices. A rapid process of commercialization and urbanization would press them to abandon most of its ecologically sound features. Studies by Soemarwoto (1985) and Michon and Mary (1990) in the greater Jakarta area indeed seem to indicate that the greater the proximity to urban centers, the more dominant are different commercial or aesthetic orientations and the more endangered are ecologically sound home-garden features such as the complex layered structure and the high index of species diversity.

Soemarwoto (1985: 215–16) points to a cultural and economic transformation changing the individual and his values. Michon and Mary's (1990) hypothesis, on the other hand, offers an alternative interpretation based on adaptation. While admitting that home gardens play "a fundamental role in the adaptation of the household economy to modern agricultural markets," they conclude on a more positive note. Adaptation of home gardens to market-oriented conditions does not assume uniformity; different types of crop associations and different conversion strategies are developed that appear to be viable economically as well as ecologically (Michon and Mary 1990: 185).

In most of their manifestations, home gardens respond to aesthetic concerns, but not only by the presence of ornamental plants. Subsistence gardeners in New Guinea have explicit aesthetic concerns even though their garden cultivated with the staple sweet potato could be considered an entirely utilitarian venture. In planting sweet potatoes they mix varieties in such a way as to combine leaves with different shades of color in a kind of checkerboard pattern, juxtaposing purple and green leaves or segmented leaves with round leaves (Kocher Schmid 1996: 158). Thus, in subsistence agriculture—and this should apply to home gardens as well—aesthetic considerations are expressed in, and incorporated within, the agricultural system. Functional and aesthetic concerns are not separate, and the emergence of a dominantly ornamental garden is a latter-day phenomenon.[6]

Conclusion: A Comment on Various Approaches

The aim of this discussion of Indonesian home gardens has been to show that sociocultural factors influence the layout and composition of home gardens. They have been identified according to various perspectives and from different theoretical approaches. At least three perspectives predominate. The first focuses on the species level and tries to identify cultural knowledge associated with particular species found in home gardens. This, of course, is a basic ethnobotanical procedure; it builds upon the identification of folk varieties and species, with their associated knowledge. At the same time, the focus on species allows one to gather folk knowledge that often reveals "sociocultural preferences." The second perspective focuses on the home garden as an agroecosystem, aiming at a functional understanding of the home garden's species inventory. The interest here is on: (i) establishing a classification of functions (economic, ornamental, food, fodder, medicinal, etc.), (ii) aggregating species into groups having a functional relevance, and (iii) associating particular functional groups with their sociocultural functions (e.g., ornamental plants with a status function). I have criticized this last step because it may lead to a residual use of "cultural use," for example, only for ritual. Moreover, the categories used to distinguish different functions may not be perceived by, or appear important to, the cultivators themselves. A third perspective on home-gardens analysis centers on macrolevel developments. It focuses on broad categories of home-garden systems associated with ethnic groups or geographical regions and compares their characteristics as a result of processes of historical and cross-cultural diffusion, agrarian intensification, and urbanization. Terra's 1953 theory on mixed gardening in Java can be seen in this context; it is an example of a speculative extrapolation from local-level data to a generalized and essentialized "culture," located beyond the home garden and its culturally informed reality.

Over time, a wealth of data coming from many detailed empirical cases studies and a number of generalizations with regard to the functional aspects of home-garden systems have come to fruition following the first and second perspective. The most important units of analysis have been the home gardens themselves, groups of related households, and whole villages. These units are empirically studied using survey, sampling, and case-study methods. Characteristic of this literature are very short sections on method, giving the impression that these are standard procedures not requiring further explanation or reflection. A number of concluding points can be made on this state of affairs. First, in order to interpret correctly empirical data pertaining to the sociocultural sphere, a more theoretical reflection and more extensive discussion of methodological issues are required. How have individual viewpoints or cultural knowledge been elicited? How have interviews been conducted? Has the differentiation of knowledge been adequately reflected in the method? The use of qualitative and interpretive methods has been fairly weak. Yet qualitative methods will make an essential contribution to revealing cultural processes, particularly in the analysis of the symbolic realm, where meanings and interpretations of cultural concepts inform home-gardeners' practices.

Methodological awareness also helps to avoid common pitfalls in analysis. A frequent shortcoming is the use of abstract concepts for local-level studies without attempting to contextualize them in the local universe of meaning. If concepts such as "household" or "status" are to be used in research, they need to be related to corresponding local categories and meanings. Equivalent or closely corresponding local terms of common usage need to be identified for research purposes. The use of important terms in the social sciences—such as, again, "household"—needs to be established on the basis of local-level phenomena.

For the task ahead it is perhaps important to remind us of Soemarwoto's words (1985): Do home gardeners "cherish" the gardens they have inherited or established, and what is their home-garden knowledge and consciousness in a dynamic environment? If a thorough analysis of the significance of cultural processes can be achieved, this will be significant for home-garden development in the context of issues of food security, nutrition, and genetic conservation.

Notes

1. Home gardens produce some paraphernalia for ritual activities that relate to the life cycle or to healing ceremonies. However, home gardens are much less of an arena for ritual activity. Suggesting an explanation for this phenomenon, Weinstock (1986: 181) emphasizes the low risk associated with home-garden production, which is usually under strong human control and thus necessitates less ritual assistance. The lesser extent to which ritual activity takes place in home gardens compared with open fields could then be interpreted as a consequence of their stability and variability. By contrast, for traditional wet rice agriculture a sequence of rituals is performed to accompany the cultivation cycle and to ensure a bountiful harvest. They underscore the synchronic and communal character of traditional rice production. It is hard to imagine a similar shared ritual system for the crops grown in home gardens, given their diversity and the dischronous nature of cultivation.

2. In a short recollection from fieldwork, I remember passing by with a group of researchers through a village in remote Bengkulu (Southern Sumatra) in 1989. We noticed that the villagers were reluctantly carrying out an instruction by the administration to surround every house compound with a bamboo fence, not a practice in this village. The order was resented because it was based on the pekarangan model of the Javanese who were at the center of state power. This small incident clearly demonstrates that home-garden blueprints can be normative models tied to particular political or development projects.

3. The term used is "permanent," which in the Indonesian context refers to the use of concrete for part or the whole of the building. "Nonpermanent" houses are built with bamboo, wood, or other traditional materials.

4. A much stricter division of crops by gender is found, for example, among the Wola of highland New Guinea (Sillitoe 1983: 172–87).

5. The manifestations of this ecological wisdom are separate from the sustainability of the system; it functions as an indicator of the whole agricultural system. The group of indicator plants also deserves special mention because it is often forgotten. These indicator plants are often used to identify the appropriate times for planting in the wetland or in other parts of the agricultural system.

6. The aesthetic preferences of the Yopno of New Guinea reflect principles that occur in the forest. Thus, the beautiful is partly expressed as an emulation of the forest (and in this sense, it could also be a source of ecological sound practice). In this context, Kocher Schmid (1996) refers to an idea of Gregory Bateson (1979: 127), who wrote with regard to aesthetic perception: "Is our reason for admiring a daisy the fact that it shows—in its form, in its growth, in its colouring, and in its death—the symptoms of being alive? Our appreciation for it is to that extent an appreciation of its similarity to ourselves." Or, as Bateson also called it, an appreciation of "a pattern which connects."

References

Abdoellah, O. S. and H. H. Isnawan. 1980. Effect of culture on home-garden structure. In J. I. Furtado, ed., *Tropical Ecology and Development: Proceedings of the Vth International Symposium of Tropical Ecology*, pp. 447–51. Kuala Lumpur, 16–21 April 1979. Kuala Lumpur: International Society of Tropical Ecology.

Ahmad, H., A. Martadihardj, and Suharto. 1980. Social and cultural aspects of home gardens. In J. I. Furtado, ed., *Tropical Ecology and Development: Proceedings of the Vth International Symposium of Tropical Ecology*, pp. 453–57. Kuala Lumpur, 16–21 April 1979. Kuala Lumpur: International Society of Tropical Ecology.

Anderson, J. N. 1980. Traditional home gardens in Southeast Asia: A prolegomenon for second generation research. In J. I. Furtado, ed., *Tropical Ecology and Development: Proceedings of the Vth International Symposium of Tropical Ecology*, pp. 441–46. Kuala Lumpur, 16–21 April 1979. Kuala Lumpur: International Society of Tropical Ecology.

Barnard, A., and J. Spencer, eds. 1996. *Encyclopedia of Social and Cultural Anthropology*. New York: Routledge.

Barth, F. 1969. *Ethnic Groups and Boundaries: The Social Organisation of Cultural Difference*. Bergen: Universitetsforlaget, and London and New York: Allen and Unwin.

Bateson, G. 1979. *Mind and Nature: A Necessary Unity*. New York: Dutton.

Christanty, L. 1990. Home gardens in tropical Asia, with special reference to Indonesia. In K. Landauer and M. Brazil, eds., *Tropical Home Gardens: Selected Papers from an International Workshop Held at the Institute of Ecology, Padjadjaran University*, pp. 9–20. Bandung, Indonesia, December 1985. Tokyo: United Nations University Press.

Christanty, L., O. S. Abdoellah, G. G. Marten, and J. Iskandar. 1986. Traditional agroforestry in West-Java: The pekarangan (homegarden) and kebun-talun (annual-perennial-rotation) cropping systems. In G. G. Marten, ed., *Traditional Agriculture in Southeast Asia: A Human Ecology Perspectiva*, pp. 132–58. Boulder, Colorado: Westview Press.

Cleveland, D. A., and D. Soleri. 1987. Household gardens as a development strategy. *Human Organization* 46 (3): 259–70.

Gessler, M., and U. Hodel. 1997. *In Situ Conservation of Plant Genetic Resources in Home Gardens of Southern Vietnam: A Report on Home Garden Surveys Undertaken in Six Different Sites in the South of Vietnam.* Serdang, Malaysia: International Plant Genetic Resources Institute, Asia, Pacific, Oceania (IPGRI APO).

Gessler, M., U. Hodel, and P. Eyzaguirre. 1996. *Home Gardens and Agrobiodiversity: Current State of Knowledge with Reference to Relevant Literature.* Working Paper. Kuala Lumpur: International Plant Genetic Resources Institute, Asia, Pacific, Oceania (IPGRI APO).

Kocher Schmid, C. 1996. Ästhetische Präferenzen im Umgang mit Pflanzen. In W. Lesch, ed., *Naturbilder: Ökologische Kommunikation Zwischen Ästhetik und Moral,* pp. 149–74. Basel, Boston, Berlin: Birkhäuser.

Landauer, K., and M. Brazil, eds. 1990. *Tropical Home Gardens: Selected Papers from an International Workshop Held at the Institute of Ecology, Padjadjaran University.* Bandung, Indonesia, 2–9 December 1985. Tokyo: United Nations University Press.

Long, N., ed. 1992. *Encounters at the Interface: A Perspective on Social Discontinuities in Rural Development.* Wageningen, The Netherlands: Pudoc.

Michon, G., and F. Mary. 1990. Transforming traditional home gardens and related systems in West Java (Bogor) and West Sumatra (Maninjau). In K. Landauer and M. Brazil, eds., *Tropical Home Gardens: Selected Papers from an International Workshop Held at the Institute of Ecology, Padjadjaran University,* pp. 169–85. Bandung, Indonesia, 2–9 December 1985. Tokyo: United Nations University.

Ochse, J. J., and G. J. A. Terra. 1934. *Geld en Producten-Huishouding, Volks-Voeding en Gezondheid in Koetowinangoen.* Buitenzorg: Departemen van Economische Zaken, Archipel Drukeriij.

Pelzer, K. J. 1945. *Pioneer Settlement in the Asiatic Tropics: Studies in Land Utilization and AgriculturalColonization in Southeastern Asia.* New York: American Geographical Society.

Raffles, T. S. 1988. *The History of Java.* Complete Text with an Introduction by John Bastin. Singapore: Oxford University Press.

Sillitoe, P. 1983. *Roots of the Earth: Crops in the Highlands of Papua New Guinea.* Manchester: Manchester University Press.

Soemarwoto, O. 1985. Constancy and change in agroecosystems. In K. L. Hutterer, A. T. Rambo, and G. Lovelace, eds., *Cultural Values and Human Ecology in Southeast Asia,* pp. 205–18. Michigan papers on South and Southeast Asia 27. Ann Arbor: University of Michigan, Center for South and Southeast Asian Studies.

Soemarwoto, O., and G. Conway. 1991. The Javanese home garden. *Journal for Farming Systems Research and Extension* 2 (3): 96–117.

Soemarwoto, O., I. Somearwoto, Karyono, E. M. Soekartadiredja, and A. Ramlan. 1975. The Javanese homegarden as an integrated ecosystem. In *Science for Better Environment,* pp. 193–97. Proceedings of the International Congress on the Human Environment. Tokyo: Asahi Evening News.

Sokolovskii, S., and V. Tishkov. 1996. Ethnicity. In A. Barnard and J. Spencer, eds., *Encyclopedia of Social and Cultural Anthropology*, pp. 190–92. London and New York: Routledge.

Stoler, A. 1981. Garden use and household economy in rural Java. In G. E. Hansen, ed., *Agricultural and Rural Development in Indonesia*, pp. 242–54. Boulder, Colorado: Westview Press.

Terra, G. J. A. 1932. De voeding der bevolking en de erfcultuur. *Koloniale Studien* 16: 552–92.

Terra, G. J. A. 1952/53. Some sociological aspects of agriculture in S.E. Asia. *Indonesie* 6: 297 and 439.

Terra, G. J. A. 1953. The distribution of mixed gardening on Java. *Landbouw* 25: 163–203.

Weinstock, J. A. 1986. Social organization and traditional agroecosystems. In G. G. Marten, ed., *Traditional Agriculture in Southeast Asia: A Human Ecology Perspective*, pp. 171–86. Boulder, Colorado: Westview Press.

three

Sampling Methods for the Study of Genetic Diversity in Home Gardens of Cuba

Zoila Fundora Mayor, Tomás Shagarodsky,
and Leonor Castiñeiras

Where Does the Diversity Lie?

Home gardens represent a dynamic system whose nutritional benefits rest directly on the unique genetic diversity they contain. Plant genetic resources must therefore be conserved through their use. In order to establish a proper in situ conservation strategy, one of the first and essential steps to undertake is the study of the dynamics and distribution of species diversity in particular home gardens and throughout the system at large. This knowledge can contribute to the in situ conservation of species and varieties that are underutilized and threatened by genetic erosion (Guarino 1995; Eyzaguirre 1998; Eyzaguirre and Linares 2001).

Because it reflects the range and diversity of its component habitats, genetic diversity can be measured at different levels. Differences among different habitats can be referred to as b diversity, while the diversity inside a site or habitat can be called a diversity. The differences in the diversity of greater areas, for example the continents, is the g diversity.

Genetic diversity is stored in the richness of species making up the plant population of a specific site, or sites, depending on the reproductive strategy of each species (Marshall and Brown 1975). It is important to know that this diversity represents only a fraction of the whole natural diversity existing out there, so we should maximize the variability to be conserved. Knowing where the diversity lies is very important for achieving success in any given conservation strategy. It is impossible to know this a priori because we only have information about a species' phenotypic variability. Obviously, the presence of the highest quantity of alleles in the conserved variability will be the exact measure of the existing diversity.

At a global level, species richness is not uniformly distributed: it increases with a decrease in latitude and decreases with an increase in altitude, except for wood trees in tropical forests. Gentry (1988) has demonstrated that in tropical forests diversity can be higher in medium altitudes than in lower areas. It should be emphasized that the b diversity is frequently higher in areas of varied topographies because environmental heterogeneity increases.

The genetic diversity of a particular sampling area depends on the measure of its species richness (Weir 1990). In the particular case of in situ conservation of cultivated plants, it contains the full inventory of all cultivated species within the study area, as well as the cultivation practices and uses associated with them. These are intimately related to the cultural inheritance of the population living in the area.

In an exhaustive study of cultivated plant diversity based on more than thirty collecting missions all over Cuba, Esquivel and his colleagues (Esquivel, Knüpffer, and Hammer, 1992) and Knüpffer (1992) reported a total of 1,045 taxa (see Table 3.1). The best-represented families were Leguminosae (164), Graminae (95), Rutaceae (55), Myrtaceae (41), and Solanaceae (35). The genera with the greatest number of cultivated species were, among others, *Citrus* (30), *Desmodium* (14), *Vigna* (12), *Erythrina* (12), and *Datura, Agave, Annona, Passiflora, Solanum*, and *Syzygium* (10 species each). In another study dealing specifically with six home gardens in the eastern zone, Esquivel and Hammer (1992b) found a total of 80 taxa, classified according to their different uses. This attests to the high diversity of cultivated species existing in Cuba.

An initial inventory of species richness allows us to select the areas with best potential for in situ conservation of biodiversity. Thus, a total of nineteen "conucos" (Cuban home gardens) were visited and, on the basis of their species richness, eleven home gardens were selected for a more in-depth study of the influences that socioeconomic, cultural, and edapho-climatic factors exerted on the in situ conservation of cultivated species variability.

Table 3.1

Families and genera represented among cultivated taxa in Cuba

Family	Taxa (n)	Genera	Taxa (n)
Leguminosae	164	*Citrus*	30
Graminae	95	*Desmodium*	14
Rutaceae	55	*Erythrina*	12
Compositae	44	*Vigna*	12
Myrtaceae	41	*Datura*	10
Salanaceae	35	*Agave*	10
Euphorbiaceae	33	*Annona*	10
Labiateae	26	*Passiflora*	10
Cucurbitaceae	22	*Solanum*	10
Malvaceae	22	*Syzygium*	10

The relative abundance of species in the home garden is a function of the available space, the diversity of plants present, their isolation, and the topography of the region. In the study areas, a number of species were present in all, or almost all, the home gardens of each area (10 out of eighty-six species in Sierra of the Rosario, and 13 out of 169 species in the Sierra San Blas), plus those that are repeated from one area to the other (23 out of 255). However, the rest of the species differed from one home garden to the next; that is, they did not repeat themselves from one garden to another. This suggests that a high species diversity exists in these areas.

Comparison among Different Areas

Another approach to the problem of measuring genetic diversity is based on a comparison of the diversity existing among different areas. In reality, the composition of species and their abundance is rarely constant in space and time. For this reason, a comparison was made, first on the basis of common species present in these areas (interspecific variability), then on the basis of different forms existing within a given species (intraspecific variability). Measurements of intraspecific variability should be carried out preliminarily on the basis of visual observation of morphologic characters, mainly flowers and fruits (Quendeba et al. 1995; Fundora et al. 1997). Once the existence of different forms is established, the characterization will be supplemented by biochemcal (Wilckens et al. 1993; Carrillo 1995), isozimatic (Simonsen and Heneen 1995; Shiraishi et al. 1994), or molecular analyses (Griffin and Palmer 1995).

A more detailed study of intraspecific variability based on morphological attributes, complemented by information from farmers at two pilot areas—Soroa, Pinar del Río Province, and Sierra San Blas, Cienfuegos Province—revealed the precise distribution of species, their frequency, and uses (see Table 3.2; Castiñeiras et al. 2000). At Pinar del Río Province, for example, we observed a total of eighty-six species, most of them cultivated. Among the best-represented species in all gardens were fruit crops such as mangoes (*Mangifera indica*), bananas and plantains (*Musa* spp.), sweet and sour oranges (*Citrus sinensis* and *Citrus aurantium*, respectively), coconuts (*Cocos nucifera*) and guavas (*Psidium guajava*). The greatest intraspecific variability was also found in fruit crops in the arboreous stratum: mangoes (7 cultivars), bananas and plantains (14), avocados (8), guavas (6), and red sapote, *Pouteria sapota* (4). In addition, sugar cane had 7 cultivars and common beans 8 in the herbaceous stratum. Some roots and tubers in the subterranean stratum, such as cassava, had 7 cultivars and cocoyam (*Xanthosoma sagittifolium*) 4 cultivars. Coffee (*Coffea arabica*) was also found in all the home gardens. It was used to prepare the usual stimulant drink, with a double purpose: inside the garden itself, for family consumption; in the zone where the garden overlaps with the forest and/or farm area, for marketing, as an additional source of income for the family.

In the Cienfuegos area, we observed 169 crop plants. Once more, the best represented species in all gardens were fruit trees: avocados (*Persea americana*), guavas (*Psidium guajava*), and sour oranges (*Citrus aurantium*). Following in importance, but also occuring in the majority of the gardens, were mangoes (*Mangifera indica*), papaya (*Carica papaya*), bananas, and plantains (*Musa* spp.). Roots and tubers such as taro, cocoyam (*Colocasia esculenta* and *Xanthosoma sagittifolium*, respectively), and cassava (*Manihot esculenta*) were also well represented. The species *Pennisetum purpureum* was cultivated for animal fodder. Again, the greatest intraspecific variability was found in mangoes (6 cultivars), bananas and plantains (11), in the arboreous and bushy strata, respectively; lima beans (5 cultivars) in the bushy stratum; cassava (4) and arrow root (2), in the subterranean stratum. Once more, coffee cultivated as a dual purpose crop had a remarkable intraspecific variability (5 cultivars). In Cienfuegos, bananas and plantains were also grown for family subsistence and as an additional source of income. A remarkable diversity of uses for all species was observed in both areas: as food (fruits, vegetables, roots and tubers, grains) as spices, medicinal plants, for living fences, for industrial purposes, and so on.

A more precise comparative analysis of the diversity of home gardens at the different locations can be performed using a statistical multivariate analysis that takes into account the number of existing cultivars, species, home gardens, area, their use, type of crop, stratum, and other variables, to measure, in a preliminary

Table 3.2

Species existing in the home gardens studied at Soroa (Pinar del Río Province) and Sierra San Blas (Cienfuegos Province)

Species	Type of crop according to use	Number of different forms	Number of home gardens
		Soroa	
C. aurantium	FR	2	6
C. sinensis	FR	2	5
C. nucifera	FR	3	6
C. arabica	ME, IN	4	6
M. indica	FR	7	6
M. esculenta	RT	7	6
P. vulgaris	GR	8	3
P. guajava	FR	6	6
S. officinarum	IN	7	6
X. sagittifolium	RT	4	4
		Cienfuegos	
C. papaya	FR	1	4
C. aurantium	FR	1	5
C. arabica	ME, IN	5	4
C. esculenta	RT	1	4
M. indica	FR	6	4
M. esculenta	RT	4	4
Musa sp.	FR	11	4
P. americana	FR	1	5
P. lunatus	GR	5	3
P. guajava	FR	1	5
S. officinarum	IN	3	4
X. sagittifolium	RT	1	4
M. arundinacea	RT	2	2

Note: FR = fruit, ME = medicinal, IN = industrial, RT = roots and tubers, GR = grain.

way, their diversity and to ordinate them. Later on, a more in-depth study can be made on the basis of the evaluated attributes to consider which species should be conserved, and in what part of the country.

It is imperative to point out that the diversity inherent in home gardens can be modified depending upon several factors. Most important are the autonomous decisions farmers make about what cultivars and species are going to persist in their garden, especially those that serve him and his family's best interests and welfare (women also participate in these decisions). Pests and diseases, natural disasters, changes in the uses of these species, and the influence of agricultural and development programs at the state level, as well as formal and participative breeding activities, can also alter home-garden diversity.

The Relationship of Diversity to the Surface Occupied by the Orchard

The diversity present at the different sites also depends upon the size of the orchard. In the eleven home gardens studied, the surface of the different properties varied markedly. Not surprisingly, a tendency exists for the variability to increase as the size of the orchards increases. Because size and environmental heterogeneity have an effect upon sampling procedures they should be taken into consideration in determining the number of individual species to be conserved. From the discussion above, two important sets of questions worth investigating readily arise:

1. What actual limits govern the surface covered by home gardens and which species should be included in an in situ conservation strategy? Can a home-garden system be framed in only one independent area having a remarkable quantity of coincident species, or should there be an overlap with other areas in the conservation strategy of some species? If an orchard does not have a defined limit can the inventory of species and its intraspecific variability be limited to the orchard area?

2. Should species of trees and bushes (fruit crops mainly) from orchards located in premontane or mountainous areas be included as components of the structure of the home gardens? Or should they, instead, be regarded as components of the natural vegetation, especially if they are located in the limits between the forest and the orchard boundaries?

Diversity of Uses

In any study of genetic diversity it is of paramount importance to register the diversity of uses associated with particular species and/or varieties, for it is the case that a good part of the observed variability among species results from the uses that the farmer gives to them (Table 3.3). When carrying out a comparison among different orchards in one or several areas a great deal of information about the sociocultural aspects of the population of the area should be obtained. In the orchards of Soroa and the Sierra San Blas, for example, a high percent of the diversity is accounted for by fruit crop trees. But, in addition, the largest proportion

Table 3.3

Inventory of species per area studied according to their uses

Uses	Pinar del Río		Cienfuegos	
	Number of species	Percentage	Number of species	Percentage
Living fences	6	6.9	4	2.4
Condiments	12	13.9	13	7.7
Fruit crops	30	34.8	30	17.8
Grains	7	8.1	8	4.7
Industrial plants	3	3.5	4	2.4
Medicinal	17	19.8	96	56.8
Roots and tubers	5	5.8	7	4.1
Vegetables	3	3.5	2	1.2
Other uses	3	3.5	5	2.9
Total	86	99.9%	169	100%

of species in Sierra San Blas is made up of medicinal plants because one of the home gardens here is dedicated mainly to their commercialization.

Population Size and the Home-Garden System

The population size needed for an effective conservation program can be considered at different levels: the number of potential sites selected on the basis of the existing species diversity, the home-garden population per site, the number of populations per species within the system, and the number of individuals to be conserved per population (Hamrick 1983; Marshall and Brown 1975; Hodgkin 2002).

For the in situ conservation of plant genetic resources it is of particular importance to apply an appropriate sampling strategy, one that allows the monitoring of the existing genetic diversity, in order to establish a solid basis for its conservation and maintenance. One of the more difficult tasks conservationists face is the proper characterization of the in situ phenotypic variability. Such a task is essential in order to define an appropriate sampling strategy, for many species have very complex genetic structures, and sampling can be carried out in many ways (Brown and Marshall 1995).

The objectives involved in the collection of plant genetic resources have changed radically in the last fifteen years as part of a new approach used in ex situ conservation of the main economic cultivars around the world. This strategy involves three elements. First, it emphasizes the collection and conservation of germplasm of the wild ancestors and weedy forms of the main crops. Second, it focuses on nationally important crops used as food, fibers, medicines, or fuel (very few of these plants are included in scientific research programs). Third, it relies on the sampling and resampling of the main crops in order to fill gaps in the collections that result from erosion or from poorly represented samples. Covering the necessities of specific breeders is one of the reasons why the handling of in situ native material may be difficult (Brown and Marshall 1995). Whatever the strategy used in conservation, one can only hope to have represented a part of the variation that is present in nature. It is important that the sample be as large as possible and contain the maximum useful variation. A sampling procedure should allow for the conservation of the maximum quantity of useful genetic variation in a limited and representative number of populations or individuals. To conserve a significant and representative part of the genetic resources of a given species, it is necessary to consider its allele richness, that is, the number of different alleles for each locus in each population. In practice, this parameter is determined first on the basis of the phenotype and then by using biochemical or molecular techniques (Brown and Marshall 1995).

The basic useful strategy employed in sampling plant materials to be conserved depends on the extent of the genetic divergence of the populations and the variation within them. As a general rule, populations with a wide distribution of alleles per locus have superior values for diversity, being genetically richer. Bigger populations, or a bigger number of populations, deserve conserving. A useful approach advocated by Marshall and Brown (1975) recognizes four allele types: (i) common, widely distributed; (ii) common, locally distributed; (iii) rare, thoroughly distributed; and (iv) rare, locally distributed. Because the value of the diversity in a population to be conserved cannot be known only through the phenotype, the value of a population sample increases with size (Brown and Marshall 1995).

Basic Sampling Strategy

When selecting the populations that should be considered for conservation, relative aspects of the environmental and edapho-climatic characteristics of the region should be kept in mind, including phytogenetic differences with respect to the main economic crops in the area. Moreover, it is crucial to determine common agricultural practices. With available time and resources in short supply it is possible to define only a limited number of areas for conservation. Experts on the region can serve as guides, thus greatly accelerating the selection of the areas.

Deciding on the number of sites to be considered and their differences with respect to physiogeographic, edaphic, cultural, and agricultural factors is crucial to a sampling strategy. If the species is more frequent, or if there is a notable polymorphism, we should use more sites. It may be adequate to begin with thirty to fifty potential sites, but this number may vary according to the target species, its abundance in those sites, and the specific goal of the sampling strategy at the time (Brown and Marshall 1995; Eyzaguirre 1998). Including at least a copy of 95 percent of the alleles for the studied species is a good policy. In order to identify more intraspecific variability among some species we chose two areas, from the thirty areas previously identified in the country, to begin our studies. Evidently, from the results we obtained, it is necessary to enlarge the number of places. The intraspecific variability found in home gardens at each site—per species represented at the gardens—was low and in some important species was almost nil. This fact suggests that it is necessary to enlarge the garden population size in the system and also to extend the study in time to insure that a great portion of the allele richness existing there is represented for conservation. After a careful analysis, we considered at last the four or five sites with the greatest amount of intraspecific variability as a first step. The next step would be to analyze home-garden population size to be integrated with each system or selected site.

The analysis of the registered data for home gardens at each selected site—taking into consideration geographic, edaphic, ethnic-cultural, phytogenetic, and agricultural factors—offers a baseline for the selection of home gardens with better potential for in situ conservation. It should also be considered whether the farmers are determined to continue cultivating their gardens, and if there is a secure familial succession. In the case of Cuba, we studied nineteen families at the pilot sites, and we selected eleven (six at Soroa and five at Cienfuegos) for further study.

The main criteria to consider in proposing the number and type of home gardens that should be integrated in the system from a phytogenetic point of view are these: (a) the existence of common species; (b) the existence of endangered species—in all gardens of the system, or in one or several of them; (c) the existence of unique species—in all gardens of the system or in one or several of them; (d) the presence of important species for the family; and (e) the presence of species that need this strategy as a complement.

Should All of These Criteria Be Considered Simultaneously?

Generally, there is a reduced number of individuals per population per species in each garden. In order to obtain an optimum representation of the existing variability, it is necessary to consider several criteria: the geographic range of the species, their distribution, local abundance, the extent of migration among populations, the duration of their life cycle, the age structure of the population, the type of reproduction, fecundity and mating system, especially if there is notable polymorphism and if there are mixed populations. In their more detailed explanation, Brown and Marshall (1995) suggest as a good starting point that the number per species should be fifty individuals from each population; if there are outbreeders, it could be thirty. Nevertheless, this raises a question: is it possible to capture the maximum intraspecific variability in a garden population or in a garden system where there are frequently three or four individuals per species per variety, particularly if we are dealing with fruit crops? Would it not be wise to conserve all, or almost all, the existing individuals? This is an important point to discuss. In the case of fruit trees and some crops with vegetative propagation such as cocoyam or bananas and plantains, it would be more reasonable to increase the number of individuals in the sample.

In the case of species of wild populations that evolved with local subpopulations, a stratified aleatory sampling technique is recommended (separate sampling of individuals in different microsites). With respect to the traditional cultivars it is common to observe a mechanical mixture that the farmer deliberately maintains. For example, the presence of more than one species in a field is demonstrated for the complex *Vigna unguiculata—Phaseolus vulgaris,* reported by Laguetti and his colleagues (Laguetti et al. 1990); different cultivars of the same *Vigna unguiculata* species is also characteristic of Cuban home gardens. It is also common to observe two or more forms of, for example, the lima bean cultigroup (*Phaseolus lunatus*), as well as intermediate forms between them, growing close in the same field or fenced cultivation (Castiñeiras et al. 1991). Species of different cultivars should be conserved in the same way that they are present in the orchard. The survival of this genetic material, and its continuous evolution, depend on farmer practices that encourage the preservation and mixture of landraces. Rare phenotypic variants in a population should also be conserved for similar reasons; they may be the result of the natural evolutionary process working at the species level. With trees, it is even more difficult to achieve representativeness. They are sometimes present in the home gardens as unique copies or, at most, the species is represented by three to five individuals for each different variety.

Crop species, like wild plants, differ in their cycle of life, ecology, and genetic attributes, and so the factors that may influence a sampling strategy for their conservation can be varied. Brown and Marshall (1995) make a thorough evaluation of these factors, considering their influence in the determination of the sampling strategy to be used in collecting missions. In a certain way, their procedure may also be valid for in situ conservation efforts.

The spatial distribution of species can also play a decisive role in the selection of the sample of the diversity of crop species and trees to be conserved. Although they can limit the number of sampled sites, the presence of physical and geographical barriers have favored the differentiation process. Species found in a narrow geographical range may need a smaller quantity of sites for their conservation, but it is probably necessary to consider a larger number of individuals in each place. The same applies to those cultivars or species that are locally rare, where it would be very difficult to find thirty to fifty individuals per population. This is the case with the malanga amarilla (*Xanthosoma sagittifolium*), which is maintained in some orchards but is distributed only locally because of different population consumption preferences. The same is true for *Annona reticulata* (cherimola), for which only a few copies are found in each home garden. In these cases, rarity can be compensated for by an increment in the number of orchards sampled.

A factor related to the previous ones is the rate of differential migration among species. For annual crops, the migration is more pervasive than for trees. Among the latter, the exchange among communities is discouraged by the considerable volume of their seeds. Sampling a smaller number of distant populations is appropriate when wide diffusion and exchange exists among the traditional cultivars of a region. If, on the contrary, cultivars have been developed in a wider range of ecological situations, it is very probable that they possess greater divergence among their populations. It would thus be convenient to consider a larger number of individuals in each population for their conservation.

Factors related to the mating system and age structure of the population are closely linked to their geographical distribution and abundance. The mating system of the species should be considered in the selection of populations and individuals to be conserved. For example, alogamous species, annual or perennial, have smaller levels of divergence among populations than the autogamous ones (Hamrick and Godt 1990). For this reason, it would be appropriate to enlarge the number of individuals to be conserved in each population in the first case, rather than to enlarge the number of populations. With respect to the autogamous species, or those which have apomixis, it would be important to include a larger number of populations in their conservation, although fewer individuals exist in each one. If they display a conspicuous level of polymorphism inside their populations, it is reasonable to increase the number of individuals to be conserved for each population. In perennial species, especially if they are alogamous, conservation should address not only mature individuals, but also the youngest cohorts, which can be genetically different from the adults.

When we deal with traditional cultivars that are often true mixtures, conserved deliberately in this way by the farmers, we should follow in our conservation efforts the customary techniques farmers employ in their production that are responsible for the microevolution of these species, especially if we are dealing with an alogamous crop (Williams 1996).

All the aforementioned methods of sampling (Hamrick and Godt 1990; Brown and Marshall 1995; Eyzaguirre 1998) raise theoretical concerns. From our experience studying two areas, we concluded that we can rarely reach the number of individuals other researchers recommended to be conserved, not even in annuals and much less in perennials, be they autogamous, alogamous, or apomictic. Therefore, it is necessary to evaluate each variant carefully, studying each concrete case in order to determine the best course to take. For some species such as cocoyam (*Xanthosoma sagittifolium*), it may be necessary to enlarge the number of local populations to be included for their conservation (that is to say, to enlarge the number of gardens per area), always looking for a larger polymorphic range. One may need to include another sector of the country having marked ecogeographic differences to complete such an objective. A system that embraces these three areas in the in situ conservation strategy for this species may provide an appropriate framework.

Methods and Tools for Field Work

The structure of a home garden consists of a diverse combination of species that are distributed in all the different vegetation strata. Annual species with short cycles are present, as well as perennial ones that have long life cycles, such as fruit trees. These play an important role in the subsistence economy of the family by supplying not only important nutrients but also multiple direct and indirect benefits (Esquivel and Hammer 1988, 1992a; Frómeta and Lima 1992; Renda et al. 1997). Annual or biannual crop plants, as well as perennial and semiperennial bushes, are distributed in the subterranean and herbaceous strata, respectively.

Appropriate tools for field work, and a correct working methodology that allows recovery of the maximum useful information for monitoring diversity, are necessary to build up a successful in situ conservation strategy for crop plants. A discussion of some aspects of the methodology employed in our project for in situ conservation of crop plants (Castiñeiras et al. 2000) developed at two geographic zones previously identified (Castiñeiras and Pico 1995) may be helpful here. Thirty previously identified areas had shown good potential for the development of this study because different elements of the Cuban landscape and agricultural and phytogenetic factors were well represented in them.

Table 3.4

Qualitative data to be collected

➤ Review of secondary sources
- Historical documents
- Official reports and statistics
- Ethnographies
➤ Direct observations
- Rapid rural appraisal techniques
- Direct observation on phenotypic variation
- Semistructured interviews
- Key individuals
- Focus groups
- Simple questionnaires
- Comparisons and analysis of differences
- Construction and analysis of maps and models
- On the home gardens sketch mapping
- Transect walks
➤ Possible future settings for work

Source: Modified from Guarino and Friis-Hansen 1995.

Field work related to the in situ conservation study of cultivated plants shares many aspects with the collection of plant genetic resources for ex situ conservation. Nevertheless, the recorded information is much richer, and more trustworthy, thanks to the continuous contact with the inhabitants of the rural communities who provide socioeconomic data on the development and conservation of this diversity. A summary of the main qualitative data that should be taken into account is found in Table 3.4 (Guarino and Friis-Hansen 1995). The data involve a survey of the pertinent historical documents, a rapid rural appraisal, the use of a baseline questionnaire, and semistructured interviews. Contrast analysis and the study of maps and transects are also useful.

Questionnaires

The study of selected areas was carried out using a baseline questionnaire that elicits information necessary for the accurate characterization of the orchards. The questionnaire consists of five parts that were modified during the development of the project.

1. It is necessary to begin by registering basic information concerning the precise geographical localization of the study area (latitude and longitude), topogra-

phy, hydrology, soil type, and climatic characteristic (precipitation and temperature). It is also important to register salient features of the natural vegetation, fauna, human activity, degree of pollution, main potentialities, and observed restrictions. We chose the areas of Sierra del Rosario in Pinar del Río, and Sierra San Blas in Cienfuegos, for definite reasons. Sierra del Rosario's Biosphere Reserve, created twenty years ago, is located in one of the more important mountainous zones at the western part of our country. Sierra San Blas is a premontane area, forming part of the Escambray's mountains, in the central part of the country.

2. The characteristics of the human population in the study area refer mainly to the attributes of the owner of the orchard and his family, his origin, birthplace, education level, and the like. This part records the final destiny of the orchard products and whether the farmer needs to supplement the production of the orchard with other agricultural products, also establishing their source. It also compiles general information about the human population of the area and its possible origins.

3. Specific data on the area refer only to the area occupied by the orchard, its dimensions, distribution of species, and presence of traditional cultivars. Here, we deal with the main problems that affect the stability of the orchard and the existing diversity of the crops. For example, we registered the presence of pests and diseases such as *Pseudosysta perseae*, which causes defoliation in avocado trees. We also noted the occurrence of hurricanes, landslides, and other climatic events (El Niño Southern Oscillation, or ENSO, phenomena) that affect crops severely, often resulting in changes in their phenology. An important factor also recorded was the predation of animals and humans on orchard crops.

4. Specific data on the plants include their scientific names, intraspecific variability, their origin, uses, and functions in the orchard. General ethnobotanic data are crucial, as are data about the methods of propagation and main agricultural practices such as weed control, harvesting, production, and seed exchange. We need to know how farmers conserve propagation material.

5. Under general questions that should be gathered is information on the expected survival of the orchard, its possible succession inside the family, and the willingness of family members to assume responsibilities for its maintenance. It is also important to investigate the relationship of the owner family with the agricultural extension services. An assessment of the main causes affecting orchard stability and permanency from the farmer's point of view is of great importance. The farmer's expressed willingness to participate in an in situ conservation strategy is paramount. Everything possible should be done to enhance his

Table 3.5

Criteria for selecting species for further research and genetic analysis in the different strata

Criteria	Stratum				
	Herbaceous	Subterranean	Arboreal	Herbaceous	Herbaceous
	Lima bean (*P. lunatus*)	Cocoyam (*X. sagittifolium*)	Red mamey (*P. sapota*)	Bananas (*Musa* sp.)	Ají y pimiento (*Capsicum* spp.)
Home gardens where the species are present	54%	73%	72%	91%	55%
Uniqueness in home gardens	Practically not found out of home gardens	Present in both home gardens and production areas	Only in home gardens, does not exist in commercial areas	Present in gardens and in the formal sector	Present in gardens and production area
Threat of genetic erosion	The existence of the species variability depends on home gardens	By virus diseases and other pests	Variability not described. The conservation depends on home gardens	Conservation of many clones depends on gardens; problems with pests and diseases (nematodes and fungi)	Problems with pests (*Thrips*) and bacterial diseases

Importance in local food security and to fulfil household needs	Medium; possible to obtain crops in drier areas where common bean can't grow	High, almost all year	Important as a possible commercial product; in several months of the year a household necessity	Important as a commercial input and a household necessity	High for both subsistence and formal sector
Population size to conduct genetic analysis; molecular markers facilities analysis	Should consider several locations with smaller number of individuals per location; molecular markers available	Necessary to sample several plants in home gardens; antecedents of molecular markers	Necessary to develop the random sampling in different parts of the trees; molecular markers available	Sampling all the individuals per each population (a few each); molecular markers available	Should consider all existing individuals per garden at expense of more diverse populations; molecular markers available.
Pantropical distribution	Yes	Yes	Yes. Tropics of Central America and the Caribbean	Yes	Yes
Type of the reproductive mechanism	Seeds, with a high percentage of outbreeding	Vegetative reproduction system	Seeds, grafted exceptionally	Vegetative reproduction system	Autogamous but with high percentage of outbreeding; propagated by seeds

awareness of the role that his home garden can play in the conservation of traditional varieties having a long-term potential for feeding the inhabitants of communities all over the country.

Identification of Species to be Conserved

To identify species that present good qualities for conservation, keeping in mind the different vegetation strata in the garden, we considered diverse criteria. From Table 3.5 we can readily appreciate why certain species were selected. The criteria used in the inclusion of each species varied, but in all cases the species chosen were considerably abundant in the orchards of both areas, fluctuating between 54 percent to 91 percent. In some instances, conserving the variability of a species depends only on its presence in the home garden; this is true for the lima bean and the red mamey. But all the identified species are important for the subsistence needs of the family of the orchard's owner. They also show great promise in fulfilling local and national nutritional requirements.

For almost all the species selected, we used isozymatic or molecular markers. This greatly facilitates following the diversity course taken by each species in the study areas and analyzing the real potential of this approach, not only for conservation, but also for the continued evolution of these species.

Germplasm Exchange

The final result of germplasm exchange in home-garden systems is a modification of the existing genetic diversity in the gardens or a restoration of the diversity that has been eroded for different reasons, including the introduction of new genetic material. The following diagram permits us to see the different levels under which the exchange can be considered (Fig. 3.1).

The first level of exchange dimension produces a gene flow that is sometimes of little importance since the existing cultivars may be very similar depending on the distance or dispersion among gardens. The flow restores common varieties that have been eroded. If the farmers exchange genotypes that were not previously present in their gardens, the gene flow acquires major importance. The second level of exchange implies, most of the time, the integration of varieties coming from the formal sector into the garden through flow. Generally, they are improved varieties that, if not managed adequately, may contribute to the erosion of traditional landraces. The third exchange level refers to the flow of forms from semiwild situations, or from feral cultivars that escaped from farmers' varieties in

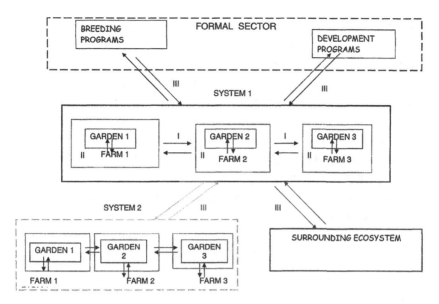

Figure 3.1. Germplasm exchange

abandoned home gardens, deep in the forest. Most of the time, these varieties are important restorers of variability and a refuge for cultivars that in home gardens nowadays tend to undergo rapid erosion because of pests, diseases, and competition with commercial varieties. This has been the case for banana clone Manzano (AAB), which is susceptible to the disease called Mal de Panamá (produced by *Fusarium oxysporum* sf. *cubense*). This fungus is almost extinct; it survives only in home gardens in mountainous zones within our country or in a semiwild state in some mountainous environments of the selected sites. In this case, import from feral or semiwild populations of banana serves to replenish the eroded genetic diversity. In all cases, the exchange flow may be reversible, with a potential danger for erosion resulting from resource overexploitation, especially at the third level.

Methodological Conclusions

Genetic diversity in home gardens must be carefully studied, starting with a preliminary survey of potential sites with an eye to the selection of sites for more in-depth studies. In the sites surveyed, we should pay attention not only to species diversity, but also to their intraspecific diversity since home gardens serve as refugia for cultivars of great usefulness to family subsistence and/or to national food security.

We should note the actual limits of a garden. Should home garden systems be framed in only one site, or should they involve several sites sharing a group of common species? May some garden systems overlap in the several species they contain, or should others remain independent?

The most important criteria to be considered in the proper selection of the study sites—the number of home gardens that should be integrated into the system and the number of populations and/or individuals or population selected for conservation—depend mainly on the target species or cultivars and their location inside the site. How should species be chosen? What aspects should be considered?

Germplasm exchange in home gardens occurs at several levels, and results in a dynamic change of the actual genetic diversity. At the third level, an imminent danger of erosion exists as a result of the introduction of new varieties coming from the formal sector. Proper measures should be taken within national conservation strategies to insure the survival of useful traditional cultivars.

Epilogue

By way of a general caveat we should note that it is not enough to do a descriptive study of the genetic diversity contained in home gardens. In Cuba, where the thrust of centralized, state-run development projects has been toward monocropping of imported species, home gardens are the only place where species diversity has been maintained in situ. Minor species occur only in these contexts. The conservation of genetic diversity ex situ, through gene banks, is not a viable alternative. Collections deteriorate and disappear. Many species—such as vegetatively propogated and tropical fruit trees—are extremely difficult to keep in such banks; thus one cannot get a measure of variability for them. Because germplasm exchange is very important, one must look at the entire home-garden system—not only at the link among home gardens, but also at the way they relate to the natural ecosystem. It is imperative that the conservation of both humanly managed home-garden systems and natural ecosystems proceed hand in hand.

References

Brown, A. H. D., and D. R. Marshall. 1995. A basic sampling strategy: Theory and practice. In L. Guarino, R. Ramantha, and R. Reid, eds., *Collecting Plant Genetic Resources Diversity: Technical Guidelines*, pp. 75–92. Cambridge: Cambridge University Press.

Carrillo, J. M. 1995. Variability for glutein proteins in Spanish *durum* wheat landraces. In *Durum Wheat Quality in the Mediterranean Region*. Proceedings of the Seminar, Zaragoza, Spain, 17–19 November 1993. Options Méditerranées, Serie A, Séminaires Méditerranéennes, 22: 143–47.

Castiñeiras, L., M. Esquivel, N. Rivero, and A. Mariño. 1991. Variabilidad de la semilla de *Phaseolus lunatus L.* en Cuba. *Revista del Jardín Botánico Nacional* 12: 109–14.

Castiñeiras, L., Z. Fundora Mayor, S. Pico, and E. Salinas. 2000. The use of home gardens as a component of the national strategy for the in situ conservation of plant genetic resources in Cuba: A pilot study. *Plant Genetic Resources Newsletter* 123: 9–18, 33.

Castiñeiras, L., and S. Pico. 1995. Home gardens as a component of a national in situ conservation strategy for crop plants: The cuban conuco. *Report of a Project.* Cuba: Instituto de Investigaciones Fundamentales en Agricultura Tropical Alejandro de Humboldt and Rome: International Plant Genetic Resources Institute.

Esquivel, M., and K. Hammer. 1988. The conuco as an important refuge of Cuban plant genetic resources. *Kulturpflanze* 36: 451–63.

Esquivel, M., and K. Hammer. 1992a. Contemporary traditional agriculture: Structure and diversity of the "conuco." In K. Hammer, M. Esquivel, and H. Knüpffer, eds., ". . . Y *Tienen Faxones y Fabas muy Diversos de los Nuestros . . . ": Origin, Evolution and Diversity of Cuban Plant Genetic Resources* 1: 174–92. Gatersleben, Germany: Institut für Planzengenetik und Kulturplanzenforschung (IPK).

Esquivel, M., and K. Hammer. 1992b. The Cuban home garden 'conuco': A perspective environment for evolution and in situ conservation of plant genetic resources. *Genetic Resources and Crop Evolution* 39: 9–22.

Esquivel, M., H. Knüpffer, and K. Hammer. 1992. Inventory of the cultivated plants. In K. Hammer, M. Esquivel, and H. Knüpffer, eds., ". . . Y *Tienen Faxones y Fabas muy Diversos de los Nuestros . . . ": Origin, Evolution and Diversity of Cuban Plant Genetic Resources*, vol. 2. Gatersleben, Germany: Institut für Planzengenetik und Kulturplanzenforschung.

Eyzaguirre, P. B. 1998. Contributions of home gardens to in situ conservation of plant genetic resources in farming systems. *Project IPGRI-GTZ.* Germany.

Eyzaguirre, P. B., and O. F. Linares. 2001. Una nueva aproximación al estudio y fomento de las huertas familiares. *Cuadernos de Pueblos y Plantas, 7. Cultivando la Biodiversidad*, pp. 30–33.

Frómeta, E., and H. Lima. 1992. Huertos frutales familiares, su aporte a la alimentación y como reservorio de germoplasma vegetal. *Agroalimentario* 1 (5): 4–5.

Fundora Mayor, Z., M. Hernández, R. López, J. López, A. Sánchez, and I. Ravelo. 1997. Variabilidad y clasificación de cultivares prospectados de maní (*Arachis hypogaea L.*). *Resúmenes del II Taller sobre Colecta y Evaluación de Recursos Fitogenéticos Nativos y Naturalizados FITOGEN '97*, Est. Exp. de Pastos y Forrajes de S. Spiritus, MINAG, 25.

Gentry, A. H. 1988. Changes in plant community diversity and floristic composition of environmental and geographical gradients. *Annals of the Missouri Botanical Gardens* 75: 1–34.

Griffin, J. D., and R. G. Palmer. 1995. Variability of thirteen isozyme loci in the USDA soybean germplasm collections. *Crop Science* 35 (3): 897–904.

Guarino, L. 1995. Assesing the threat of genetic erosion. In L. Guarino, Ramantha Rao, and R. Reid, eds., *Collecting Plant Genetic Resources Diversity: Technical Guidelines*, pp. 67–74. Cambridge: Cambridge University Press.

Guarino, L., and E. Friis-Hansen. 1995. Collecting plant genetic resources and documenting associated indigenous knowledge in the field: A participatory approach. In *Collecting Plant Genetic Resources Diversity: Technical Guidelines*, pp. 345–65. Cambridge: Cambridge University Press.

Hamrick, J. L. 1983. The distribution of genetic variation within and among natural plant populations. In C. M. Schonewald-Cox, S. M. Chambers, B. MacBryde, and L. Thomas, eds, *Genetics and Wild Populations Management*, pp. 335–48. Menlo Park, Calif.: Benjamin Cummings.

Hamrick, J. L., and M. J. Godt. 1990. Allozyme diversity in plant species. In A. H. D. Brown, M. T. Clegg, A. L. Kahler, and B. S. Weir, eds., *Plant Population Genetics, Breeding, and Genetic Resources*, pp. 43–63. Sunderland, Massachusetts: Sinauer Associates.

Hodgkin, T. 2002. Home gardens and the maintenance of genetic diversity. In J. W. Watson and P. B. Eyzaguirre, eds., *Proceedings of the Second International Homegardens Workshop: Contribution of Home Gardens to the in situ Conservation of Plant Genetic Resources in Farming Systems*. 14–18 and 17–19 July 2001. Witzenhausen, Federal Republic of Germany. Rome: International Plant Genetic Resources Institute.

Knüpffer, H. 1992. The database of cultivated plants of Cuba. In K. Hammer, M. Esquivel, and H. Knüpffer, eds., "*. . . Y Tienen Faxones y Fabas muy Diversos de los Nuestros . . .*": *Origin, Evolution and Diversity of Cuban Plant Genetic Resources*, vol. 1. Gatersleben, Germany: Institut für Planzengenetik und Kulturplanzenforschung (IPK).

Laguetti, G., S. Padulosi, K. Hammer, S. Cifarelli, and P. Perrino 1990. Cowpea (*Vigna unguiculata* (L.) Walp.). Germplasm collection in Southern Italy and preliminary evaluation. In N. Q. Ng and L. M. Monll, eds. *Cowpea Genetic Resources*, pp. 46–57. Ibadan, Nigeria: International Institute of Tropical Agriculture.

Marshall, D. R., and A. H. D. Brown. 1975. Optimum sampling strategies in genetic conservation. In O. H. Frankel and J. G. Hawkes, eds. *Crop Genetic Resources for Today and Tomorrow*, p. 80. Cambridge: Cambridge University Press.

Quendeba, B., G. Ejeta, W. W. Hanna, and A. K. Kumar. 1995. Diversity among African pearl millet landrace populations. *Crop Science* 35 (3): 919–24.

Renda, A., E. Calzadilla, M. Jiménez, and J. Sánchez. 1997. *La Agroforestería en Cuba*. Red Latinoamericana de Cooperación Técnica en Sistemas Agroforestales, Dirección Recursos Forestales, FAO, Roma; Oficina Regional de la FAO para América Latina y el Caribe, Santiago de Chile.

Shiraishi, S., N. H. Latiff, S. Miyatake, Y. Ochiai, and T. Furukashi. 1994. Population-genetical studies on *Dryobalanops* (Kapur) species. *Bulletin of the Forestry and Forest Products Research Institute* (Iburaki) 366: 107–14.

Simonsen, V., and W. K. Heneen. 1995. Genetic variation within and among different cultivars and landraces of *Brassica campestris* L. and *Brassica oleraceae* L. based on isozymes. *Theoretical and Applied Genetics* 91 (2): 346–52.

Weir, B. S. 1990. *Genetic Data Analysis: Methods for Discrete Population Genetic Data*. Sunderland, Massachusetts: Sinauer Associates.

Wilckens, E. R., J. T. Vidal, H. F. Hevia, C. A. M. Gutiérrez, and V. M. Tapia. 1993. Exploration of genetic variation in chilean sweet potatoes (*Ipomoea batatas* (L.) Lam) I. Vegetative morphology. *Agrociencia* 9 (2): 87–90.

Williams, D. E. 1996. Aboriginal farming system provides clues to peanut evolution. In B. Pickersgill and J. M. Locke, eds., *Legumes of Economic Importance*, pp. 11–17. Advances in Legume Systematics 8. Kew, U.K.: Royal Botanic Gardens.

Part 2

Country Studies

four

Vietnamese Home Gardens
Cultural and Crop Diversity

Luu Ngoc Trinh

Home gardens, or *vuon nha*, have a long tradition in Vietnam, where they have always been important as a source of livelihood for farming families, especially those that are poor. In this chapter I will show that ethnic differences between the Kinh dominant group and the Tho ethnic minority account for major contrasts in crop-genetic repertoire. Another important differentiating factor is ecology. There have also been two important directions of change operating at the same time, enrichment and erosion of plant-genetic diversity. Both processes must be taken into account to evaluate future trends in home-garden biodiversity.

Natural Conditions for Agriculture in Vietnam

Having an area of 330,000 km² and a population near 80 million inhabitants, Vietnam is situated in Southeast Asia. The country stretches from 8°30′ to 23°30′ N latitude, with three-fourths of the territory being comprised of mountains and highlands, ensuring that climatic and soil characteristics are complex and diversified. In the winter, the monsoon winds blow from Central Asia to Vietnam through mountain passes, resulting in cold temperatures in North Vietnam. The Haivan Pass at 16° N latitude prevents the winter northeast monsoon from spreading into the southern part of Vietnam, resulting in two clearly distinct climatic zones. North of the Haivan Pass, there are two distinct annual seasons: the cold winter and the humid, hot summer, with complex weather fluctuations resulting in many natural calamities such as typhoons and flooding. South of the Haivan Pass, climatic conditions are considerably more stable: humid and hot all year round, with flooding and typhoons rarely observed. Nevertheless, distinct dry and rainy seasons do exist in the South.

In Vietnam, one finds two densely populated deltas: the Red River Delta in the North, and the Mekong River Delta in the South. Soils here are among the most fertile in the world. Average annual precipitation in Vietnam is quite high, ranging from 1,700 to 2,000 mm; coupled with extensive river systems, this country is rich in water resources.

From north to south, Vietnam can be divided into 7 agroecological zones (see map, Fig. 4.1). The northeast zone (1) consists primarily of mountains and midlands having a subtropical climate. Temperate conditions are found in the high mountains, where it is dry cold in early winter and wet cold in late winter because of light precipitation from the middle of January until April. The northwest zone (2) is mainly mountainous and has a subtropical climate. The Red River Delta, including the Ma River Delta, is a vast plain zone (3) having ferrite soils and a subtropical climate (dry cold in early winter and wet cold in late winter). The north central zone (4) is mainly mountainous, with only a narrow strip of cultivable but nonfertile soil; harsh climatic conditions here are the result of the hot and dry winds that flow from Laos. The coastal south central zone (5) is characterized by fertile soils and a tropical climate. The central plateau (6) has fertile soils and a tropical climate with distinct dry and rainy seasons. Severe water deficiencies mark the dry season. The Mekong River Delta (7) is the largest plain in the country; it is characterized by fertile soils, plentiful water resources, and a typical tropical climate. Partly because of differences in ecology and partly because of ethnic and socioeconomic factors, the particular features of crop-genetic resources vary among agroecological zones, as does home-garden structure. Several sites representing the major ecozones of the country were chosen for study. Nho Quan was chosen to represent the northeast and northwest zones, as well as the Red River Delta (zones 1–3), because it has a rich plant-genetic diversity that results from its location in a transition zone between the mountains and the delta of the big river,

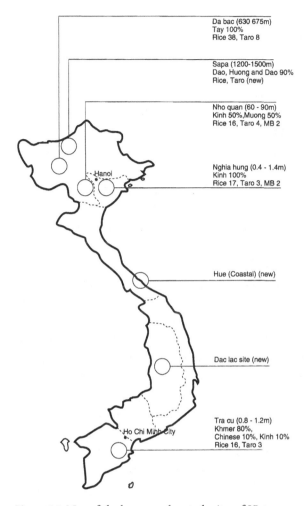

Da bac (630 675m)
Tay 100%
Rice 38, Taro 8

Sapa (1200-1500m)
Dao, Huong and Dao 90%
Rice, Taro (new)

Nho quan (60 - 90m)
Kinh 50%,Muong 50%
Rice 16, Taro 4, MB 2

Nghia hung (0.4 - 1.4m)
Kinh 100%
Rice 17, Taro 3, MB 2

Hue (Coastal) (new)

Dac lac site (new)

Tra cu (0.8 - 1.2m)
Khmer 80%,
Chinese 10%, Kinh 10%
Rice 16, Taro 3

Hanoi

Ho Chi Minh City

Figure 4.1. Map of the home-garden study sites of Vietnam

where the home-garden tradition is centuries old. Here, the dominant ethnic group is the Kinh. The Nghia Dan site is representative of north-central Vietnam (zone 4); it is located at a high elevation, far from any urban center. The dominant group here is the Tho ethnic minority. The third site, in the district of Thuan An, is in the suburbs of Ho Chi Minh City (zones 5 and 6). It is experiencing the effects of urbanization and industrial activity. Our final site, the community of Nhon Ngiah, in Chau Thanh, is representative of the Mekong River Basin (zone 7). The families in this and the Thuan An community belong to the Kinh ethnic group. Nhon Ngiah's inhabitants have a rich gardening tradition, cultivating multistoried gardens with high diversity.

Ethnic and Socioeconomic Conditions

The Vietnamese people belong to very diverse cultural traditions. In the country live 54 nationalities, each possessing a separate language, different histories, particular characteristics, and unique cultural behaviors (ethnicities are referred to as nationalities in Communist states). Nevertheless, the Kinh are the major nationality, accounting for over 80 percent of the population. The languages of the 54 nationalities are classified into groups of the Austronesian-Asian, Austronesian, and Sino-Tibetan families (Van, Son, and Hung 1993). Each ethnic group lives in a defined geographical area, practices a particular farming system, and has specific food preferences. Ethnic diversity is one of the main axes of differentiation in crop-genetic repertoire. Crops growing in home gardens differ among different ethnic groups.

The government of Vietnam is focusing on the integration of minorities by educating children from minority communities in the Vietnamese language and encouraging assimilation. As a result, in many places differences between minority groups and the Kinh majority have become negligible. In isolated communities such as Nghia Dan, however, marked cultural differences can still be observed that translate into structural and compositional differences in home gardens. Ethnic minorities in Vietnam tend to practice a method of gardening that is less intensive than the traditional gardens of the Kinh majority, and they invest less time and resources in gardens. In terms of medicinal plants, the gardens of minority groups are often more diverse but, in terms of vegetables, much less diverse. There is a tradition in many minority groups of collecting greens and vegetables from the forest, so there is less need for intensive cultivation of vegetables such as spinach, cabbage, watercress, and tomatoes. Ethnic groups in general eat less of the common species of vegetables, partly because of the rural-urban divide. Urban residents often eat more processed food, and the diversity available in cities is dictated by the predominant cultural tastes. Rural people eat many different kinds of plants, often collected from forests, to satisfy their vitamin and mineral requirements.

The Vietnamese economy is predominantly agricultural, based on paddy production. The agricultural sector accounts for 36.6 percent of the national income, employs about 70 percent of the total labor force, and represents 26 percent of Vietnam's total exports. The diversity and richness of plant-genetic resources are important factors for the development of an agricultural production capable of sustaining an ever growing population (2.0 percent–2.5 percent per year). Plant-genetic resources consist of three main components: indigenous species, intro-

A woman home gardener in Vietnam showing the taro varieties that she grows under pomelo trees. Photo by P. Eyzaguirre

Home gardens in Vietnam are rich in starchy staples such as banana, taro, and sweet potatoes, with local banana varieties highly prized for taste. Photo by P. Eyzaguirre

duced species from South China, and introduced species from southern Asia (Pham Hoang Ho 1991). According to preliminary data, Vietnam possesses about seven hundred crop species belonging to seventy genera. In addition, there exist hundreds of underutilized species.

The entire region is enormously rich in useful plant species (Khi 1996), with an impressive number having been domesticated here: rice, banana, and taro are the most successful early domesticates. As many as 40 species are reported to have originated in Southeast Asia; many of them and their wild relatives occur in Vietnam. Famous Vietnamese rice varieties are known for their high grain quality, such as Tam in the North, Nanghuong in the South, and Gie in Central Vietnam. There are also various specific types of fruits such as hungyen longan, thanhha litchi, xadoai orange, doanhung pomelo, that are considered delicacies.

Home Gardens in Vietnam

There is a proverb in the Vietnamese language: "Benefits are found first in home ponds with fish-breeding, second in home gardens [without ponds], and third in field cultivation." In 1997, the total area covered by home gardens in Vietnam was estimated at approximately 200,000 ha, or around 4.0 percent of the total cultivated area. In 1997, home gardens, home ponds, and home husbandry accounted for 30 percent of total agricultural production in Vietnam.

Table 4.1 gives district-level general site information and lists major contrasts between sites, including prevalent ecosystems, altitude, level of home-garden commercialization, proximity to an urban center, and ethnic diversity. Not surprisingly, ethnic minorities comprise the greatest percentage of surveyed households in the Nghia Dan site. Religious diversity is low because Vietnam is a predominantly Buddhist country. Table 4.2 shows statistics on the actual households that were surveyed, generally reflecting district trends. The oldest home-garden sites were not in the areas that necessarily have the longest history of settlement because the southern sites appear to contain the oldest gardens. The average age of home gardens in Thuan An, in the suburbs of Ho Chi Minh City, is 38.9 years, and at Chau Thanh, in the Mekong Delta, it is 30 years. The northern and central sites contain home gardens of the average age of 25 and 21.5 years, respectively. This was explained by the fact that the home gardens in the Mekong area, especially those at Thuan An, where there was a strong American presence during the 1960s and 1970s, were less affected by the war with the United States than some areas in the North. Displacement and destruction resulting from war meant that many home gardens were reestablished after the American war ended in 1975

Table 4.1

Descriptive general data on Vietnamese home garden sites (from district-level data)

Geographical location	North	Central	South	Mekong Delta
Province	Ninh Binh	Nghe An	Binh Duong	Can Tho
District	Nho Quan	Nghia Dan	Thuan An	Chau Thanh
Ecosystem	Red River Delta: tropical to subtropical	Midlands: tropical and subtropical	Lowlands: tropical	Mekong Delta: tropical
Altitude	60 masl	80 masl	10 masl	1 masl
Average temperature	26° C	23.4° C	26.6° C	29.5° C
Mean annual rainfall	1,900 mm	1,573.4 mm	1,388 mm	1,500–1,800 mm
Major soil types	Loam and sandy soil	Bazan	Alluvial clay	Clay
Latitude	107°23′ N	105°10′–105°34′N	106°55′–107°04′N	105°30′–105°45′ N
Longitude	21°5′ E	19°00′–19°32′E	10°70′–10°62′E	10°05′–10°20′ E

Land-use data (ha)				
Total land	49,862		7,200	40,604
Total agricultural land	15,623	25,476	4,489	35,512
Area under rice	6,525	3,400	1,838	20,635
Area under crops other than rice	1,285	7,300	2,651	14,877
Forest plantation	8,098	3,455	135	83
Natural forest	5,606	10,414	425	—
Major agricultural products	Rice, corn, sweet potato, anona	Rice, citrus, black bean, cassava, yam, banana	Rice, coconut, jackfruit, banana, pomelo, luffa	Rice, orange, pomelo, longan, kumquat, banana, spinach

Demographic data				
Official age of communes (yrs.), time settled	Settled more than 1,000 years ago	1,000 years	Around 300 years	Around 300 years
Population	14,251	185,200	99,892	280,837
Density (persons/ha)	1.09		13.9	6.9
Ethnic groups	Muong: 11% Kinh 89%	Kinh 3.6% Tho 96.4%	Kinh 98% Khmer and Hoa 2%	Kinh 99.7% Khmer and Hoa 0.3%
Religion	Buddhist 95% Catholic 5%	Animist 4% Buddhist 96%	Buddhist 98% Ancestor worship and Cao Dai 2%	Buddhist 100%

Table 4.2

Characteristics of surveyed households by site

Site	Number	Ethnic groups in survey	Average age of home gardens	Average number of people	Average number of breadwinners	Highest level of education
Nho Quan	30	Kinh 93% Muong 7%	25	5.2	2.9	9–12
Nghia Dan	30	Kinh 13% Tho 87%	21.5	5.3	2.3	6–8
Thuan An	35	Kinh 100%	38.9	5.7	3.2	6–8
Chau Thanh	21	Kinh 100%	30	5.1	3	6–8

(hence, an average age of 25). At Nghia Dan, in the midlands and semimountainous region of Central Vietnam, the area was sparsely settled until 10–15 years ago, when overpopulation in neighboring districts spurred migration into the area. Fifty percent of families now living in the district migrated during that period; this is one reason why the average age of home gardens at this site is lower than at other sites. The family size, between five and six persons, is fairly constant across sites. People at the Nho Quan site seemed to have a slightly higher average level of education; at least one member of the household had reached grades 9–12. At the other sites, secondary education (grades 6–8) seemed to have been achieved by at least one member of the household.

Home-garden size is largest in Chau Thanh, followed by Thuan An, Nghia Dan, and Nho Quan (Table 4.3). At Chau Thanh in the southern Mekong Delta, gardeners focus on commercial fruit production and need large areas for orchards. At Nho Quan, on the other hand, home gardeners focus on raising crops for home consumption. This fact, coupled with alternative sources of income through rice production, leads to smaller areas for home gardens at the Red River Delta site. At Thuan An, home-garden size is limited by the scarcity of available space that results from high population density; nevertheless, gardens still figure prominently in family subsistence and market production. In Nghia Dan, there are fewer space constraints for home gardens, so there is a wide variation in their size, ranging from 200 m² to 10,000 m². A family's total rice-field holdings here seem to be roughly twice as large as home-garden holdings in Nho Quan and Thuan An. The opposite is true of Nghia Dan, where the home garden is twice the size of the rice fields In the case of Chau Thanh, in the Mekong Delta, however, home gardens are very large and are equal in size to rice-field lands. The small field

Table 4.3

Area of home gardens and field land

Site (district)	Home garden		Paddy/field land		Total
	Average size (m²)	Range (m²)	Average size (m²)	Range (m²)	Total farm land (m²)
Nho Quan	1,407.9	500–3,200	3,841.7	1,260–13,358	5,249.6
Nghia Dan	2,771.7	200–10,000	1,208.3	250–2,500	3,980
Thuan An	2,822.9	800–7,200	5,588.6	0–40,000	8,411.5
Chau Thanh	7,500	2,000–22,000	8,571	2,000–22,000	16,071

size and large home-garden size in Nghia Dan is explained by the presence of low mountains without optimal rice-growing land (i.e., without flat valley land with plentiful water). The conditions for growing rice are much less favorable in Nghia Dan than in the other sites, and because available field land is constrained, rice is not as important a crop here. Families focus instead on home-garden production for household subsistence.

Table 4.4 shows the percent of land allocated by the household to home gardens, field land, and ponds. The importance of home gardens to households in Nghia Dan is underscored by the fact that they make up almost 70 percent of their landholdings. In Nho Quan and Thuan An, home gardens comprise 27 and 34 percent, respectively, of a family's holdings, approximately half of which is allocated to rice fields. In Chau Thanh, 47 percent of land is used for home gardens, and 53 percent of land is taken up by field crops such as rice.

A tradition of making sustainable home gardens exists in Vietnam; the extent of their sustainability is hypothetically dependent on their degree of complexity and commercialization. Home gardens in highland and mountainous areas inhabited by many ethnic minorities tend to maintain complexity of structure and

Table 4.4

Allocation of land (percent of total)

Site	Home garden	Field crops/rice
Nho Quan	26.8	73.2
Nghia Dan	69.6	30.4
Thuan An	33.6	66.4
Chau Thanh	46.7	53.3

Pomello, a traditional Vietnamese home-garden crop, now important commercially; most varieties maintained by households

diversity of species. They are characterized by a large surface area and numerous crop species: fruit trees, vegetables, medicinal plants, wood trees, and spices. These larger home gardens are often oriented toward the subsistence of the household and tend to provide a low income per unit area.

One danger to the preservation of crop-genetic diversity is market pressure to commercialize these spaces, with a consequent decrease in the number of crop species. More commercialized home gardens exist in the plain-delta areas adjacent to intensive rice production, where the Kinh people comprise the majority population. The more commercialized home garden is characterized by small areas, stable but reduced number of crop species—mainly vegetables, spices, and fruit trees—and a very high economic value per unit of land. They are often planted with litchi, longan, citrus, plum, and apricot in the Red River Delta; with mango, citrus, longan, rambutan, and anonas in the Mekong River Delta; and with coffee and cashew in the Central Plateau and east part of the South Plain Delta. Much of the multistory complexity of highland home gardens is absent from the delta home gardens.

Species diversity per household is highest at the southern sites, where an average of 53.9 species are found in a home garden of Chau Thanh and 50.3 species in a home garden of Thuan An (Table 4.5). An average Nho Quan home garden

Table 4.5

Average plant diversity at each site

Region	Site (district)	Average number of species per garden	Range of species per site	Average garden size (m²)	Average number of species (100 m²)
Northern mountains: subtropical to temperate	Nho Quan	38.6	27–54	1,407.9	2.7417
Central midlands: tropical and subtropical	Nghia Dan	23.4	12–42	2,771.7	0.8442
Southern lowland: tropical	Thuan An	50.3	36–78	2,822.9	1.7819
Mekong Delta: tropical	Chau Thanh	53.9	20–103	7,500	0.7187

contained 38.6 species. The Nghia Dan home gardens were the least diverse, containing 23.4 species on average. The range of species found in gardens was also higher in the Mekong Delta, where home gardens contain 20–103 species in Chau Thanh. Seventy-eight species was the maximum number found per household at Thuan An, while in Nho Quan and Nghia Dan households it was 54 and 42, respectively. The high diversity of species in Chau Thanh could be attributed to the much larger areas of home gardens at this site, so it is useful to look at diversity per 100 m² as well. Using this measure, Nho Quan was the most diverse, with 2.7 species per 100 m², followed by Thuan An with 1.8 species and Nghia Dan with 0.8 species. Although Chau Thanh was the most diverse in terms of numbers of species per home garden, it was the least diverse in terms of space, containing only 0.7 species per 100 m².

The Evolution of Crop-Genetic Resources in Vietnam

Population growth and inappropriate agricultural intensification schemes have brought irreversible loss of crop-genetic resources at an alarming rate. Many special traditional crop varieties are being replaced by new high-yield varieties with a narrow genetic base, leading to erosion of landraces that are lower in yield but rich in variability. Deforestation, changing land-use patterns, and other associated factors also pose a serious threat to traditional crops.

During the last three decades, crop-genetic resources in Vietnam have suffered major changes in two opposite directions: toward enrichment and toward erosion. Thanks to agricultural development schemes and cultural exchanges, Vietnamese plant-genetic resources have become more diversified. Numerous economically valuable crop species have recently been introduced into Vietnam, such as grape, cashew, okra, avocado, stevia, and dragon fruit. The genetic diversity of numerous annual crop species has also been remarkably enriched by germplasm exchange and cultivar introduction from various international research institutions and from countries enjoying sound scientific-technical cooperation relationships with Vietnam. Most important are rice germplasm introduced from South China, Taiwan, and South Korea through the International Rice Research Institute (IRRI), Philippines; maize from Thailand through Centro Internacional de Mejoramiento de Maíz y Trigo (CIMMYT), Mexico; and food legumes including groundnut from India through the International Crop Research Institute for the Semi-Arid Tropics (ICRISAT).

The second trend, toward crop erosion, can be attributed to several factors:

1. The Green Revolution, and the intensive farming processes it brought, had negative effects on the survival of traditional crops. The expansion of irrigation systems and the widespread adoption of chemical fertilizers made possible a transformation from extensive to intensive farming. Countless traditional cultivars adapted to local ecological conditions have been replaced by a few, newly developed, intensive varieties. Many crop varieties have thus disappeared forever because insufficient attention has been paid to their collection and preservation.

2. Population increase, and ever growing food demands, have resulted in the setting up of development targets such as increasing single-crop yield. Crop resources are therefore being reduced and narrowed. In upland areas, population pressure leads everywhere to the burning of the forest for shifting cultivation of rice; thus, crop- and tree-genetic resources are being damaged or destroyed on a large scale.

3. Long wars, bombs, and herbicides have caused Vietnam to lose over two million hectares of forest. Together with the destruction of such large forest areas, hundreds of species of crops, forest trees, and medicinal plants have disappeared forever.

4. The economic revitalization of Vietnam started in 1988 but has been a practical success only since 1990. Agricultural production in Vietnam has witnessed a new period of rapid development based on a gradual process of crop diversification. People's demand for fruits and vegetables has visibly increased. As a consequence of developments in husbandry, production of crops for animal food has also been augmented.

Summary and Conclusions

Information from various agroecological areas of Vietnam and from two ethnic groups show that both natural and cultural factors account for much of the diversity in home-garden composition (Hé 1991). Some of the differences can also be accounted for by trends in the market. Commercialization is affecting species composition, as witnessed by the home gardens of Chau Thanh and Thuan, whose trees yield fruit for sale. In contrast, very little of what is produced in the Nho Quan or the Nghia Dan's gardens is sold; most of it is consumed by the family.

Genetic erosion is less pronounced in subsistence than in commercial gardens. Similarly, traditional gardens are constantly being enriched by species introduced from other home gardens or from the forest. This argues for the importance of protecting and encouraging in situ conservation of genetic resources in species-rich gardens that enhance to the family's welfare (Trinh 1996a, b).

References

Hé, P. H. 1991. *The Plants of Vietnam* [in Vietnamese]. Santa Ana, CA.: Mekong Printing.

Hoang Ho, Pham. 1991. *C©ycá* [in Vietnamese]. Santa Ana, CA: Mekong Printing.

Khi, N. 1996. Report of the Project Director. In *Plant Genetic Resources in Vietnam*, pp. 10–26. Proceeding of the National Workshop on Plant Genetic Resources, March 28–30, 1995. Hanoi, Vietnam.

Trinh, L. N. 1996a. Crop genetic resources in Indochina and available approaches for its conservation. Report presented at the Fourth Ministry of Agriculture, Forestry, and Fisheries (MAFF) Workshop on Plant Genetic Resources, Tsukuba, Japan, 22–24 October 1996.

Trinh, L. N. 1996b. Ex-situ and in-situ conservation of plant genetic resources in Vietnam: Importance and criteria to be considered in their implementation. Abstract of posters, Second International Crop Science Congress (ICSC), New Delhi, India, 17–23 November 1996.

Van, D. N., C. T. Son, and L. Hung, eds. 1993. *Ethnic Minorities in Vietnam*. Hanoi: Gioi Publishers.

five

Managing Diversity in Various Ecosystems

Home Gardens of Nepal

Pratap Shrestha, Resham Gautam,
Ram Bahadur Rana, and Bhuwon Sthapit

Broadly speaking, a home garden encompasses the traditional land-use practices that take place around a homestead, where several species of plants are cultivated and maintained by members of the household, primarily for their own consumption. In Nepal, however, the home-garden concept is not clearly defined and often overlaps its surrounding agroecosystems. Home gardens in the plains of southern Nepal are called *bari,* that is, the fenced area around the house, and in the hills are called *ghar-bari,* the nonirrigated land around the house, usually enclosed with a live fence. Home gardens are thus differentiated from larger production systems called *pakho-bari,* the nonirrigated uplands dominated by maize, and *khar-bari,* uncultivated land where thatch grass, livestock grasses, and a few multipurpose trees are grown.

This chapter is intentionally descriptive. We explore the various kinds of regional home gardens that exist and their structures and uses, highlighting the multiple roles that home gardens play in the livelihood options of the Nepalese people. We focus on the major contributions gardens make to the conservation of plant-genetic resources. Detailed information on the many positive aspects of this rich and promising system is essential if home gardens are to become a central component of future national development efforts. All too often experts promote cultivation alternatives that are ill-defined and inadequately described. Our purpose is to convince the reader that the Nepalese home garden is a wise choice in the effort to improve the health and welfare of the inhabitants of this mountainous kingdom.

Background

Nepal is located between 26° 22' N and 30° 27' N latitude and 80° 4' E and 88° 12' E longitude. It extends from the terai, or Indo-Gangetic plains, in the south, with an altitude of about 60 meters above sea level, to Mount Everest, the highest peak in the world, in the north. The country is divided into five ecological regions, namely, the Himalayas (more than 4,000 masl), the high hills or mountains (2,000–4,000 masl), the mid hills (1,500–2,000 masl), the siwalik (300–1,500 masl), and the terai (below 300 masl). Climatic conditions vary sharply across these ecological regions, from hot tropical in the south to freezing alpine in the north. The extreme variation in altitude, the complex topography, the varied climate, and the diverse sociocultural composition and farming practices of the communities have contributed to the evolution of a markedly differentiated natural flora and fauna and of a multitude of cultivated crop species. Nepal's great biodiversity is attested to by the fact that its share of the world's flowering plants exceeds 2 percent, whereas its land area comprises no more than a tenth of a percent of the total world area (Ryman 1992).

Nearly 81 percent of the Nepalese rely on agriculture for their livelihood (Centre Bureau of Statistics [CBS] 1999), but most farming systems are subsistence-oriented. Farmers are predominantly smallholders, with an average holding of less than one hectare of cultivated land per household (CBS 1999). Because of large family size (5.6 person per household) and low productivity for food crops (less than 2 metric tons per hectare for major cereals), the majority of rural households experience periods of food shortage during the year. Farmers adopt a variety of coping strategies, including collecting wild and uncultivated foods during the months of scarcity (Local Initiatives for Biodiversity Research and Development [LI-BIRD] 1999). One of the most useful strategies to ensure food security is to make a garden on land adjacent to the homestead.

The Importance of Home Gardens in Nepal

Home gardens in Nepal have multiple uses: as a source of livelihood, for firewood and timber, for spices and medicinal plants, for green manure, and for pesticides. In rural areas, where about 90 percent of the total population lives (CBS 1999), home gardens are an important source of food, supplying most of the vegetables and fruits required by the family. Home gardens are also maintained in urban areas, but information on them is almost nonexistent. A survey of the western hills of Nepal indicates that 85 percent to 94 percent of households rely entirely on home gardens for their year-round supply of vegetables (Shrestha and Gurung 1997). Similarly, 57 percent to 81 percent of households plant fruit trees in their home garden. Maize grown in home gardens is harvested and eaten green, to supplement the declining stock of the preceding year's harvest. Similarly, corms of taro, yam, phul tarul (a flower plant with an edible yamlike root), and potato supplement staple cereals and thus prolong the availability of food all year-round. In the hills, many seasonal vegetables growing wild, for example, githa, bhyakur (*Dioscorea deltoidea*), lude (*Amaranthus viridis*), niuro (*Dryopteris* spp.), jaluka (a wild taro), sisnu (*Urtica ardens*), among others, also supplement the staple crops eaten by the household.

Fruit and vegetable species grown in home gardens have multiple uses and different rates of maturation, contributing to the year-round availability and diversity of sources of micronutrients in the daily diet. For example, pumpkin (*Cucurbita moschata*) is grown for its shoot, flower, and fruit; chayote (*Sechium edule*) for its tender shoot, fruit, and yamlike root; and taro (*Colocasia esculenta*) for its leaves, petioles, corm, and cormels. Home gardens also provide a number of green leafy vegetables that are rich in micronutrients (Agte et al. 2000). Home-garden crops, vegetables, and fruits are largely grown organically, providing safe and healthy food for household consumption. In the terai and in the hill areas with market access, people also sell vegetables and fruits grown in their home gardens to supplement their cash income. These crops commonly include pumpkin, sponge gourd (*Luffa cylindrica*), bottle gourd, cucumber, chayote, taro, oal (*Amorphophallus campanulatus*), and amaranthus in the vegetable category; and guava, mango, lychee, banana, pineapple, badahar (*Artocarpus lakoocha*), amala, bayar, jackfruit, tamarind, peach, plum, and many others in the fruit category.

A variety of trees are well integrated into the home-garden systems of Nepal (Table 5.1), particularly in the terai and middle hills regions. Trees have multiple uses; they provide food, fodder, firewood, and timber for household use. Where

Table 5.1

Distribution of vegetables, fruits, and staple food crops species in home gardens in three contrasting physiographic regions of Nepal

Common name	Scientific name	Stratum	Parts used	Main uses
Amaranthus	*Amaranthus* spp.	H	Grains	Crops
Peanut	*Arachis hypogea*	M	Grains	Crops
Canola	*Brassica compestris* var. *toria*	T	Grains	Crops
Pigeonpea	*Cajanus cajan*	M, T	Grains	Crops
Finger millet	*Eleusine coracana*	M	Grains	Crops
Soya bean	*Glycine max*	H, M	Grains	Crops
Sweet potato	*Ipomoea batatus*	M, T	Leaf, plant, tubers	Crops
Millet	*Pennisetum* spp.	H	Grains	Crops
Sugarcane	*Saccharum officinarum*	M, T	Stalk	Crops
Foxtail millet	*Setaria italica*	H	Grains	Crops
Potato	*Solanum tuberosum*	H, T	Tubers	Crops
Sorghum	*Sorghum bicolor*	M	Grains	Crops
Maize	*Zea mays*	H, M, T	Grains	Crops
Aanta (Nepali)		T	Fruit	Fruits
Hairpha (Nepali)		T	Fruit	Fruits
Sapodilla	*Manilkara zapota*	T	Fruit	Fruits
Bael	*Aegle marmelos*	T	Nut	Fruits
Chiuri (Nepali)	*Aesandra butyracea*	M	Fruit	Fruits
Pineapple	*Ananas comosus*	M	Fruit	Fruits
Wild custard apple	*Annona* spp.	H, M	Fruit	Fruits
Bettlenut	*Areca catechu*	T	Nut	Fruits
Jackfruit	*Artocarpus heterophyllus*	M, T	Fruit	Fruits
Papaya	*Carica papaia*	M	Fruit	Fruits
Lime	*Citrus aurantiifolia*	T	Fruit	Fruits
Sweet lime	*Citrus limettioides*	M	Fruit	Fruits
Lemon	*Citrus limon*	M	Fruit	Fruits
Pomello	*Citrus maxima*	T	Fruit	Fruits
Tasi	*Citrus* spp.	H, M	Fruit	Fruits
Coconut	*Cocos lucifera*	T	Nut	Fruits
Persimmon	*Diospyros virginiana*	T	Fruit	Fruits
Emblic	*Emblica officinalis*	T	Fruit	Fruits
Strawberry	*Fragaria vesca*	M	Fruit	Fruits
Walnut	*Juglans regia*		Nut	Fruits
Litchi	*Litchi chinensis*	T	Fruit	Fruits
Apple	*Malus* spp.	H	Fruit	Fruits
Mango	*Mangifera indica*	M, T	Fruit	Fruits
White mulberry	*Morus alba*	M	Fruit	Fruits
Banana	*Musa* spp.	M, T	Fruit	Fruits
Box myrtle (kaphal)	*Myrica esculenta*	M	Fruit	Fruits
Date palm	*Phoenix dactytifera*	T	Fruit	Fruits
Almond	*Prunus amygdalus*	H	Fruit	Fruits
Apricot	*Prunus armeniaca*	H	Fruit	Fruits
Plum	*Prunus domestica*	T	Fruit	Fruits

Table 5.1 continued

Common name	Scientific name	Stratum	Parts used	Main uses
Peach	*Prunus persica*	M	Fruit	Fruits
Guava	*Psidium guajava*	M, T	Fruit	Fruits
Pomegranate	*Punica granatum*	M	Fruit	Fruits
Pear	*Pyrus communis*	M	Fruit	Fruits
Blackberry	*Rubus* spp.	M	Fruit	Fruits
Jaman	*Syzygium cumini*	M	Fruit	Fruits
Kalojamun (Nepali)	*Syzygium* spp.	T	Fruit	Fruits
Tamarind	*Tamarindus indica*	T	Fruit	Fruits
Grape	*Vitis vinifera*	M, T	Fruit	Fruits
Jujube	*Ziziphus* spp.	M	Fruit	Fruits
Okra	*Abelmoschus esculentum*	M, T	Fruit	Vegetable
Shallots	*Allium ascalonicum*	M	Bulb	Vegetable
Onion	*Allium cepa*	H, M, T	Bulb, plant	Vegetable
Chive	*Allium schoenoprasum*	T	Plant	Vegetable
Armale	*Allium* spp.	H	Leaf, plant	Vegetable
Cholecha (Nepali)	*Allium* spp.	M, T	Plant	Vegetable
Ginari (Nepali)	*Amaranthus* spp.	M, T	Leaf, plant	Vegetable
Latte (Nepali)	*Amaranthus* spp.	M, T	Leaf, plant	Vegetable
Pigweed, green amaranth	*Amaranthus viridis*	T	Leaf, plant	Vegetable
Oal	*Amorphophallus campanulatus*	H, M, T	Root	Vegetable
Cane (bamboo)	*Arundinaria* spp.		Shoot	Vegetable
Asparagus	*Asparagus officinalis*	M	Shoot, root	Vegetable
Bamboo shoot	*Bambusa* spp.	H, M, T	Shoot	Vegetable
Ashgourd	*Benincasa hispida*	M, T	Fruit	Vegetable
Swiss chard	*Beta vulgaris* var. *cicla*	M, T	Leaf	Vegetable
Rayo	*Brassica juncea* var. *rayo*	M, T	Leaf	Vegetable
Cauliflower	*Brassica oleracea* var. *botrytis*	M	Flower	Vegetable
Broccoli	*Brassica oleracea* var. *broccoli*	H, M, T	Flower	Vegetable
Cabbage	*Brassica oleracea* var. *capitata*	H, M, T	Head	Vegetable
Turnip	*Brassica rapa*		Root	Vegetable
Yellow sarson	*Brassica rapa* subsp. *Trilocularis* var. *Sarson*	H, M, T	Leaf, twig	Vegetable
Chillies	*Capsicum annuum*	H, M, T	Fruit	Vegetable
Sweet pepper	*Capsicum annuum* var. *grossum*	H, M, T	Fruit	Vegetable
Goosefoot	*Chenopodium album*	H, M, T	Leaf, plant	Vegetable
Taro	*Colocasia esculenta*		Corm, stalk, leaf	Vegetable
Jute	*Corchorus* spp.	T	Young plant	Vegetable
Coriander	*Coriandrum sativum*	T	Leaf	Vegetable

Continued on next page

Table 5.1 continued

Common name	Scientific name	Stratum	Parts used	Main uses
Cucumber	*Cucumis sativus*	M	Fruit	Vegetable
Pumpkin	*Cucurbita moschata*	M	Fruits	Vegetable
Korila gourd	*Cyclanthera pedata*	M	Fruit	Vegetable
Tree tomato	*Cyphomandra betacea*		Fruit	Vegetable
Carrot	*Daucus carota*	H, M, T	Root	Vegetable
Yam	*Dioscorea* spp.		Root	Vegetable
Neuro fern	*Diplazium* spp.	H, M, T	Shoot	Vegetable
Hiude simi	*Dolichos lablab*	M	Fruit	Vegetable
Buckwheat	*Fagopyrum esculentum*	H, M, T	Young plant	Vegetable
Purple moonflower	*Ipomoea musicata*	M	Leaf, plant	Vegetable
Lettuce	*Lactuca sativa*	M, T	Leaf, plant	Vegetable
Bottle gourd	*Lagenaria siceraria*	H, M	Fruit	Vegetable
Cress	*Lepidium sativum*	M, T	Plant	Vegetable
Ridgegourd	*Luffa acutangola*	H	Fruit	Vegetable
Sponge gourd	*Luffa cylindrica*	M	Fruit	Vegetable
Tomato	*Lycopersicon esculentum*		Fruit	Vegetable
Cherry tomato	*Lycopersicon* spp.	M, T	Fruit	Vegetable
Chinese mallow	*Malva verticillata*	M	Leaf, plant	Vegetable
Bitter gourd	*Momordica charantia*	H, M, T	Fruit	Vegetable
Chinese bitter-cucumber	*Momordica cochinchinensis*	M	Fruit	Vegetable
Drumstick-tree, horseradish-tree	*Moringa oleifera*	M, T	Fruit	Vegetable
Watercress	*Nasturtium officinale*	M	Plant	Vegetable
Beans	*Phaseolus* spp.	T	Fruit	Vegetable
Pea	*Pisum sativum*	M	Fruit	Vegetable
Waterweed	*Polygonum* spp.		Twig	Vegetable
Radish	*Raphanus sativus*	M, T	Root, leaf	Vegetable
Chayote	*Sechium edule*	M, T	Fruit, root	Vegetable
Aubergine	*Solanum melongena*	T	Fruit	Vegetable
Potato	*Solanum tuberosum*	H, M	Tuber	Vegetable
Spinach	*Spinacia oleracea*	M, T	Leaf, twig	Vegetable
Snakegourd	*Trichosanthusanguina*	H	Fruit	Vegetable
Stinging Nettle	*Urtica* spp.	H, M, T	Twig	Vegetable
Faba bean	*Vicia faba*	T	Fruit	Vegetable
Cowpea	*Vigna unguiculata*	M, T	Fruit, pod	Vegetable

H = high mountain, M = mid/low hills and valleys, T = terai and inner terai

Physiographic region:

    1. High mountain: rain-shadow areas above 3,000 masl

    2. Mid/low hills and valleys: hill environment between 300–3,000 masl

    3. Inner terai and terai: plain environment below 300 masl

Source: Modified from Sthapit 2000.

livestock is an integral part of the farming system and is generally kept within the homestead, fodder trees are a prominent feature of the home gardens; this is especially true in the middle hills. The twigs and branches of fodder trees left after feeding the domestic animals are used as firewood for cooking. Timber and firewood trees, however, are limited in type and number. Home-garden trees are also commonly used to support the trailing vines of a number of vegetables (beans, yams, chayote, gourds, pumpkin, cucumber, etc.). They provide a variety of foods, such as flower buds (e.g., koiralo, *Bauhinia variegata*), leaf buds (kavro, *Ficus lacor*), siplican (*Crataeva religiosa*), vegetables (drumstick, *Moringa oleifera*), katahar (*Artocarpus heterophyllus*), and fruits (e.g., badahar, *Artocarpus lakoocha*), kimbu (*Morus* spp.), kaphal, (*Myrica esculenta*). These products are used to prepare special Nepalese dishes that are considered a great delicacy.

Nepalese cuisine uses a variety of spices; in fact, the taste and delicacy of Nepalese dishes depends on the proper use of special mixes of a number of spices. Thus, various spices, such as chilli, ginger, turmeric, cinnamon, garlic, shallot, onion, fenugreek, coriander, timur (*Xanthoxylum armatum*), and many others, are found in Nepalese home gardens (Table 5.2). As they have very poor access to modern medicines and medical facilities, people also keep a number of medicinal plants in their home gardens (Tables 5.2 and 5.3). Of these, tulasi (*Ocimum sanctum*), babari (*Ocimum basilicum*), marathi, pudina (*Mentha spicate*), ginger, timur, and bojo (*Acorus calamus*) are commonly used to cure colds, coughs, and stomach disorders, whereas *Rawolfolia serpentine* is used to cure snakebite. Traditional healers (*dhami* and *jhakri*) and medical practitioners (*vaidya*) maintain a range of medicinal plants in their home gardens to use in the treatment of various illnesses.

A number of plant species used for green manure, to improve soil fertility, and for pesticides, to control crop and storage pests (Table 5.2), are grown in home gardens, especially those of the middle hills. Asuro (*Adhatoda vasica*), titepati (*Artemisia vulgaris*), khirro (*Sapium insigne*), and ankhitare (*Walsura trijuga*) are common green manure crops planted along the boundary lines as live fences; they are used as green mulch and green manure, both inside the home garden as well as in the rice nursery. The leaves and stems of titepati, and the leaves, bark, and seeds of bakaino (*Melia azedarach*) and neem (*Azadirachta indica*), as well as the fruit of timur and the rhizomes of bojo, are used to control a variety of crop and storage pests. Since a majority of farmers use very little or no chemical fertilizers and pesticides in their home gardens, these species play an important role in maintaining soil fertility and controlling insect pests.

Table 5.2

Distribution of herbs and spices, medicinal, fodder, and other multipurpose tree species in home gardens in three contrasting physiographic regions of Nepal

Common name	Scientific name	Stratum	Parts used	Main uses
Elephant yam	*Amorphophallus campanulatus*	T	Rhizome	Cultural
Bhimsenpati	*Buddleja asiatica*	M		Cultural
Katus	*Castanopsis* spp.	M	Fruit	Cultural
Coconut	*Cocus lucifera*	T	Fruit	Cultural
Dubo	*Cynadon dactylone*	M, T	Plant	Cultural
Blue marbletree	*Elaeocarpus ganitrus*	T	Tree, fruit	Cultural
Banyan tree	*Ficus benghalensis*	M, T	Tree	Cultural
Pipal	*Ficus religiosa*	M	Tree	Cultural
Simrik/rohini	*Malotus phillippensis*	M	Fruit	Cultural
Fodder cane	*Saccharum spontaneum*	M		Cultural
Malabar-nut	*Adhatoda vasica*	M		Green manure, pesticide
Ceylon rosewood	*Albizia odoritissima*	M		Green manure, pesticide
Siris	*Albizia* spp.	M		Green manure, pesticide
Garlic pear	*Crataeva religiosa*	M		Green manure, pesticide
Banmara	*Eupatorium* spp.	M		Green manure, pesticide
Bardalo	*Ficus clavata*	M, T		Green manure, pesticide
Niger	*Guizotia abyssinica*			Green manure, pesticide
Chinaberry	*Melia azedarach*	M		Green manure, pesticide
Oregano	*Origanum vulgare*	M		Green manure, pesticide
Khirro	*Sapium insigne*	M, T		Green manure, pesticide
Dhaincha	*Sesbania*	M		Green manure, pesticide
Ankhitare	*Walsura trijuga*			Green manure, pesticide
Tithonia	*Tithonia diversifolia*	M		Green manure, pesticides
Titepati	*Artimisia vulgaris*	M	Plant	Green manure, pesticides, Cultural
Marathi		M	Flower, leaf	Medical
Asparagus	*Asparagus officinalis*	M	Root, shoot	Medical
Marijuana	*Cannabis sativa*	M	Seed	Medical
Dhaturo	*Datura* spp.	M, T	Seed	Medical
Githa	*Dioscorea* spp.	M	Root	Medical
Bhayakur	*Dioscorea deltoidea*	T	Root	Medical
Pudina	*Mentha* spp.	M, T	Leaf, plant	Medical
Sweet basil	*Ocimum basilicum*	M, T	Leaf, plant	Medical
Holy basil	*Ocimum sanctum*	M, T	Whole plant	Medical
Java pepper	*Piper cubeba*	M, T	Fruit, root	Medical
Jangali methi	*Trigonella emodi*	H	Leaf, seed	Medical
Kohan		T		Spices
Shallot	*Allium ascalonicum*	M	Leaf, plant, fruit	Spices
Onion	*Allium cepa*	H, M	Bulb, plant	Spices

Table 5.2 continued

Common name	Scientific name	Stratum	Parts used	Main uses
Jimbu	*Allium hypsistum*	H, T	Leaf	Spices
Garlic	*Allium sativum*	H, M	Bulb, leaf	Spices
Bhotelasun	*Allium* spp.	M	Leaf, bulb	Spices
Chillies	*Capsicum annuum*	H, M, T	Fruit	Spices
Coriander	*Coriandru sativum*	H, T	Leaf, fruit	Spices
Cumin	*Cuminum cyminum*	T	Seed	Spices
Turmeric	*Curcuma longa*	M	Rhizome	Spices
Cardamom	*Elettaria cardamomum*	M	Fruit	Spices
Perilla	*Perilla frutescens*	M	Seed	Spices
Seasame	*Sesamum indicum*	M, T	Seed	Spices
Bishop's weed	*Trachyspermum ammi*	T	Seed	Spices
Fenugreek	*Trigonnela* spp.	H, M, T	Seed	Spices
Saffron	*Crocus sativus*	H	Fruit	Spices, medical
Fennel	*Foeniculum vulgare*	M, T	Seed	Spices, medical
Opium	*Papaver somniferum*	H	Seed, fruit nectars	Spices, medical
Winged prickly ash	*Zanthoxylum armatum*	H, M, T	Fruit, fruit, leaf	Spices, medical
Ginger	*Zinziber officinale*	M, T	Rhizome	Spices, medical, cultural
Dhanyaro		M		Tree/shrubs for fodder
Monkeyfruit	*Artocarpus lakoocha*	M		Tree/shrubs for fodder
Camel's foot	*Bauhinia purpurea*	M		Tree/shrubs for fodder
Chuletro	*Brassaiosis* spp.	M, T		Tree/shrubs for fodder
Faledo	*Erythrina* spp.	M		Tree/shrubs for fodder
Khaniyo	*Ficus cunia*	M		Tree/shrubs for fodder
Dudhilo	*Ficus nemoralis*	M		Tree/shrubs for fodder
Roxburgh fig	*Ficus roxburghii*	M		Tree/shrubs for fodder
Bhotepipal, jimhar	*Ficus* spp.	H, T		Tree/shrubs for fodder
Fasro	*Grewia optiva*	M		Tree/shrubs for fodder
Kutmero	*Litsea polyantha*	M		Tree/shrubs for fodder
Kaulo	*Machilus gamblei*	M		Tree/shrubs for fodder
Kimbu	*Morus alba*	M		Tree/shrubs for fodder
Kaphal	*Myrica esculenta*	M		Tree/shrubs for fodder
Gigari	*Premna barbata*	M		Tree/shrubs for fodder
Ring-cup oak	*Quercus glauca*	M		Tree/shrubs for fodder
Babylon weeping willow	*Salix babylonica*	H, M		Tree/shrubs for fodder
Gogan	*Saurauia napaulensis*	M		Tree/shrubs for fodder
Harro	*Teminalia chebula*	M		Tree/shrubs for fodder
Behra	*Terminalia belerico*	M		Tree/shrubs for fodder
Amriso	*Thysanolaens maxima*	M		Tree/shrubs for fodder
Bael	*Aegle marmelos*	T	Leaf, fruit	Tree/shrubs for other

Continued on next page

Table 5.2 continued

Common name	Scientific name	Stratum	Parts used	Main uses
Kadam	*Anthocephalus cadamba*		Tree, fruit	Tree/shrubs for other
Nigalo	*Arundinaria spp.*	M	Shoot	Tree/shrubs for other
Indian lilac	*Azadirachta indica*		Tree	Tree/shrubs for other
Mountian ebony	*Bauhinia variegata*	M	Flower	Tree/shrubs for other
Red silk cottontree	*Bombax malabaricum*	M	Fruit	Tree/shrubs for other
Toon, red cedar	*Cedrela toona*	M		Tree/shrubs for other
Camphor	*Cinnamomum camphora*	M	Tree	Tree/shrubs for other
Indian bark	*Cinnamomum tamala*	M, T	Bark, leaf	Tree/shrubs for other
Spider tree	*Crataeva unilocularis*	M	Shoot	Tree/shrubs for other
Tamabans	*Dendrocalamus* spp.	M	Shoot	Tree/shrubs for other
Amala	*Emblica officinalis*	M, T	Fruit	Tree/shrubs for other
Fig	*Ficus carica*	M	Fruit	Tree/shrubs for other
Pakhuri	*Ficus glaberrima*	M		Tree/shrubs for other
Spotted fig	*Ficus lacor*	M, T	Shoot	Tree/shrubs for other
Indian lilac	*Melia azadirachta*	M	Seed, trunk	Tree/shrubs for other
Drumstick	*Mringa oleifera*		Fruit	Tree/shrubs for other
Castor	*Ricinus communis*	T	Seed	Tree/shrubs for other
Chinese soapberry	*Sapindus mukorossi*	M, T	Fruit	Tree/shrubs for other
Sal	*Shorea robusta*		Leaf, tree	Tree/shrubs for other
Lapsi	*Choerospondia axillaris*	M, T	Fruit	Tree/shrubs for other

H = high mountain, M = mid/low hills and valleys, T = terai and inner terai

Physiographic region:

   1. High mountain: rain-shadow areas above 3,000 masl

   2. Mid/low hills and valleys: hill environment between 300–3,000 masl

   3. Inner Terai and Terai: plain environment below 300 masl

Source: Modified from Sthapit 2000.

Cultural and Religious Use

Home gardens harbor a number of plant species that play an important role in the cultural and religious life of the inhabitants of particular communities in different parts of the country (see the study by Gurung and Vaidya 1998 on the western hills of Nepal). Nigalo (*Drepanostachyum* spp.), tusa (young bamboo shoots), and bamboo tama (fermented young shoots) are important delicacies for hill people, whereas these same species are mostly used as construction materials by people in the terai. Newars, a dominant ethnic group of the Kathmandu Valley, specifically maintain cholecha (*Allium* spp.), black soybean, garlic, shallot, chamsur (*Lepidium sativum*), and red turnip in their home gardens to use in their ceremonies and feasts. Hill people in Eastern and Western Nepal tend to keep

Table 5.3

Selected home-garden species used for traditional medicine in Nepal

Local name	Scientific name	Medicinal value reported
Asuro	*Adhatoda vasica*	• Used to prepare expectorant and antispasmodic medicine to treat chronic bronchitis, asthma, anthelminthic, applied over fresh wounds, rheumatic joints and inflammatory swellings
Bojo	*Acorus calamus*	• The rhizome is roasted in fire and used against dry cough • Promotes memory longevity and good voice • Liberates sinus • Use for piles, constipation, colic pains, epilepsy, urine disorder, infections, etc. • Use for storage pest as insecticide
Harro/ barro	*Terminalia chebula/* *T. bellerica*	• Dry fruits roasted in fire and used against cough and cold • Tonic, laxative • When half ripe it has purgative value whereas when fully ripe it has astringent value, kernel-narcotic value
Koiralo	*Bauhinia variegata*	• Juice of flower is used to treat dysentery and diarrhea
Neem	*Azadirachta indica*	• Twigs used for toothbrush • Leaves used for repellent for rice moth • Juice of neem leaves mixed with salt and black pepper to cure intestinal worms • Juice and oil extracts used for venereal, skin diseases, jaundice, malaria, dysentery and diarrhea • Neem seed oil used for sprains, toothache, and earache • Neem trees repel mosquitoes from the garden • Antidotal and diuretic value
Sajiwan	*Jatropha curcas*	• Extracts used for mud-borne disease between gaps of toes during paddy transplanting • Used as toothbrush
Sattuwa	*Paris polyphylla*	• Juice extract from root is used against poison and gas formations
Sisnu	*Utrica* spp.	• Bark is used to treat gout • Juice of leaf mixed with curd to treat dysentery • A decoction of leaves usful for treating sexual disease, gonorrhea
Soph	*Foeniculum vulgare* (Fennel)	• Stimulant • Vermicide • Aromatic and anti-inflammatory
Timur	*Litsea citrata* (Sil timur)	• Soup of timur is used against diarrhea and gas formation
	Xanthoxylum *armatum* (Raye timur)	• Soup of raye timur mixed with jimu, garlic, and turmeric is used for gastric treatment
Tulasi	*Ocimum basilicum*	• Leaves used for various kinds of fever, bronchitis, stomach, gastric disorder of children and earache • Mosquito repellent • Stimulating expectorant

Sources: Rajbhandary et al. 1995; Manandhar 1989; Kandel and Wagley 1999; Pratap and Sthapit 1998.

broad leaf mustard, garlic, tree tomatoes (*Cyphomandra betacea*), cherry tomatoes, chayote, and radishes in their home gardens, which they use for cooking. On the other hand, oal, lapha sag and patuwa sag (leafy vegetables), and drumstick are delicacies to the terai people. Banana, sugarcane, and ginger are also carefully maintained in the home garden in the terai, where they are specifically required for use in the chhat festival, one of the most important religious ceremonies here. Similarly, food prepared from oal, a commonly grown vegetable in the terai home gardens, is a must at one of the many local ceremonies taking place in eastern terai.

Nepal is a multiethnic and multicultural country, and people are deeply religious. Not surprisingly, some plant species are kept in home gardens mostly for their religious use. For example, tulasi (*Ocimum sanctum*) is regarded as a sacred plant, the incarnation of the god Vishnu, and therefore is planted on a built structure called *matha* and is worshipped and watered daily. Dubo (*Cynadon dactylone*) is another species required for daily worship (*puja*), and for other religious occasions. Many home gardeners in the terai keep bel (*Aegle marmelos*) for its leaves, which they specially offer to the god Shiva. Many households, especially those in urban areas, have now also started to plant pipal (*Ficus religiosa*), regarded as an incarnation of Vishnu, for their daily worship. The Brahmin and Chhetri ethnic groups are very particular about maintaining these plant species in their home gardens.

Space to Introduce New Species and Maintain Unique Old Species

Home gardens provide space for the introduction of new species and the domestication of wild ones. They also serve as experimental plots where people breed new varieties of crops and test different management practices. Rana *bagaincha* (palace gardens) are the classical example of how new species are introduced into home gardens (Kaini 1995; Pandey 1994). During the Rana regime (1846–1950), rulers in Kathmandu and other parts of Nepal introduced a number of new fruit, vegetable, and ornamental plant species and varieties into their palace gardens. Important landlords (previously called *jamindar*) did the same in the home gardens and *phulbari* (orchards). Nowadays, people who travel frequently for reasons of work to different parts of the country or to India have introduced a number of new species of fruits, vegetables, spices, flowers, and medicinal plants into their gardens. They have brought coffee, tea, cardamom, avocado, cashew nut, and different varieties of grapes into the hills, and coconut, betel nut, and black pepper into the terai. Similarly, a variety of fodder trees, cinnamon, marathi, sal (*Shorea robusta*), and lapsi (*Choerospondia axillaris*) are some of the other introduced species. In short, home gardens have served as a good venue for the introduction, enhancement, and in situ maintenance of a wide range of genetic diversity.

Home gardens have also been privileged places where community members maintain unique plant species, either introduced, nearly lost, or endangered. Our own observations and anecdotal reports show a number of such cases, to wit madale kankro (a large-sized cucumber used especially for pickling), dalle kankro (the oval-shaped cucumber), basaune ghiraula (the aromatic sponge gourd; Pandey et al. 2001), jire khursani (a small hot chilli), koira (a local turnip variety; Lohar et al. 1993), and thulo cauli (a large-sized local green cauliflower). Rana palace gardens contain a number of such cultivars. Home gardens, therefore, play an important role in the conservation of unique and/or rare plant species that are not found in the larger ecosystem and are on the verge of extinction.

Creating an Attractive Homestead Environment

Some tree and plant species are specifically planted in the home garden to improve the environment around the homestead. These include ashoka (*Saraca indica*), neem, kadam (*Anthocephalus cadamba*), gulmohar (*Delonix regia*), rudraksha (*Elaeocarpus ganitrus*), and a number of ornamentals, both trees and shrubs. These trees provide shade and clean air to the homestead, and they beautify the surroundings. Ashoka, neem, and tulasi are also believed to repel insects.

Home gardens in Nepal have always been a symbol of social status. Their size, rich species composition, attractive layout, and cleanliness are a source of pride to their owners. Wealthy families have bigger home gardens, a larger number of unique plant species, and a greater diversity than poorer families (Rana, Rijal et al. 2000). Rana palace gardens in and outside of Kathmandu and the big gardens and *bagaincha* (fruit orchards) of *jamindar* (landlords) were purposely designed to include a considerable diversity of plant species, reflecting the high status of their makers. The social value placed on home gardens has helped to diversify and maintain a wide range of plant species in the community.

Types and Features of Home Gardens in Nepal

The typology, species diversity, and other features of home gardens are not well documented. Our observations indicate that there is great diversity in the types, composition, and structure of home gardens in Nepal as we travel from east to west and from south to north. An attempt is made here to characterize the Nepalese home gardens.

The different types of home gardens observed in various parts of Nepal are listed in Table 5.4. This typology, using the terms local people employ to refer to different home gardens and their related structures, is based largely on their loca-

Table 5.4

Types of home gardens reported in different parts of Nepal

Types of home gardens	Ecoregion	Location in relation to house	Composition	Structure
1. Bari	Terai (plains)	Close to house	Vegetable dominant but mixed with fruits, multipurpose trees, and flowers	More than 3 layers, intensive, and varying size
2. Ghar-bari	Hills	Close to house	Vegetable dominant but mixed with fruits, multipurpose trees, and flowers	More than 3 layers, intensive, and varying size
3. Goth-bari	Hills	Away from house but close to goth	Vegetable dominant but mixed with fruits, multipurpose trees, and flowers	About 3 layers, less intensive, and varying size
4. Tarkari bari	Terai (plains)	Away from house	Largely vegetables with limited number and types of vegetables	About 2 layers with intensive ground layer
5. Dumna	Inner terai, midwestern Nepal	Away from house	Largely vegetables with limited number and types of vegetables	About 2 layers with intensive ground layer
6. Karesa bari	Hills and valleys	Close to house	Mostly vegetables of modern varieties and seasonal in nature	Single layer
7. Bagaincha	Hills and valleys	Close to as well as away from house	Mostly fruits of single species but often mixed with few other fruits and vegetables	Mostly single layer and less intensive
8. Phulbari	Terai (plains)	Close to as well as away from house	Mostly fruits of single species but often mixed with few other fruits and vegetables	Mostly single layer and less intensive

tion in relation to the house and on their composition. If we adhere to the generally accepted definition of home gardens, that is, a fenced or protected area around a homestead where crops, vegetables, fruits, medicines, spices, fodder, and other plant species are integrated integrated, then only bari and ghar-bari truly represent Nepalese home gardens. However, other garden types also share some features and uses with home gardens and are therefore described here as their variants.

Bari, literally meaning fenced area in the terai, and *ghar-bari*, literally meaning fenced area around a house in the hills, are the most common types of home gardens found in Nepal. These home gardens are maintained around the homesteads and are generally fenced to keep the livestock away. *Goth-bari*, literally meaning fenced area around an animal shed (*goth*), is an imitation of ghar-bari in the hills. People not limited in their space around their houses keep animals near cultivated land, at a convenient distance away from the family home. The goth-bari is also used to grow a number of vegetables, fruits, and fodder trees. *Tarkari bari*, literally meaning fenced vegetable-growing area, is maintained by farmers belonging to the Koiri ethnic group who are traditionally engaged in commercial vegetable farming in the terai region of Eastern Nepal. The tarkari bari is generally located away from the home but close to the village for ease of supervision and is usually made when the bari home garden is very small. *Dumna*, locally meaning upland, is similar to tarkari bari and is maintained by farmers of the Tharu ethnic community in mid to far Western Nepal. Dumna is also located away from home, generally on a slightly raised area in the middle of a rice field that is unfenced. *Karesa bari*, literally meaning garden located behind the house, and otherwise called "kitchen garden," is introduced terminology used by development agencies, both governmental and nongovernmental, to refer to an area set apart within the homestead for year-round vegetable production. It is, therefore, a subsystem of a home garden where seasonal and mostly modern and exotic varieties of vegetables are promoted with the primary objective of meeting the nutritional requirements of the family.

Bagaincha in valleys and hills and phulbari in the terai and inner terai regions are basically fruit orchards that may be close to or inside the homestead or away from the home altogether but close to the village. Rana bagaincha in the Kathmandu Valley and *suntala bagaincha* (orange orchard) in the middle hills are examples of bagaincha; mango orchards in terai are examples of phulbari. Bagaincha and phulbari orchards located close to or inside the homestead share many features with bari and ghar-bari; they can be regarded as fruit-dominated home gardens.

In terms of composition, the common types of Nepalese home gardens, such as bari and ghar-bari, are dominated by vegetables; many types and varieties of vegetables are integrated with spices, medicinal plants, fruits, and multipurpose trees of various types. These home gardens hold a great diversity of plant species having multiple uses; they are purposely maintained to meet the diverse needs of the family (Table 5.1). Our survey of twenty-nine households in the Kaski district of Western Nepal (see map, Fig. 5.1) showed that, on average, people maintained about fourteen species of vegetables, five species of fruits, and five species of fod-

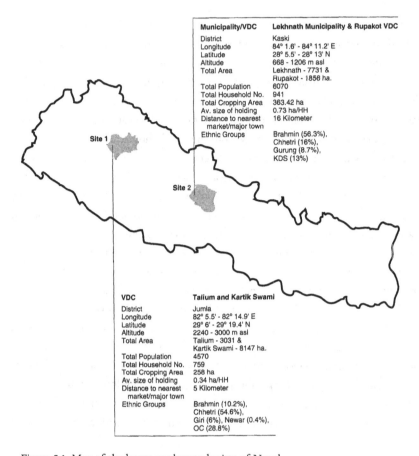

Municipality/VDC	Lekhnath Municipality & Rupakot VDC
District	Kaski
Longitude	84° 1.6' - 84° 11.2' E
Latitude	28° 5.5' - 28° 13' N
Altitude	668 - 1206 m asl
Total Area	Lekhnath - 7731 & Rupakot - 1856 ha.
Total Population	6070
Total Household No.	941
Total Cropping Area	363.42 ha
Av. size of holding	0.73 ha/HH
Distance to nearest market/major town	16 Kilometer
Ethnic Groups	Brahmin (56.3%), Chhetri (16%), Gurung (8.7%), KDS (13%)

VDC	Talium and Kartik Swami
District	Jumla
Longitude	82° 5.5' - 82° 14.9' E
Latitude	29° 6' - 29° 19.4' N
Altitude	2240 - 3000 m asl
Total Area	Talium - 3031 & Kartik Swami - 8147 ha.
Total Population	4570
Total Household No.	759
Total Cropping Area	258 ha
Av. size of holding	0.34 ha/HH
Distance to nearest market/major town	5 Kilometer
Ethnic Groups	Brahmin (10.2%), Chhetri (54.6%), Giri (6%), Newar (0.4%), OC (28.8%)

Figure 5.1. Map of the home-garden study sites of Nepal

der trees in their home gardens. Although commercial varieties of vegetables are increasingly finding their way into home gardens, indigenous vegetables and their varieties are still dominant, a striking feature of Nepalese home gardens. Similarly, maintenance of a large number of preferred perennial vegetables such as yam, taro, chayote, drumstick, tree tomato, and the like, as well as vegetable varieties of aubergine, taro, tomatoes, chillies, and vegetatively propagated thulo cauli is another interesting feature of the these home gardens. The addition of fodder-tree species is a unique feature of home gardens in the hills, whereas the incorporation of fruit and shade trees is a characteristic of terai home gardens.

The species composition of goth-bari is more or less similar to that of bari/ ghar-bari, but it is less intensive; that is, it has less species diversity and is planted less densely. Tarkari bari and dumna are similar in composition; they consist mostly of annual and perennial vegetables, with none or very few trees on the

boundary. Similarly, bagaincha and phulbari are basically fruit orchards dominated by a single fruit species; for example, orange in hill bagaincha, and mango
in terai phulbari. However, intravarietal diversity exits in these gardens. For example, Rana bagainchas in the Kathmandu Valley, consist of a variety of fruits,
and many mango phulbaris in the terai consist of a good number of other trees
such as jackfruit, badahar, jamun, sapota (*Achras sapota*), and coconut.

The high species diversity of bari/ghar-bari is structured into a multilayered
system. The species found in these home gardens are systematically arranged in
close association with each other within a small area in more than three vertical
layers. Tall trees are usually placed along the boundary of the home garden to
serve as live fences and to avoid shading the larger area. Experienced farmers have
expert knowledge about the compatibility of different home-garden plant species
and how to orient them in a symbiotic relationship. The principal features of lay-
ering plant species follow a pattern: The top layer consists of large fruit trees (such
as mango, jackfruit, jamun, guava, pear, peach, etc.), fodder trees, and other
multipurpose trees. The middle layer consists of shrublike species of fruits (papaya, banana, citrus, etc.), vegetables (tree tomato, drumstick, cassava, etc.), and
climbers (gourds, yam, chayote, cucumber, pumpkin, beans, etc.). The lower layer
consists largely of vegetables (okra, chillies, aubergine, cauliflower, taro, etc.),
spices (ginger, turmeric, coriander, etc.), and herbs (tulasi, babari, marathi, etc.).
The ground layer consists of creepers (sweet potato, lahare sag, etc.), root crops
(radish, turnip, carrot, etc.), and spices (coriander, marathi, etc.). Species number
and diversity decrease as one moves from the lower layer to the top layer, and
farmers do this purposely and carefully to avoid plant competition for light and
nutrients. Tarkari bari, dumna, and karesa bari are less intensively layered; they
usually have ground and lower layers, though in a very few instances a middle
layer consisting of fruit trees such as papaya, guava, and banana has been added.
Bagaincha and phulbari generally have a top layer and a weakly integrated middle
layer. However, when established within the homestead, these gardens have all
four layers, as in the bari/ghar-bari home gardens.

Except for bagaincha and phulbari, intensive care and management are the
common features of most types of home gardens. Since home gardens are located around the house, family members are able to pay great attention and lav-
ish care on the plants grown there. Home gardens receive heavy applications of
animal manure, and the soil is consequently more fertile than in the larger ecosystem. Lohar and his colleagues (1993) have estimated that farmers in the western
hills of Nepal use more than 50 metric tons per hectare of animal manure in their
home gardens. Leaf litter and crop by-products are used as mulching, and ashes

from the kitchen also go into the home garden to fertilize the soil. Home gardens in Nepal are generally managed with low external inputs; the use of chemical fertilizers and pesticides is negligible or almost nonexistent. Therefore, their production, which is largely organic, is healthy and safe. Even commercial vegetable farmers grow organic vegetables in their home gardens for family consumption.

Seeds and planting materials for home gardens are maintained by the garden owners themselves (Rana, Joshi, and Lohar 1998; Shrestha 1998: 143–52). Planting materials brought in from the outside are obtained through exchange within as well as outside the community (Shrestha 1998; Subedi et al. 2001). Our own observations and a limited study (Rana, Joshi, and Lohar 1998; Baniya et al. 2001) show that farmers select seeds and planting materials, going as far as breeding—that is, selecting from naturally created variation—as well as crossing to generate diversity in the existing stock of home-garden species. Diversity in varieties of chilli in home gardens is a result of such processes. Baniya and his colleagues (2001) found that farmers use different plant parts in their selection for different varieties of taro.

Women are generally the custodians of home gardens; they devote much time and care to their management. Men also contribute to the maintenance of home gardens, but their role is more important in the introduction of new species and varieties. Thus, men tend to introduce exotic commercial fruit trees into the home garden, whereas women prefer to maintain traditional vegetables and other plant species that are required on a regular basis for cooking. The gender dimension of home-garden activities, however, needs more future attention.

Plant species found in home gardens have diverse and multiple uses; they meet household requirements for food, spices, medicines, fodder, firewood, timber, and so forth. Home-garden production systems are, therefore, subsistence-oriented; plant species are carefully selected to be available throughout the year, as well as to satisfy taste and food habits. However, in communities that have access to markets, home-garden production is often semicommercial; part of the produce is sold in the market to supplement the cash income of the family. In such home gardens, commercial vegetables, fruits, and spices are dominant, often gradually displacing the indigenous species (Rana, Joshi, and Lohar 1998). Urban home gardens, however, should not be seen as synonymous with semicommercial home gardens. Urban home gardens represent a different home-garden system, but they share important resemblances with rural home gardens. Even though the details of this system have yet to be fully understood, it has been observed that urban home gardens maintain many indigenous plant species that are not commonly available in the market.

Factors Affecting the Composition and Structure of Nepalese Home Gardens

Our observations show considerable variation in the composition and structure of home gardens in Nepal. Major factors causing this variation are discussed below.

The agroecology of a particular region and location has been found to influence to a great extent the species composition and structural layout in home gardens. For example, tropical plants such as mango, coconut, papaya, oal, and others are common in home gardens of the terai, whereas subtropical to temperate species such as peach, pear, and chayote are common in the home gardens of the hilly regions. The number of vertical layers in the home gardens decreases with the increase in altitude, to allow light and heat to reach the lower layers. Thus, home gardens in high hills have none, or very few, top tree layers, as compared with terai home gardens, which have densely arranged top tree layers.

A number of studies indicate that wealthy households maintain more diversity in their home gardens than poorer households (Rana, Rijal et al. 2000; Rana, Shrestha, et al. 2000: 117–26). The fact that home-garden diversity shows a strong positive correlation with the size of the home garden has also been reported from a number of countries (IPGRI 1998).

A typical home garden in the low hills or plains of Nepal

Home gardens of a Gurung community in the high mountains of Nepal

Ethnicity and cultural attitudes toward food are closely associated; these in turn have also been observed to influence the choice of species planted in home gardens: tasi (a citrus species) and cholecha are cultivated by the Newars people; bhote lasun (a garlic variety) and rayo sag (broad leaf mustard) by highlanders; and oal, lapha sag (*Malva verticillata*), and patuwa sag (*Corchorus* spp.) by terai families. Similarly, tulasi is always kept in the home gardens of Brahmin and Chhetri households for its religious and medicinal values.

We have already mentioned that women play an important role in the management of home gardens. Because women are primarily responsible for the daily preparation of meals for the family, deciding what to cook and how, they have a large say in the composition and structure of the home gardens. They make sure that tomatoes, chilli, garlic, coriander, mint, and leafy vegetables are always present. Women also promote diversity by bringing new plant species from their parental home. Gender roles, however, also depend on the ethnic and cultural background of the farmers. In the terai ethnic communities, for example, men and women play equally important roles in the management of home gardens and the introduction of new diversity into them (Subedi et al. 2001).

As farmers come to learn more about new species, they become increasingly interested in introducing them into their home gardens; the appearance of the neem tree in many parts of the lower hills is a good example. Knowledge has also encouraged the domestication of some medicinal plants and spices otherwise found only in the wild. Farmers also keep a number of varieties of the same species having different uses, as in case of taro (Rijal et al. 2001).

The mobility of the people and their exposure to new places and novel information have also influenced the composition of their home gardens. Rana palace gardens are an example. Subedi and his colleagues (2001) have found that key farmers, with connections and contacts outside the community, maintain a higher plant diversity than more sedentary farmers. Similarly, *lahures,* that is, people working in the Indian and British Gurkha armies, have adopted a number of exotic plant species. Study tours for farmers, nowadays increasingly being organized by development agencies, have also helped farmers to diversify their gardens.

Migration is another factor that has helped to introduce new plant species into an area. In Chitwan Valley, which is full of migrants from all over Nepal, immigrants have introduced a wide range of plant species. The same is true in other parts of Nepal. Food crops such as buckwheat, niger, and a number of fodder trees and green manure crops—asuro in Chitwan and inner terai, bhote lasun in the lower hills, and broad leaf mustard in terai—are good examples of this trend. Because food habits and associated uses persist, people carry a variety of plant species when they migrate to a new area. If these plant species survive, they will certainly find their way into the home gardens of other persons in the community.

Access to markets encourages people living in periurban areas and close to roads to maintain semicommercial home gardens whose composition is influenced by what crops sell well. For example, commercial vegetables that are seasonally available, such as cauliflower, cabbage, okra, radish, and beans, are common in such gardens, whereas perennial vegetables are more characteristic of traditional home gardens. Commercial gardens integrate fewer fruit trees and are less layered in structure because the emphasis is rather on short-duration and high-input vegetables. Diversity in such home gardens is also low and is continually declining (Rana, Joshi, and Lohar 1998). Commercialization of home-grown crops has also eroded indigenous management practices and associated knowledge. Access to markets, however, can also lead to the promotion and conservation, especially in urban home gardens, of indigenous plant species that are not readily available in the market.

The composition and structure of home gardens are increasingly being influenced by development activities that are expected to improve family nutrition and/or increase the family income in areas with accessible markets. These programs have been focusing on year-round production of seasonal, modern and exotic vegetable varieties, often undermining the functions and value of traditional vegetables. Even though such development activities have increased the vegetable diversity of home gardens in rural areas, their sustainability has suffered from deficient networks of seed supply. In most cases of commercial production, it has actually reduced the overall genetic diversity of the traditional home gardens. Because very little or no consideration is given to the introduction of fruits and other multipurpose trees and plant species, development activities have promoted single-layered, less intensive home gardens.

Research and Development Issues

Despite the significant contribution they make to the livelihood of rural people, and though they play an important role in the conservation of a wide range of plant-genetic resources, home gardens are a highly neglected area of research and development, ignored in the agenda of both formal and informal institutions. It has not even been considered a subject worthy of scientific research. And because home-garden production has never been included in the Nepalese national statistics, their contribution as a food source has been sadly undervalued. In this context, it is worth discussing relevant research and development issues.

Scientific and systematic information on home-garden production in Nepal is totally lacking, and this has prevented the inclusion of home gardens in national strategies focused on food security, improved family nutrition, and conservation of plant-genetic resources. A concerted effort to document the characteristic features and types, structure and composition, inherent species and varietal diversity, and ecological and social setting of home gardens is therefore urgently required. In addition, answers to the following research questions would help to refine conservation and development strategies implemented through home gardens.

1. Do home gardens retain varietal and species diversity not commonly found in the larger agroecosystems? The answer to this question is vital in deciding whether home gardens can be useful units for in situ conservation of plant-genetic resources. A study conducted in the western hills of Nepal by Rijal and his colleagues (2001) shows that more than twenty varieties of taro are maintained collectively in the home gardens of a single community. A majority of these varieties are grown in a small area; two of them, however, namely, hatipau and khari, which have multiple uses and market value, are grown in a large area outside the home garden. Similarly, only one or two varieties of sponge gourd are grown per

household, but at the community level four to five varieties have been maintained (Pandey et al. 2001). The social network within a community plays a significant role in the exchange of information and genetic materials, thus enhancing the in situ conservation of plant-genetic resources (Subedi et al. 2001). Such preliminary studies show that a conservation strategy is possible if home gardens are considered at the community level.

2. How do ecological factors influence the structure and composition of home gardens? To a large extent, ecological factors such as altitude, soil, climate, seasonality, stress, and abundance of plant species set limit to the occurrence and diversity of crops. The effect of such factors on the structure, composition, and distribution of species diversity in home gardens in different agroecological zones needs to be explored and compared.

3. How do socioeconomic factors affect the various components of home gardens? Socioeconomic factors have an important influence on the behavior of those who manage the home garden. Gessler, Hodel, and Eyzaguirre (1998) have documented a number of factors, such as labor availability, level of on-farm returns, outside employment, and migration that have influenced home-garden composition. Understanding the socioeconomic background of farmers and their decision-making patterns is, therefore, crucial in designing proper in situ conservation activities. Income distribution, ethnicity, profession, dietary preferences, and market forces are key factors that must be taken into account in order to assess when and how people value and maintain genetic diversity in their home gardens.

4. How do commercialization and crop introduction and improvement affect species and varietal diversity in home gardens? In most cases, commercialization has promoted monoculture crop production, causing a decrease in the genetic diversity of the system. Similarly, crop introduction and improvement of crops may have a positive or negative impact on the diversity within a locality. New crops may inject new diversity into the system, but if they are more profitable and productive, they might marginalize traditional and less productive varieties.

5. What development interventions enhance home-garden biodiversity and improve family nutrition and income? The maintenance of biodiversity in home gardens reflects the farmers' multiple objectives. It is increasingly being recognized that in rural Nepal home gardens are the main source of micronutrients for the family, especially for women and children. A majority of development interventions seem to conflict with the goals of enhancing home-garden biodiversity. But if carefully designed, such projects are likely to support farmers' goals of maintaining and enhancing biodiversity in their home gardens.

National Strategies

Home gardens have never been a top priority in national strategies for agricultural development in Nepal. Nevertheless, development agencies—both governmental and nongovernmental—have often used them to promote their family nutrition and income-generating programs. Unfortunately, these programs suffer from the classic development mentality and top-down approach that cause serious anomalies and conflicts.

Development programs focused on nutrition tend to promote the indiscriminate introduction of exotic and/or improved species and varieties of vegetables without reference to people's actual needs or their home-garden management systems. Introduced species are mostly seasonal and short-lived. They have single uses and therefore do not fill people's requirement for perennial species with multiple uses. For example, chilli, aubergine, tomatoes, and amaranths provide a continuous supply of vegetables throughout the year, which seasonal species do not. Traditionally, people have included in their gardens a number of vegetable species that have good processing qualities and long-duration storage value. For example, pumpkin, chayote, taro, and ash gourd are processed and stored foods that can be used in the dry season, when there is a scarcity of vegetables. This aspect has been completely ignored by development planners. Moreover, experts have focused most of their attention on vegetables, whereas traditional home gardeners give equal value to other species such as spices, medicinal plants, fruits, and multipurpose trees. Misguided development interventions have the potential to reduce home-garden biodiversity and narrow their micronutrient base.

Moreover, the vegetable and other plant species introduced into home gardens by most development agents often require external inputs in the form of chemical fertilizers and pesticides. In contrast, local home-garden species thrive well with inputs of animal manure and locally made organic pesticides. Similarly, many introduced species have difficulty in producing seeds, while some are hybrids, making them dependent on external sources. These are not easily and cheaply accessible to rural peoples, thus gradually reducing the control over seeds exerted by household members. Traditional home-garden species, on the other hand, are easy to seed, including vegetable species that are perennial and others, such as chilli, aubergine, and tomatoes, that have been selected to perform well under perennial management. Local farmers have developed unique seed-management practices, such as the vegetative propagation of thulo cauli and variety-specific propagation techniques for taro. Thus, many traditional home-garden species are the result of continuous selection, adaptation, and local breeding efforts. Most "developers" have been unable to recognize these aspects, with the result that such innovations have been discouraged. Similarly, traditional home gardeners use management practices such as multilayering that maximize the use of space and increase and diversify production. Many introduced species, however, have failed to adapt to such management regimes.

Often, new plant species and varieties promoted through development programs require new management knowledge; the resulting knowledge gap has often been one of the reasons why such programs fail. Farmers who plant traditional home gardens, on the other hand, have a vast store of knowledge concerning how to use different plant species, including their compatibility in a multilayered production system, their soil-fertility and pest-control requirements, their plant propagation and seed properties, and their storage and processing capacities. Despite farmers' proven competence, their knowledge and practices are rarely given the consideration they merit. Not surprisingly, development programs have contributed to the erosion of indigenous knowledge and eventually to the genetic erosion of many traditional home-garden species.

Development strategies for home gardens need, therefore, to be redefined in such a way as to combine livelihood goals with conservation goals. New development interventions should build on the traditional knowledge and practices of home-garden managers. Well-designed programs may have a positive impact on both food security and the conservation of agrobiodiversity (Joshi et al. 1997). A holistic approach needs to be adopted to capitalize on use value, to strengthen the seed supply system, and to increase access to information and germplasm. Experiences from in situ crop conservation initiatives show that community mobilization is a useful strategy to link development and conservation objectives.

Conclusions

Home gardens are an important component of the Nepalese farming system. Unfortunately, they have long been a neglected area for research and development. Because information is so limited, the scientific study of the home-garden systems in Nepal is urgently required. Such a study will contribute in at least three important ways: (a) it will reveal research areas and agendas necessary to generate home-garden technologies that are compatible with the traditional systems; (b) it will chart development strategies and actions that further enrich indigenous home-garden systems; and (c) it will supply planners and policymakers with appropriate information so they can include home gardens in national development and conservation strategies. Unquestionably, then, home gardens provide an excellent context for the in situ conservation of plant-genetic resources.

Acknowledgments

We are grateful to Dr. Anil Subedi, executive director, Local Initiatives for Biodiversity Research and Development (LI-BIRD), and Dr. Pablo Eyzaguirre, senior social scientist, International Plant Genetic Resources Institute (IPGRI), for encouraging us to write this paper. We are also thankful to Deutsche Stiftung für Internationale Entwicklung (DSE), Germany, for supporting our participation in the workshop.

References

Agte, V. V., K. V. Tarwadi, S. Mengale, and S. A. Chiplonkar. 2000. Potential of traditionally cooked green leafy vegetables as natural sources for supplementation of eight micronutrients in vegetarian diets. *Journal of Food Composition and Analysis*, 13: 885–91.

Baniya, B. K., A. Subedi, R. B. Rana, R. K. Tiwari, and P. Chaudhary. 2001. Planting material management of taro in Kaski Districts of Nepal. Paper presented at the First National Workshop, Strengthening the Scientific Basis of in situ Conservation of Agricultural Biodiversity on-Farm, 24–26 April 2001, Lumle, Kaski, Nepal.

Centre, Bureau of Statistics (CBS). 1999. *Statistical Year Book of Nepal*. Centre, Bureau of Statistics, Kathmandu, Nepal.

Gessler, M., U. Hodel, and P. Eyzaguirre. 1998. Home gardens and agrobiodiversity: Current state of knowledge with reference to relevant literatures. Discussion paper. Rome: International Plant Genetic Resources Institute (IPGRI).

Gurung, J. B., and A. Vaidya. 1998. The benefits to agrobiodiversity of the wide range of food cultures in Nepal. In T. Pratap and B. R. Sthapit, eds., *Managing Agrobiodiversity: Farmers' Changing Perspectives and Institutional Responses in the Hindu Kush–Himalayan Region*, pp. 55–60. Kathmandu, Nepal: International Centre for Integrated Mountain Development (ICIMOD) and International Plant Genetic Resources Institute (IPGRI).

International Plant Genetic Resources Institute (IPGRI). 1998. Contribution of home gardens to in situ conservation of plant genetic resources in farming systems. An unpublished project proposal. Rome: International Plant Genetic Resources Institute (IPGRI).

Joshi, K. D., M. Subedi, R. B. Rana, K. B. Kadayat, and B. R. Sthapit. 1997. Enhancing on-farm varietal diversity through participatory variety selection: A case of *Chaite* rice in Nepal. *Experimental Agriculture* 33: 1–10.

Kaini, B. R. 1995. Status of fruit plant genetic resources in Nepal. In M. P. Upadhyaya,

H. K. Sainju, B. K. Baniya, and M. S. Bista, eds., *Plant Genetic Resources: Nepalese Perspectives*. Kathmandu, Nepal: Nepal Agricultural Research Council (NARC) and International Plant Genetic Resources Institute (IPGRI), Kathmandu, Nepal.

Kandel, D. D., and M. P. Wagley. 1999. *Some Salient Indigenous Technology Practice for Watershed Management in Nepal*. Rome and Kathmandu: Food and Agricultural Organization (FAO) and His Majesty's Government of Nepal (HMGN).

Local Initiatives for Biodiversity Research and Development (LI-BIRD). 1999. Developing baseline census profile of foster child families and assessing domain-wise situation to support future development interventions by PLAN. Makawanpur: Main report Cluster II (draft). A consultancy report. Local Initiatives for Biodiversity Research and Development (LI-BIRD), Nepal.

Lohar, D. P., B. R. Roka, B. Adhikari, L. K. Amatya, T. B. Subedi, G. B. Gurung, S. R. Ghimire, R. B. Rana, D. K. Saraf, and B. K. Dhakal. 1993. Survey on indigenous horticulture in Baglung and Syangja districts. *LARC Working Paper* No. 93/18. Lumle Agricultural Research Center, Lumle, Kaski, Nepal.

Manandhar, N. P. 1989. *Useful Wild Plants of Nepal*. Nepal Research Centre Publication no. 14. Godawari, Nepal: Botanical Survey and Herbarium.

Pandey, I. P. 1994. Indigenous methods of sustainable vegetable production in the Kathmandu Valley, Nepal. Food and Agriculture Organization of the United Nations (FAO), Regional Office for Asia and the Pacific (RAPA), Publication no. 29. Bangkok, Thailand.

Pandey, Y. R., D. K. Rijal, and M. P. Upadhyay. 2001. In situ characterization of morphological traits of sponge gourd at Begnas ecosite, Kaski, Nepal. Paper presented at the First National Workshop Strengthening the Scientific Basis of in situ Conservation of Agricultural Biodiversity on-Farm, 24–26 April 2001, Lumle, Kaski, Nepal.

Pratap, T., and B. R. Sthapit, eds. 1998. *Managing Agrobiodiversity: Farmers' Changing Perspectives and Institutional Responses in the Hindu Kush–Himalayan Region*. Kathmandu and Rome: International Centre for Integrated Mountain Development (ICIMOD) and International Plant Genetic Resources Institute (IPGRI).

Rajbhandary, T. K., N. R. Joshi, T. Shrestha, S. K. G. Joshi, and B. Acharya. 1995. *Medicinal Plants of Nepal for Ayurvedic Drugs*. Kathmandu, Nepal: Ministry of Forest and Soil Conservation (MoFSC) and His Majesty's Government of Nepal (HMGN).

Rana, R. B., K. D. Joshi, and D. P. Lohar. 1998. On-farm conservation of indigenous vegetables by strengthening community-based seed banking in Seti River Valley, Pokhara, Nepal. *LI-BIRD Technical Paper* No. 3. Local Initiatives for Biodiversity Research and Development (LI-BIRD), Pokhara Nepal.

Rana, R. B., D. K. Rijal, D. Gauchan, B. R. Sthapit, A. Subedi, M. P. Upadhyay, Y. R. Pandey, and D. I. Jarvis. 2000a. *In Situ Crop Conservation: Findings of Agro-ecological, Crop Diversity and Socio-economic Baseline Surveys of Begnas Eco-site, Kaski, Nepal*. National Partners Working Paper no. 2/2000. Nepal Agricultural Research Council and Local Initiatives for Biodiversity Research and Development (LI-BIRD), Nepal; International Plant Genetic Resource Institute (IPGRI), Rome, Italy.

Rana, R. B., P. K. Shrestha, D. K. Rijal, A. Subedi, and B. R. Sthapit. 2000b. Understanding farmers' knowledge systems and decision-making: Participatory techniques for rapid biodiversity assessment and intensive data plots in Nepal. In E. Friis-Hansen and B. R. Sthapit, eds., *Participatory Approaches to the Conservation and Use of Plant Genetic Resources*. Rome: International Plant Genetic Resource Institute (IPGRI).

Rijal, D. K, R. B. Rana, B. R. Sthapit, and D. I. Jarvis. 2001. The use of taro local varieties in contrasting production systems in Nepal: I. Extent and distribution of taro varieties. Paper presented at the First National Workshop, Strengthening the Scientific Basis of in situ Conservation of Agricultural Biodiversity on-Farm, 24–26 April, 2001, Lumle, Kaski, Nepal.

Ryman, J. C. 1992. Life support: Conserving biological diversity. Worldwatch Institute, paper no. 108. Washington D.C.

Shrestha, P. K., and T. B. Gurung. 1997. Baseline survey report of Lumle Agricultural Research Center's horticulture outreach research sites. *LARC Working Paper* No. 97/42. Lumle Agricultural Research Center, Lumle, Kaski, Nepal.

Shrestha, P. K. 1998. Gene, gender, and generation: Role of traditional seed supply systems in on-farm biodiversity conservation in Nepal. In T. Pratap and B. R. Sthapit, eds., *Managing Agrobiodiversity: Farmers' Changing Perspectives and Institutional Responses in the Hindu Kush–Himalayan Region*, pp. 143–52. Kathmandu, Nepal: International Centre for Integrated Mountain Development (ICIMOD) and International Plant Genetic Resources Institute (IPGRI).

Sthapit, B. R. 2000. Extent and distribution of species diversity in Nepalese homegardens. Unpublished report.

Subedi, A., P. Chaudhary, B. K. Baniya, R. B. Rana, D. K. Rijal, R. K. Tiwari, and B. R. Sthapit. 2001. Who maintains crop genetic diversity and how? Implications for on-farm conservation and participatory plant breeding. Paper presented at the First National Workshop, Strengthening the Scientific Basis of in situ Conservation of Agricultural Biodiversity on-Farm, 24–26 April, 2001, Lumle, Kaski, Nepal.

six

The Enset-Based Home
Gardens of Ethiopia

Zemede Asfaw

Ethiopia is a land of ancient indigenous agricultural practices with an amazingly rich plant lore and numerous cultivated ancient species and varieties. To date, crop agriculture in Ethiopia relies heavily on indigenous species and varieties that evolved over the millennia under the influence of human and natural selection pressures. A considerable number of the crops cultivated in Ethiopia are known to have been domesticated within its boundaries. As a well-known Vavilovian center of crop-species domestication and evolution, Ethiopia has successfully produced and conserved distinct varieties and/or clones of many crops, among them enset (*Ensete ventricosum (Wew.)* Cheesman). Crops introduced during the early periods of agricultural innovation and interchange were favored by the prevailing agroclimatic and sociocultural conditions, resulting in their quick adoption, diffusion, integration, and diversification (Westphal 1975). Many traditional crops are cultivated today according to ancient practices and indigenous know-how.

The small-scale farming premises around homes, from which traditional rural farming families draw a significant proportion of their annual livelihood, are known by the generic term *home garden* (Zemede Asfaw 2000: 137). A home gar-den is a dynamic farming system, serving multiple purposes in the production and conservation of the biodiversity of crops and useful plants (Millat-e-Mustafa 1998). It is the best place to preserve the long tradition of Ethiopia's agriculture and its ancient crops. Here, experts can determine the many linkages, interac-tions, and interdependences that exist between wild and cultivated plant popula-tions (Zemede Asfaw 2001).

The results of a survey conducted in 1993 (Asfaw 1997a) revealed that home gardens are widespread throughout the country in different regions and agro-ecologic zones. On the average, about 60 percent of the households surveyed had home gardens; these were found in rural (81 percent), peri-urban (69 percent), and urban (56 percent) settings. Home gardens are most common in the middle altitudes of the south and southwestern sectors of the country. In parts of the southern region where the enset-based vegeculture abounds, all rural households cultivate home gardens, although they are fewer and more limited in scope and importance in the small-cereal–dominated northern and central highlands. While the survey showed that enset is one of the species frequently encountered in home gardens of the lowlands, midlands, and highlands—having been recorded in about 80 percent of the 111 home gardens studied—its special role as a major staple and costaple in the southern and southwestern parts has been well recog-nized (Westphal 1975, Brandt 1996, Taye Bizuneh 1996). The fact that the enset area contains a special type of home garden was noted from the results of the sur-vey and led to the present study.

The primary role that enset plays in defining the agroecology of the home-garden system is a key component of this chapter. I pay special attention to the enset-based home gardens of Kefa, Welayta, and Gurage. In this chapter, I will characterize and compare the home gardens of these areas in which enset is the most conspicuous and most valued species. The status, role, and diversity of other plants associated with enset, including cultivated as well as weedy and voluntary plants found within the general ecological complex, are reported. The impor-tance of this approach is that it demonstrates how entire systems can be con-structed around a dominant plant with multiple uses and associations. It high-lights the contributions that a sophisticated tradition of plant management and use can make in efforts to improve and conserve the biodiversity of useful native species in a home-garden setting. Unfortunately, no meaningful ethnobotanical investigation of this complex yet exists, and the system is poorly understood by modern science. The limited scientific studies carried out so far have focused mainly on enset as an agricultural commodity, without paying attention to the traditional system and its indigenous knowledge base. I hope this study goes some way toward correcting this imbalance.

How Enset Is Grown in Ethiopia

Within the enset agrosystem of Ethiopia, four general subsystems are usually recognized on the basis of environmental factors, agronomic features, cultural practices, and the extent to which enset is an important food. The four subtypes include: (a) the complex where enset is the main crop and the major staple, found mainly in Gurage and Sidama; (b) the complex where it is a costaple with cereals and tuber crops, found in Welayta and Gamo; (c) the complex where cereals are the most important crops, with enset and root crops taking a secondary role, found among the Oromo people of southwestern Ethiopia; and (d) the complex where root and tuber crops are of prime dietary importance, cereals are of secondary importance, and enset has a relatively minor role, found in Kefa and Sheko in the southwest (Westphal 1975, Brandt et al. 1997).

Enset is in the Musa family and, therefore, is a close relative of the banana. It is propagated vegetatively, using suckers whose production is initiated by removing the above-ground part of a two- to four-year-old plant; the remaining stub is then covered with soil. Removal of the apical bud initiates the growth of the lateral buds, otherwise dormant, found at ground level, where they join suckers growing around the periphery of the rootstock. The young suckers are usually ready for transplanting after about a year. In cities, and outside the enset-farming zone, where only one or two specimens are planted in the home garden for ornamental purpose and/or for nonfood utility purposes, the enset plant, once transplanted, is left in the same place. Its mature leaves are periodically cut and used until the plant flowers, gives fruit, gets old, and dies a natural death as a monocarpic species. In places where enset is grown primarily for food, that is, in the enset-based farming area, the young plant is dug out and transplanted again in well prepared soil. This can be done up to four times, depending on the social group cultivating it, the household's needs, and the availability of resources such as land, labor, capital, farmyard manure (associated with the availability of livestock), or on other food crops present. In these areas, the enset plant is harvested and processed for food at different stages of its growth, most often just before it begins to flower. It needs to be emphasized that enset cultivation is very complex; it has developed special characteristics in some localities, and differences exist not only between localities but also between households within the same hamlet. Regional comparisons are made on the basis of personal observations and data from

Table 6.1

Similarities and differences in the ways enset is grown in the various areas

Growth Feature	Kefa zone	Welayta zone	Gurage zone	Around Dilla in the Sidama zone
Propagation	Vegetatively by suckers	Vegetatively by suckers	Vegetatively by suckers	Vegetatively by suckers
Transplanting	Generally once	Can vary between 2–3 times	Can be done as many as 4 times	Limited
Intercropping	Polycultural; few spots with dense stands of enset of different ages	Polycultural; more spots with dense stands of enset of various ages	Rare; enset in pure stands in different plots of different ages	With maize and kale in the early stages and coffee; also some fruit crops, legumes, etc.
Mixing growth stages in a plot	Very frequently practiced	Less commonly practiced	Not practiced	Rarely practiced
Spacing	Dense at places, but also spots with dispersed plants, where intercropping with various root and tuber crops is practiced	Dense stands, with intercropping at different spots and during different growth stages	Dense during younger stages and widely apart during later stages; young enset usually intercropped with kale	Very dense when grown as pure stands, and dispersed when intercropped
Soil preparation	Limited preparation	Extensive preparation	Very extensive preparation	Extensive preparation
Manuring	Limited manuring when plot is on shallow rocky soil	Reasonable manuring	Heavy manuring	Reasonable manuring
Harvesting	Step-by-step so the canopy structure of enset looks intact on the same spot year after year	Step-by-step harvesting ensures presence of maturing enset in the same spot year after year	Many plants harvested at once, or during one season, until all are harvested and a new generation of young suckers are transplanted in the space left open	Mostly early, to leave space for the coffee that is grown vertically and horizontally and requires more space
Clones	Many types occur; farmers select and propagate those considered best	Many types; the best types are selected	Many types; the best types are elected	Many types; the best types are selected

the available literature (e.g., Judith 1974, Westphal 1975, Brandt et al. 1997, As-naketch Woldetensaye 1997). Table 6.1 shows similarities and differences in the ways enset is grown in various areas.

The Antiquity of Home Gardens in Ethiopia

Historical records have shown that the home-garden agrosystem has been an important component of human subsistence strategies since the Neolithic (Soleri and Cleveland 1989). Its antiquity is in evidence from paintings, papyrus illustrations, and texts of the third millennium BC in the Near East (Brownrigg 1985). The term itself is all-inclusive, covering processes and interactions among household members, between them and domestic animals, crops cultivated around the homestead, and the land where all these organisms interact with the abiotic components of the ecosystem. All these elements are parts of a self-contained ecosystem and a self-sufficient resource acquisition facility.

Early agriculture in tropical Africa coexisted with the forest, causing minimum environmental interference. Crops were planted within the forest and near residential areas, and many natural trees were spared. Considering the long history of agriculture in Ethiopia (Harlan 1969, Westphal 1975, Ehret 1979, Brandt 1984, Brandt 1996), and the everlasting presence of ancient crop domesticates in home gardens, it is safe to assume that gardening was probably the earliest form of farming ever practiced in the country. The enset-based home gardens of Ethiopia recall this early agriculture; they fit the description of a peasant cultivation system that is known for its high species-diversity indices (Benneh 1974). Approximately two hundred useful species survive in and around home gardens in Ethiopia, and enset-based home gardens have most of them.

Study Area and Methods

An estimated 10–15 million people in Ethiopia are said to depend on enset as their main staple or costaple, together with maize, other cereals, and tuber crops (Taye Bizuneh 1996). Because of its importance, we conducted an initial survey and observed enset home gardens in different parts of Ethiopia in the years between 1991 and 1993 (Zemede Asfaw 1997a; Zemede Asfaw and Nigatu 1995). In another study we focused on crop associations within home gardens of southern Ethiopia (Zemede Asfaw and Woldu 1997) and followed that by further research on selected areas of the south and southwest, where home gardens abound (Zemede Asfaw 1999 a, b).

The present study looks specifically at the enset culture zone of Ethiopia, which extends over a vast area, from the southwest, where *Ensete ventricosum* also occurs in the wild state, to the northeast, where it has been far removed from its natural wet forest habitat. We have emphasized the characteristics of home gardens where this key species is conspicuous, of high use value, and important in determining the management options of the farmers who care for this crop.

The three contrasting areas within the enset zone, namely, Kefa, Welayta, and Gurage, were selected, and their home gardens studied from the perspective of their crop composition, structure, and traditional management. In the home gardens of the three areas *Ensete ventricosum,* and the other species that go along with it, are dominant. But some features, such as climate, crop species, traditional management practices, and overall garden structures also separate these areas. Kefa is located at 70°16′ N and 360°14′ E, Welayta at 60°49′ N and 370°45′ E, and Gurage at 80°22′ N and 380°35′ E. The mean annual rainfall of Kefa is above 1,500 mm, and that of Welayta and Gurage about 1,000 mm. Welayta is found on the humid side, and Gurage on the subhumid side, of the 1,000 mm isohyte. The home gardens of these zones were studied and compared with respect to their structure and the crop species and varieties cultivated in them by the local people. The study also touched upon informal plants that are commonly found in proximity to the home gardens, including wild and/or weedy relatives, as well as protected or tolerated useful plants. Making comparisons within and between zones is necessary, because the status of enset as a staple or costaple varies among them.

Most local people in the three study areas belong to the Kefa, Welayta, and Gurage ethnic groups. The Kefa and Welayta are in the Omotic language group, whereas the Gurage are in the Semitic group. The lives of these people revolve around the enset culture. Their house sites are conspicuously marked by the presence of dense stands of enset. Not surprisingly, their practices for managing this crop are very elaborate.

We conducted our preliminary study in order to define the characteristic features, and the key position of enset and other major crops and varieties found in this farming complex, in the various zones (Zemede Asfaw 1997a). The data for the present study was collected between August and September in 1999–2001, during various field trips made to different parts of the southern region. These months correspond to the rainy season, when the enset zone receives maximum rainfall and the area is fully vegetated. Having the plants in their flowering and fruiting stage facilitates their proper identification and enables us to record all useful annual and perennial plants found in the gardens. Many mature home gardens were inspected, and the crops encountered were noted, whether or not the species was typical of the area's enset-based home gardens. Useful species planted to serve as a live fence were also recorded. More in-depth observations, recording, and sketching was done in selected home gardens distributed along a stretch running from the southwestern margin of the enset zone, to the northeast, spreading over altitudinal gradients ranging 1,500–3,000 masl. A rich array of field data was gathered through direct observation, recording, plant collecting, and discussions with household members and key informants in semistructured interviews. The home gardens were sketched, and the use values of the enset clones in the gardens were recorded. Elderly farmers were asked many questions about the enset farming system, including the crops cultivated as companions and admixtures with it. Informants were also asked to describe specific aspects of enset, including its husbandry, diversity, and ways of identifying the different clones. Between twenty and forty clones were usually named, and farmers in each area described their most diagnostic characteristics. This data revealed the farmers' rich ethnobotanical knowledge. The species recorded from home gardens in the three areas were tabulated, and their presence in each area was noted. Those species present were scored on a five-point scale; the most typical were given a score of 5, and the others lower scores. An area where a given crop was not recorded was given a value of 0. Then, the similarities between the home gardens of Kefa, Welayta, and Gurage was computed using Pearson's correlation coefficient and Russel's dissimilarity and discriminant analysis. From this analysis we produced dendrograms showing the rate of home gardening of the different areas and crops.

General Features of Ethiopian Home Gardens

Ethiopian home gardens are of different sizes and shapes. They are located at the back, front, or sides of the house, or they may completely encircle the dwelling, as is usually the case in areas where they are most developed. In the enset zone, home gardens are almost exclusively of the latter, encircling, type. Home gardens include the main house, animal pens, grain stores, drying areas, and plots with many garden species. Each is seen as a functional unit, surrounded by a fence that is frequently reinforced by multipurpose tree and shrub species.

Many indigenous crops of Ethiopia are cultivated in home gardens, and spontaneous wild populations of some species occur in the natural ecosystems (Zemede Asfaw 1997a, b, 1999a, b). Some of the crops maintained in these home gardens, including enset, are not known as crops elsewhere. Hence, focusing on enset-based home gardens means drawing attention to a hitherto neglected global resource.

The home garden is the only place where meaningful conservation of indigenous key species and endemic crops, as well as the others found in association, could ever be attempted. In a study undertaken in the southern and southwestern parts of Ethiopia (Zemede Asfaw 1999a), 112 crop species were recorded, of which 69 were recovered only from home gardens, 26 from both home gardens and fields, and 17 from fields only. This and other findings demonstrate the key role of home gardens in conserving crop species and associated useful plants. The enset-based home gardens were described by Westphal (1975) as the hoe and enset complex and were discussed and analyzed later by Okigbo (1990) under the rubric of tropical home gardens. In Ethiopia, this unique agricultural system is generally considered to be part of an enset-based agriculture by contemporary agricultural experts (cf. Tsedeke et al. 1996).

In Ethiopia, home gardens are cultivated everywhere; they are more frequent and developed in the south and southwest, where root and tuber crops, vegetables, spices, and fruits predominate (Westphal 1975, Okigbo 1990, Zemede Asfaw and Nigatu 1995). They are less common and rather rudimentary, in the cereal-dominated small zone of the northern and central highlands. Plant diversity in Ethiopian home gardens can be seen under the three categories of garden crops, live-fence species, and useful wild plants in the vicinity of home gardens. The crops belong to many taxonomic and horticultural groups and have different growth forms. The live-fence species are multipurpose trees and shrubs used as reinforcement; they also provide additional benefits to the households. The useful wild and semiwild plants that are tolerated or encouraged provide edible tubers, leafy vegetables, and fruits, as well as traditional medicines.

Home gardens are found in close proximity to dwellings, which are usually constructed on high ground to allow a clear view of the surrounding countryside where the crop fields and grazing lands are situated. Villages are therefore built on raised, well-drained land, allowing farmers to supervise their fields closely, even at a distance. The regular accumulation of domestic waste around the home improves the fertility of the soil, and for this reason families in the semiarid central Rift Valley periodically shift their house location, to leave their old, improved site for the cultivation of field crops. These families soon establish new home gardens by taking seeds, seedlings, cuttings, and other planting materials from the vacated sites.

Different types of home gardens can be defined according to their position, size, and purpose. Common Ethiopian home-garden types are backyards (48 percent), front yards (26 percent), side yards (13 percent); and those that almost encircle the house (13 percent; Zemede Asfaw 1997a). Various combinations of the above types also exist, such as back and sides, back and one side, front and sides, and so on. In urban areas gardens are mostly of the backyard type, but in rural villages and peri-urban towns gardens combine traits of back, front, and side yard types.

The many vernacular names for home garden—*yeguaro ersha* and *eddo* in the Amharic and Oromic languages, respectively—mean the backyard farm, emphasizing the closeness of the structure to the house, and the private nature of the holding. In some areas gardens are enclosed by fences, but in others they merge with crop fields. The gardens of roadside houses are usually of the backyard or side yard type. When the house is located adjacent to a stream, the garden is usually situated at the back of the house, next to the stream, where water can be obtained to irrigate seedlings during the dry season, for example. Even if irrigation is not practiced, the mere location of gardens in depressions bordering streams usually provides a suitable microenvironment.

The size of home gardens varies; some are less than 20 m², whereas a few may reach up to 6,000 m² and merge with the crop fields. In rural and semirural settings home gardens are widespread, large in size, and relatively diverse. In these areas, the staple crops (root and tuber crops) are produced in the home garden itself. The typical garden of the enset zone belongs in this category.

Differences in the Enset-Based Home Gardens of Three Areas

Enset-based home gardens in Ethiopia are characterized by the conspicuous presence of *Ensete ventricosum,* which is clearly visible from a distance. A bunch of enset stands is often a reliable marker for a settlement. A closer examination of enset-based home gardens reveals differences along a gradient, going from the southwestern to the northeastern border of this plant's distribution. These are described in terms of three enset subculture zones, namely, Kefa, Welayta, and Gurage, as examples.

In Kefa, the home garden is a traditional form of agroforestry linked to the surrounding ecosystem through useful trees, domesticated plants, and a canopylike structure. It is referred to as the *daaddegoyo,* meaning the homestead farm in the Kefa language. Many tall trees (e.g., *Cordia africana, Ficus sur, Erythrina brucei, Phoenix reclinata,* etc.) are found mostly on the outer margins of the home garden, where they encounter spontaneous populations in the adjacent forest (see Table 6.2). These trees, together with thick stands of maturing enset and banana plants, constitute the upper layer of the daaddegoyo. The middle layer is occupied by coffee, citruses, sugarcane, tree tomato, *Rhamnus prinoides,* and other species. This layer can also include climbers such as yams, aerial yam, *Coccinia abyssinica, Sechium edule,* climbing beans, and other crops. The lower stratum is composed of

A home garden in Kefa, Ethiopia, showing the enset plants

herbs such as sweet basil, peppers and chillies, false cardamom, ginger, rue, and fennel, as well as roots, tubers, and vegetables, including taro and *Xanthosoma sagittifolium*, kale, cabbage, tobacco, pumpkins, *Plectranthus edulis*, tomato, potato, and sweet potato. Shade-loving species are assigned to covered spaces within the garden. The general pattern within the mature home gardens of the Kefa shows that, on the average, plant size increases with distance from the house and biological diversity is highest near homes. Further out, diversity is reduced, becoming almost a single species at the extreme end of the garden. A cross-section from the back of the house to the end of the garden shows typical zoning. A small circle immediately behind the house (zone A) contains primarily small-sized species such as *Ruta chalepensis, Cymbopogon citratus, Ocimum basilicum, Foeniculum vulgare,* and *Astemisia afra*. The next two zones (B and C) account for about 90 percent of the species in the entire home garden, and the last circle (D) has only a few species, but larger populations of each in a wider area. The area occupied by individual crops increases with distance from the house, grading into more extensive plots of one or two species at the end. Thus, species number generally decreases away from the house, while number of individuals of a single species increases. A similar pattern is reported for cultivated landscapes in Africa (Okigbo 1994).

The small circle just behind the house maintains more species per unit area, including spices, medicinal plants, vegetables, and aromatic plants that provide good fragrance to the house surroundings. Their primary use, however, is for

Table 6.2

Crops and other frequently utilized plants recorded in enset-based home gardens

No.	Common name	Scientific name	Region
1		*Aeollanthus sp.*	K
2		*Aframomum corrorima*	K
4	Agave	*Agave americana*	G
5	Onion	*Allium cepa*	K, W, G
6	Garlic	*Allium sativum*	K, W, G
7	Quonoa	*Amaranthus caudatus*	K, W, G
8	Amaranthus	*Amaranthus hybridus*	K, W, G
9	Pinapple	*Ananas comosus*	K, W
10	Custard apple	*Annona cherimola*	W, G
11	Wormwood	*Artemisia absinthium*	K, W
12		*Artemisia afra*	K, W
13		*Arundinaria alpina*	K, W, G
14	Giant reed	*Arundo donax*	K, W, G
15	Beets	*Beta vulgaris*	K, W, G
16	Abyssinian mustard	*Brassica carinata*	K, W, G
18	Kale	*Brassica integrifolia*	W, G
19	Rape, sweet	*Brassica napus*	W, G
20	Mustard	*Brassica nigra*	K, W, G
21	Kales, collards, cauliflower, broccoli	*Brassica oleracea*	K, W, G
22	Cabbage	*Brassica oleracea / capitata*	K, W, G
23	Pigeon pea	*Cajanus cajan*	K, W, G
24	Jackbean	*Canavalia africana*	K, W, G
25	Bell pepper	*Capsicum annuum*	K, W, G
28	Tabasco pepper	*Capsicum frutescens* (small fruit)	K, W, G
29	Papaya	*Carica papaya*	K, W, G
30	Egyptian carissa	*Carissa edulis*	W, G
31	Safflower	*Carthamus tinctorius*	K, W, G
32	White sapote	*Casimiroa edulis*	W, G
33	Khat	*Catha edulis*	K, W, G
34	Lime	*Citrus aurantiifolia*	K, W, G
35	Sweet orange	*Citrus aurantium*	K, W, G
36	Tangerine	*Citrus reticulata*	K, W, G
37	Orange	*Citrus sinensis*	K, W, G
38		*Coccinia abyssinica*	K
40	Coffee	*Coffea arabica*	K, W, G
42	Taro	*Colocasia esculenta*	K, W
43		*Cordia africana*	K, W, G
44	Coriander	*Coriandrum sativum*	K, W, G
45	Mulangu	*Croton macrostachyus*	K, W, G
46	Cucumber	*Cucurbita pepo*	K, W, G
47	Turmeric	*Curcuma domestica*	K
48	Lemongrass, West Indian	*Cymbopogon citratus*	K, W, G

Continued on next page

Table 6.2 continued

No.	Common name	Scientific name	Region
49	Tree tomato	*Cyphomandra betacea*	K
50	Indian apple, sacred datura	*Datura inoxia*	K, W
51	Carrot	*Daucus carota*	K, W, G
52	Asian yam	*Dioscorea alata*	K, W
53	Aerial yam	*Dioscorea bulbifera*	K, W
54	Yellow yam	*Dioscorea cayenensis-rotundata*	K, W
55		*Dracaena steudneri*	K
56		*Echinops kebericho*	K, W
57	Finger millet	*Eleusine coracana*	K, W, G
58	Enset	*Ensete ventricosum*	K, W, G
59	Loquat	*Eriobotrya japonica*	W
60		*Euphorbia cotinifolia*	K, W
61	Erythrina	*Erythrina brucei*	K, W
62	Eucalyptus	*Eucalyptus* spp.	K, W, G
63	Candelabra tree	*Euphorbia candelabrum*	K, W, G
65	Poinsettia	*Euphorbia pulcherrima*	K, W, G
66		*Ficus sur*	W, G
67	Fennel	*Foeniculum vulgare*	K, W, G
68	Strawberry	*Fragaria* sp.	K, W, G
69	Cotton	*Gossypium* spp.	K, W, G
70	Sunflower	*Helianthus annuus*	K, W, G
71	Sweet potato	*Ipomoea batatas*	K, W, G
72	Bitter heart	*Iresine herbstii*	K
73	Lablab bean	*Lablab purpureus*	K
74	Lettuce	*Lactuca sativa*	K, W, G
75	Bottlegourd	*Lagenaria siceraria*	K, W, G
76	Garden cress	*Lepidium sativum*	K, W, G
77	Flax	*Linum usitatissimum*	K, W, G
78	Coseret	*Lippia adoensis*	K, W, G
79	Tomato	*Lycopersicon esculentum*	K, W, G
80	Mango	*Mangifera indica*	K, W
81	Manroc	*Manihot esculenta*	K, W
82	Horseradish tree	*Moringa stenopetala*	W
83	Plantain banana	*Musa paradisiaca*	K, W, G
84	Myrtle	*Myrtus communis*	G
85	Tobacco	*Nicotiana tabacum*	K, W, G
86	Black cumin	*Nigella sativa*	K, W, G
87	Basil	*Ocimum basilicum*	K, W, G
88	Dama kesseh	*Ocimum lamiifolium*	K, W, G
89	Olive	*Olea europaea* ssp. *Cuspidata*	K, W, G
90	Passion fruit	*Passiflora edulis*	K, G
91	Avocado	*Persea americana*	K, W, G
92	Runner bean	*Phaseolus coccineus*	K

Table 6.2 continued

No.	Common name	Scientific name	Region
93	Lima bean	*Phaseolus lunatus*	K, W, G
94	Common bean	*Phaseolus vulgaris*	K, W, G
95	Senegal date palm	*Phoenix reclinata*	K, W, G
96	Cape gooseberry	*Physalis peruviana*	K, W, G
98	Bospepper	*Piper capense*	K
99	Oromo dinich	*Plectranthus edulis*	K, W
100	Peach	*Prunus persica*	K, W, G
101	Guava	*Psidium guajava*	K, W, G
102	Pomegranate	*Punica granatum*	K, W, G
103		*Pycnostachys dawei*	K, W
104	Buckthorn	*Rhamnus prinoides*	K, W, G
105	Castorbean	*Ricinus communis*	K, W, G
106	Abyssinian rose	*Rosa abyssinica*	W, G
107	Rosemary	*Rosmarinus officinalis*	W, G
108	Blackberry	*Rubus* spp.	K, W, G
109		*Rumex abyssinicus*	K, W, G
110	Fringed rue	*Ruta chalepensis*	K, W, G
111	Sugar	*Saccharum officinarum*	K, W, G
112	Sage	*Salvia leucantha*	K, W, G
113	Chayote	*Sechium edule*	K
114	Eggplant	*Solanum dasyphyllum*	K, W
115	Nightshade	*Solanum nigrum*	K, W
116	Potato	*Solanum tuberosum*	K, W, G
117	Sorgum, sweet	*Sorghum bicolor* (sweet)	K
118	Fenugreek	*Trigonella foenum-graecum*	K, W, G
119	Bitterleaf	*Vernonia amygdalina*	K, W, G
120	Fava bean	*Vicia faba*	K
121	Cowpea	*Vigna unguiculata*	K, W, G
122		*Vigna membranacea*	K
123	Grape	*Vitis vinifera*	K, W, G
124	New cocoyam	*Xanthosoma sagittifolium*	K, W
125	Maize	*Zea mays*	K, W, G
126	Ginger	*Zingiber officinale*	K, W
		Total number of species	K = 113
			W = 101
			G = 85

Note: See Figure 6.2. Many ornamentals, and other less important tolerated or protected species, are not included.

K = in Daaddegoyo (Kefa home gardens)

W = in Darincha (Welayta home gardens)

G = in Guaro/Guara (Gurage home gardens)

food preparation and health care. Where animal urine and droppings run into the garden, crops like enset, coffee, and tobacco profit from these fertilizers. Spices and vegetables, however, are placed on the clean side of the garden immediately behind the house. The parcel of land containing these plants is the domain of women, who take responsibility for propagating, managing, harvesting, and using the produce, including selling it and giving it to friends and relatives. Women's share of garden duties is usually significant. Women spend much time around homes, selecting seeds, cleaning and weeding, and in many ways influencing day-to-day farm activities. Their tasks are all essential, making them key actors in production and livelihood relations.

The outer circle of the garden (zone D), on the other hand, is dominated by enset, which forms a circular grove around the house, completely enclosing it and hiding the other crops. People believe that the enset grove of able farmers must render the house invisible from far away. The grove also detains the smoke coming from the house, distributing it all over the garden to repel insect pests. It is asserted that the smoke has a positive impact on the growth and development of enset. Some species maintained as thick live fences (e.g., *Pycnostachys abyssinica*) also emit fragrances that people believe repel insect pests. These assertions need to be demonstrated in a scientific way.

In the Kefa home gardens, young enset plants are accommodated in the open spaces created after the harvest and removal of old plants. The enset ring, therefore, remains constant, as young plants grow to maturity and old ones are harvested. Hence, it is a kind of permanent culture found in the same place year after year, even though each individual plant has a lifespan of three to four years. The staggered planting of enset suckers means that when one specimen is harvested there is already another one to take its place. Thus, the gradual planting and harvesting of enset does not change the overall appearance of the home garden.

In Welayta, the second subcultural area, home gardens make up a kind of forest patch dominated by enset, usually sitting amidst open cereal crop fields. Gardens are very traditional and are locally referred to as *darincha*, meaning homestead farm in the Welayta language. Scattered trees grow in association with the conspicuous enset stands. Usually, a thick stand of enset is found on one or two sides of the house, the other sides being taken up by other crops. The enset garden may shift its position slightly when young plants are placed on the margins, instead of being fitted into the gap created when maturing plants are harvested. Adding a plot of young enset plants periodically may enlarge the area occupied by the crop. Thus, a bigger stand of maturing enset and a smaller one of juvenile enset on the sides are common features of the enset-based home gardens of Welayta. Along with the patchy stand of enset, many other crops are grown in the garden: vegetables, including potato, yams, taro, beans, kale, cabbage, pumpkin, sugarcane, sweet potato, peppers and chillies, *Plectranthus edulis*, bottle gourd, and coffee); fruit trees, including citruses, papaya, avocado, custard apple, mango, banana, guava, and casmir; and spices, such as garlic, onion, shallot, basil, rue, and others. The proportion of fruit trees grown here is considerable, especially when compared with the home gardens of Kefa. A home garden in Welayta is distinguished by the piece of land generously left as a green meadow in front of the house, to serve as a playground for the children, as a family resting spot, and as a place for social events. Land scarcity, further aggravated by population growth, is eroding this tradition; some families have started claiming their space for gardening, eliminating this culturally valued and ecologically sound free space.

In the third area under consideration, Gurage, home gardens are also very traditional, being referred to as the *guara-guaro,* meaning the backside or the back farm. The enset-based home gardens in this zone are distinguished by patches of *Ensete ventricosum* at successive stages of growth. Plants approaching maturity, plants at intermediate stages, and young suckers are found in these groves. The plot of plants at the younger stages accommodates many herbaceous crops, including *Brassica carinata*, peppers and chillies, tomato, potato, garlic, onion, shallot, basil, rue, and maize. Most home gardens also contain a good number of coffee bushes and chat, banana, papaya, guava, and citrus trees; other crops, for example sugarcane, pumpkin, bottle gourd, are also present. The gap created when maturing enset is harvested is used for intercropping maize, kale, and other crops of the family's choosing. There is more crop diversity on the wetter side of the Gurage zone than on the drier side facing the Rift Valley. In this wetter zone, homesteads are distinguishable from a distance by patches of enset on one side, and *Eucalyptus* spp. on the other side.

Slightly different versions of the enset-based home garden are observable in other parts, as in Dilla, for example, where enset is grown as a temporary crop intercropped with coffee, which gradually grows in height and breadth, claiming the entire space. In most cases, enset is initially intercropped with coffee and maize. Then the maize is harvested within a season, and the enset within three to four years; by that time the coffee has grown vertically and horizontally to become a veritable coffee garden. Hence, enset-based home gardens in this culture serve as a sort of transitional system in the development of a permanent coffee plantation. Though coffee is the most valued key species in climax home gardens of this type, other crops are accommodated in a limited space. Moreover, the cultural and economic significance of enset as the main food crop still holds.

Distinct age classes of enset are found in separate subplots in the Gurage area. In Welayta, the fast growth of this species may blur age differences in a short time, but age can still be determined from the thickness of the pseudostem. In Kefa, suckers are fitted into available spaces within the existing plot; hence no distinct subplots exist as such, but the age of individual plants can still be determined. Open spaces within enset plots are planted with enset or other species. The management of the home gardens in all three areas revolves around the cultural practices that govern enset cultivation.

Other Useful Plants in the Enset-Based Home Gardens of Kefa, Welayta, and Gurage

The enset-dominated home gardens contain the highest number of crops and other useful plant species in the Ethiopian system. Although their overall aspect is the same, differences in the crops grown, their mixes, their proportions, structure, and management exist, depending on the agroecology, the relations with the land, and the cultural and individual preferences.

Generally, a conservative figure of about 50 percent similarity holds among the home gardens of the three areas; the major indicator of this similarity is the abundant presence of *Ensete ventricosum*. This means that about half (74) of the 126 species of home-garden plants listed in Table 6.2 occur in all the three home-garden types. In fact, the overall similarity is greater because the major species occur abundantly in all three places. Home gardens of Welayta and Gurage showed about 86 percent similarity, whereas those of Kefa and Welayta showed about 82 percent similarity, and those of Kefa and Gurage about 71 percent similarity. Gurage gardens contained 85 of the species (67 percent), Welayta gardens 101 (80 percent), and Kefa gardens 113 (90 percent). Many ornamentals and other less important tolerated or protected species are not included in these numbers. The same general pattern was obtained when a brief comparison was made with enset-based home gardens of the Sidama people (a Cushitic language family) around Dilla, a town in southern Ethiopia.

Other Differences in the Enset-Based Home Gardens of Kefa, Welayta, and Gurage

In general, the diversity and frequency of trees around the home garden decreases from Kefa to Welayta, and Gurage. In the latter, species of *Eucalyptus* dominate as a homestead tree. Furthermore, the frequency of separate plots of varying ages of enset increases from the Kefa to the Welayta and Gurage home gardens. The need for animal manure also generally increases from Kefa to Welayta and Gurage. Hence, Kefa seems to be a more natural environment for the cultivation of *Ensete venrticosum*, followed by Welayta and Gurage, where intensive management is required. This suggests the possible origin of enset in environments like those of Kefa, rather than those of Gurage and Welayta. Taking the useful plant species present as markers of similarities and differences, the home gardens of the three areas are differentiated by distance factors, as shown in Figure 6.1.

Out of the 85 species recorded in Gurage home gardens, 81 also occur in Welayta and 75 occur in Kefa. Hence, Welayta home gardens are closer to Gurage home gardens than they are to Kefa home gardens. Out of the 101 species found in Welayta home gardens, 94 are found in Kefa. About 59 percent of the total species are found in all three areas. The number of species they have in common and the calculated similarity coefficients are shown in Table 6.3.

Although they share many similarities when viewed at the macro level, the home gardens of the three areas also contain differences that are not so easy to describe and explain. Part of the difference can be accounted for by the variation in crop association; the agroclimatic and cultural factors account for the remaining differences. Overall, Kefa home gardens contain more species diversity than home gardens in the other two areas. A good number of the species found in the enset-based home gardens of Kefa are not found in the other areas; 20 species found in Kefa were not recorded from the other areas (Table 6.4). The 20 species fall into

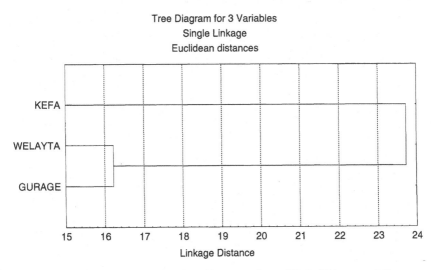

Figure 6.1. Distances between enset-based home gardens of Kefa, Welayta, and Gurage

Table 6.3

Number of species and similarity coefficients between home gardens of the three areas based on data for the archetypal species

Number	Combinations of home gardens	Number of species in common	Similarity (%)	Sfrenson's similarity coefficient (%)	Major indicators of similarity other than *Ensete ventricosum*
1	Home gardens of Kefa and Welayta	94	41	88	Presence of *Dioscorea* spp., *Plectranthus edulis*, *Solanum dasyphyllum*, *Xanthosoma sagittifolium*
2	Home gardens of Kefa and Gurage	75	18	76	Presence of many ubiquitous species and *Passiflora edulis* found in the two areas
3	Home gardens of Welayta and Gurage	81	71	86	Presence of *Annona cherimola, Casimiroa edulis*
4	Home gardens of Kefa, Welayta, and Gurage	74		50	Presence of many ubiquitous species found in all the three areas

different categories; some are conventional home-garden crops, some are plants maintained as live fences, some are spontaneous populations of crop species found in the adjacent environment, and some are feral crops found outside the home gardens. Furthermore, species believed to have been introduced from elsewhere into Kefa home gardens have also managed to escape into the natural ecosystem. The species that are unique to Kefa home gardens distinguish them

Table 6.4

Species recorded only from the Kefa home gardens

Aeollanthus sp.	*Euphorbia cotinifolia*
Aframomum corrorima	*Iresine herbstii*
Aframomum corrorima (wild)	*Lablab purpureus*
Coccinia abyssinica	*Phaseolus coccineus*
Coffea arabica (wild)	*Piper capense*
Colocasia esculenta (escape from cultivation)	*Pycnostachys abyssinica*
Curcuma domestica	*Sechium edule*
Cyphomandra betacea	*Sorghum bicolor* (sweet)
Dracaena steudneri	*Vigna membranacea*
Ensete ventricosum (wild type is rare in home gardens)	

A young, wild enset plant

from those of Welayta and Gurage. *Moringa stenopetala*, which is encountered in only a few home gardens in Welayta, is the key home-garden species in the adjacent area of Arbaminch and its surroundings. The species that are unique to Kefa are good markers for enset-based home gardens here.

Kefa home gardens are firmly linked to the surrounding natural ecosystem (Table 6.5). Some of their major components are Ethiopian domesticates, others are African plants, and the rest are from other parts of the world. Therefore, Kefa home gardens are important for finding crops that are unique to Ethiopia.

Table 6.5
Some crops that are occur in Kefa home gardens and the surrounding natural ecosystem and their putative places of origin

Crops	Origin
Aframomum corrorima	Ethiopia
Coffea arabica	Ethiopia
Echinops kebericho	Ethiopia
Ensete ventricosum	Ethiopia
Ocimum lamiifolium	Ethiopia
Rhamnus prinoides	Ethiopia
Solanum dasyphyllum	Tropical Africa

Among the crop species introduced from elsewhere that have escaped into the surrounding areas are: *Psidium guajava, Passiflora edulis, Colocasia esculenta, Xanthosoma sagittifolium*. Thus, the biological interaction (Zemede Asfaw and Desissa 1999) between home gardens and the natural environment is significant and must be respected and maintained for the health of both the managed and the natural ecosystem. Maintenance of home-garden biodiversity in environments like Kefa must go hand in hand with maintenance of the natural forest ecosystem. Home-garden genetic diversity should be seen as part and parcel of the genetic diversity of the surrounding forests and other natural ecosystems.

The pattern of covariation and cooccurrence of a crop (interpreted from the dendrogram in Fig. 6.2), reveals many of similarities in the complex of crops and their associations. Although they are numerous, crops in the enset-based home gardens are husbanded together, and farmers tend to regard them as a package.

Biodiversity Conservation in Enset-Based Home Gardens

The enset-based home gardens are privileged sites for the in situ conservation of botanical diversity. This includes a large collection of crop species, intraspecific categories, and many useful plants. The plants conserved in home gardens in Ethiopia include many endemic and indigenous forms, as well as other forms introduced during the agricultural history of the country. People's cultural practices and indigenous knowledge play a key role in preserving the biological diversity in time and space. Although the value of home-garden products to the household is tremendous, the critical role this system plays in biodiversity conservation (Nguyen 1995, Gesseler et al. 1996, 1997, Godbole 1998) and environmental health has not been sufficiently emphasized. The enset-based home garden is a key place for the generation, evolution, and conservation of botanical diversity. What, then, is the future of home gardens? Can they continue as they are or will they change, and how? A strong cultural attachment to home gardens is clearly evident; they are deep-rooted in the cultures of the peoples who make them. But existing agricultural dynamics, coupled with other pressures on the land, spell a dim future for the system. Left on their own, home gardens may gradually shift to a monoculture of cereal grains. Expansion of maize cultivation and the planting of fruit trees appear to be major threats to the home-garden agrosystem. For these reasons, a strong cultural preference for home gardening needs to be backed up by policy, research, and development-oriented initiatives.

Conservation of the home-garden agrosystem must rest on a collectivist strategy whereby farming communities generate and maintain the species and genetic

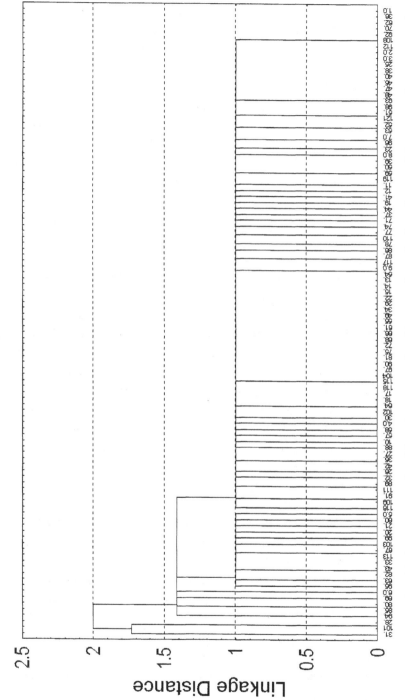

Tree Diagram for 105 Cases

Single Linkage

Euclidean distances

Figure 6.2. Groups of useful plant species produced from data on enset-based home gardens of Kefa, Welayta, and Gurage (numbers correspond to the species numbers in Table 6.2)

diversity of the system. The various approaches, methods, preferences, and perspectives of farmers contribute to the diversity of species, varieties, and genetic stocks. No modern system can adequately replace home gardens as a viable conservation option. Only one choice exists, and that is to promote and enhance traditional home gardening in the enset-based system of Ethiopia. The international scientific community and other responsible agencies must see that this crop and its system are preserved in the only place on earth where it could ever be done. Such actions would avoid howling about the lost crops of the world.

Conclusions

In this study we examined the characteristics of the enset-based home gardens of Ethiopia, emphasizing the overall features of the system. A distinctive feature of enset-based home gardens is the abundance of *Ensete ventricosum* as a major component. Because it is the most valued crop of the home gardens in the areas discussed and because the enset system has been viable for generations, our analysis and discussion have concentrated on this species. Overall garden structure is dependent on what is done by way of managing enset; most other crops in this system are made to fit into their structure. The vertical and horizontal structure of the garden, and its temporal pattern, depend on the management of *Ensete ventricosum*. This species provides a framework for other crops that are fitted into this production system. The area of land it occupies and the number of individual plants per garden also point to the use value and cultural significance of the enset species. With respect to the useful plants of the home gardens and its environs, there is a high degree of similarity between the home gardens of Kefa, Welayta, and Gurage.

The enset-based home gardens of Ethiopia are a special category in that they produce most of the things needed at home, thus serving as a food security system for the family. Even if differences exist in the intensity of cropping patterns, in the level of crop mixing, the productivity, and the skill of management and utilization, enset gardens are everywhere important. The results I have presented are meant to draw attention to an important farming system that still maintains the bulk of Ethiopia's agricultural diversity and the useful plants that are associated with it. These data have also shown indirectly that more in-depth analyses and synthesis of these home gardens is justified. It has been observed that over the years cereal-based agriculture is gradually replacing enset groves in some areas. It is imperative, therefore, that a conservation strategy be put in place so that enset survives as a viable system.

To conclude, some key questions can be posed. Would home gardens in general, and enset-based home gardens in particular, persist in the face of changing socioeconomic relations? Can the outside world be made to turn a keen eye to further research on the development and optimal utilization of this species? Can the diversity of useful plants that the enset system harbors be provided with a future? The day could come when the unfavorable attitudes toward enset that were held in the past would begin moving in the reverse direction, to favor its long awaited and potentially rewarding future.

References

Asnaketch Woldetensaye. 1997. The ecology and production of *Ensete ventricosum* in Ethiopia. Acta Universitatis Agriculturae Sueciae. *Agraria* 78. Swedish University of Agricultural Science.

Benneh, G. 1974. The ecology of peasant farming systems in Ghana: Environment in Africa. *Environment and Regional Planning Research Bulletin* (Dakar, Senegal) 1(1): 35–49.

Brandt, S. A. 1984. New perspectives on the origins of food production in Ethiopia. In J. D. Clark and S. A. Brandt, eds., *From Hunters to Farmers: The Causes and Consequences of Food Production in Africa*, pp. 173–90. Berkeley: University of California Press.

Brandt, S. A. 1996. A model for the origins and evolution of enset food production. In A. Tsedeke, C. Hiebsch, S. A. Brandt, and S. Gebremariam, eds., *Enset-Based Sustainable Agriculture in Ethiopia*, pp. 36–46. Proceedings of an International Workshop on Enset, 1993. Addis Ababa, Ethiopia: Institute of Agricultural Research.

Brandt, S. A., A. Spring, C. Hiebsch, J. T. McCabe, E. Tabogie, M. Diro, G. Wolde-Michael, G. Yntiso, M. Shigeta, and S. Tesfaye. 1997. *The Tree against Hunger: Enset-Based Agricultural System in Ethiopia*. Washington, D.C.: American Association for the Advancement of Science, vol. 56.

Brownrigg, L. 1985. *Home Gardening in International Development*. Washington, D.C.: League for International Food Education.

Ehret, C. 1979. On the antiquity of agriculture in Ethiopia. *Journal of African History* 20: 166–77.

Godbole, A. 1998. Home gardens: Traditional systems for maintenance of biodiversity. In A. Rastogi, A. Godbole, and S. Pei, eds., *Applied Ethnobotany in Natural Resource Management: Traditional Home Gardens*, pp. 9–12. Kathmandu, Nepal: International Centre for Integrated Mountain Development.

Harlan, J. R. 1969. Ethiopia: A centre of diversity. *Economic Botany* 23: 309–14.

Judith, O. 1974. The versatile enset plant: Its use in Gamu highlands. *Journal of Ethiopian Studies* 12: 147–58.

Millat-e-Mustafa, M. 1998. An approach towards analysis of home gardens. In A. Rastogi, A. Godbole, and S. Pei, eds., *Applied Ethnobotany in Natural Resource Management: Tra-*

ditional Home Gardens, pp. 39–47. Kathmandu, Nepal: International Centre for Integrated Mountain Development.

Nguyen, X. Q. 1995. Home-garden systems in Vietnam. In P. Halladay and D. A. Gilmour, eds., *Conserving Biodiversity Outside Protected Areas: The Role of Traditional Agroecosystems*, pp. 153–64. Gland, Switzerland: International Union of Conservation of Nature and Natural Resources (IUCN), The World Conservation Unit.

Okigbo, B. N. 1990. Home gardens in tropical Africa. In K. Landauer and M. Brazil, eds., *Tropical Home Gardens*, pp. 21–40. Tokyo, Japan: United Nations University Press.

Okigbo, B. N. 1994. Conservation and use of germplasm in African traditional agriculture and use systems. In A. Putter, ed., *Safeguarding the Genetic Basis of Africa's Traditional Crops*, pp. 15–38. Wageningen, The Netherlands: Technical Centre for Agriculture and Rural Cooperation and Rome: International Plant Genetic Resources Institute (IPGRI).

Soleri, D., and D. A. Cleveland. 1989. Dryland household gardens in development. *Arid Lands Newsletter* 29: 5–10.

Taye Bizuneh. 1996. An overview on enset research and future technological needs for enhancing its production and utilization. In A. Tsedeke, S. C. Hiebsh, A. Brandt, and S. Gebremariam, eds., *Enset-based Agriculture in Ethiopia*, pp. 1–14. Proceedings of an International Workshop on Enset (1993). Addis Ababa, Ethiopia: Institute of Agricultural Research.

Tsedeke, A., S. C. Hiebsh, S. A. Brandt, and S. Gebremariam, eds. 1996. *Enset-Based Agriculture in Ethiopia*. Proceedings from an International Workshop on Enset, 1993. Addis Ababa, Ethiopia: Institute of Agricultural Research.

Westphal, E. 1975. Agricultural systems in Ethiopia. *Agricultural Research Report* 826. Wageningen, The Netherlands: Centre for Agricultural Publishing and Documentation.

Zemede Asfaw. 1997a. Survey of indigenous food crops, their preparations and home gardens in Ethiopia: Indigenous African food crops and useful plants. *Resources Utilization Assessment Series*, B. N. Okigbo, series ed., No. B6. United Nations University, Institute for Natural Resources in Africa, Nairobi: International Centre of Insect Physiology and Ecology (ICIPE) Science Press.

Zemede Asfaw. 1997b. Conservation and use of traditional vegetation in Ethiopia. In *Proceedings of the IPGRI International Workshop on Genetic Resources of Traditional Vegetables in Africa*, pp. 57–65. Nairobi, Kenya: International Plant Genetic Resources Institute (IPGRI).

Zemede Asfaw. 1999a. Ethnobotany of nations, nationalities and peoples in Gambella, Benishangul-Gumuz and southern regions of Ethiopia. A Research Report submitted to the Research and Publications Office of Addis Ababa University, Addis Ababa.

Zemede Asfaw. 1999b. How they cope in the Ethiopian drylands: Indigenous modes of living that evolved under uncertainties of the arid and semi-arid Ethiopian rift system. *Dryland Biodiversity, Biannual Newsletter of the Research Programme on Sustainable Use of Dryland Biodiversity* 3: 2–8.3.

Zemede Asfaw. 2000. Home garden biodiversity in Ethiopia. Abstract, Paper of the International Conference: Ethiopia, a Biodiversity Challenge. Biological Society of Ethiopia and Linnean Society of London, 2–4 February, Addis Ababa.

Zemede Asfaw. 2001. Origin and evolution of rural home gardens in Ethiopia. In I. Friis and O. Ryding, eds., *Biodiversity Research in the Horn of Africa*, pp. 273–86. Proceedings of the Third International Symposium on the Flora of Ethiopia and Eritrea. Danke Videnskabers Selsk 54.

Zemede Asfaw and D. Desissa. 1999. Interactions and interdependence between the agrobiodiversity and the wild biodiversity. Ninth Annual Conference of the Biological Society of Ethiopia Abstracts, p. 25. 3–5 February 1999, Awassa, Ethiopia.

Zemede Asfaw and A. Nigatu. 1995. Home gardens in Ethiopia: Characteristics and plant diversity. *Sinet: Ethiopian Journal of Science* 18(2): 235–66.

Zemede Asfaw and Z. Woldu. 1997. Crop associations of home-gardens in Welayta and Gurage in Southern Ethiopia. *Sinet: Ethiopian Journal of Science* 20(1): 73–90.

seven

Aspects of Home-Garden Cultivation in Ghana

Regional Differences in Ecology and Society

S. O. Bennett-Lartey, G. S. Ayernor, Carol M. Markwei,
I. K. Asante, D. K. Abbiw, S. K. Boateng,
V. M. Anchirinah, and P. Ekpe

Home gardens occur in all the agroecological zones of Ghana. They are a long-established tradition founded by the Basel missionaries. Located around home-steads, these gardens are planted with fruit trees, vegetables, and other crops. They have been classified in several groups. Asare, Oppong, and Twum-Ampofo (1990) sorted the home gardens they surveyed in the humid tropical forests of Ghana into three categories, but the criteria they used in their classification were not clearly defined. Owusu and his colleagues (1994) classified home gardens according to their structural characteristics, grouping them into four categories. In the first category are extensively managed, multistoried home gardens with tree crops; plants in this type of garden were randomly spaced. In the second category are intensively managed, multistoried home gardens with tree crops. This type of garden differs from the first type in that crops receive greater attention and are generally readily marketable, for example, avocado pear and pineapple. In the third category are extensively managed, multistoried home gardens without trees.

These are essentially similar to mixed crop farms. And in the fourth and last category are intensively managed, single-story home gardens that generally consist of stands of purely marketable, nonnative vegetables. Theirs is the only study in existence that is concerned specifically with home gardens although there are a number of other, more general studies of the edible crops and medicinal and woody plants of Ghana (Irvine 1930, 1961; Dokosi 1969; Abbiw 1990).

Unfortunately, neither Asare, Oppong, and Twum-Ampofo (1990) nor Owusu and his colleagues (1994) addressed the problem of how much intraspecific variation is represented by crops grown in home gardens and how useful they are for in situ conservation of species. The current study addresses both these questions. The primary objective of this study, therefore, is to document the species and intraspecies diversity in home gardens, including the biological, cultural, and socioeconomic factors that govern their distribution and maintenance. A secondary objective is to discuss the usefulness of home gardens as reservoirs of genetic diversity.

Methodology

In order to capture as much of the variation in home gardens as possible, we carried out a rapid rural appraisal, mapping out important areas of home-garden cultivation within the country and identifying various forms of cultivation. The survey involved informal discussion with farmers as well as interviews with extension officers and other key informants. Random stops were made in villages and towns to assess home-garden production practices with the help of a checklist.

Based on the result of the rapid rural appraisal, several regions or agroecological zones were selected for more extensive study (Table 7.1; Dickson and Banneh

Table 7.1

Agroecological zones, political regions, and districts selected for the study of home gardens

Agroecological zone	Region	District
Moist semideciduous forest	Eastern	East Akim, New Juaben
Moist evergreen and southern marginal forest	Western and central	Ahanta West, Cape Coast,
Sekondi-Takoradi, Agona		
Guinea savannah	Northern	West Dagomba, Tolon Kumbungu
Sudan savannah	Upper east	Bolgatanga, Bongo

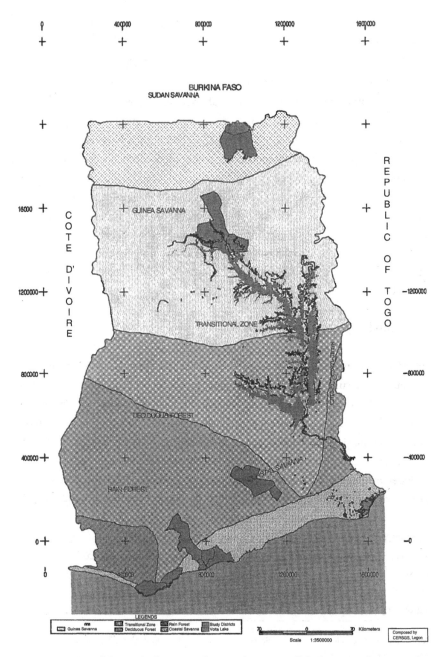

Figure 7.1. Map of the study districts and vegetation zones of the home-garden survey in Ghana

1988). These were the upper east (Sudan savanna), the northern (Guinea savanna), the eastern (moist, semideciduous forest), the western (evergreen forest), and the central (moist, semideciduous forest) regions (see map, Fig. 7.1). Project sites and home gardens were randomly selected from lists of districts and villages/towns within these regions.

For the formal survey, we compiled an exhaustive list of villages stratified into urban, peri-urban, and rural areas. We then randomly selected and surveyed a total of five per district. After assembling a complete list of home-garden farmers from all the villages, we again randomly selected ten farmers from each village and administered pretested questionnaires to them in order to obtain information on the socioeconomic aspects of home-garden cultivation. From species inventories for the various agroecological zones we selected three crops, namely, plantain (*Musa* sp.), yam (*Dioscorea* spp.), and millet (*Pennisetum* sp.) for detailed study. The criteria used in the selection were the importance of the crop to the household economy, its prevalence in home gardens, and its importance in the national food and nutrition system. Studies of these crop species and their varieties, including their management and use, were then carried out in five home gardens per village in order to illustrate some of the criteria that governed regional differences in cultural and ecological preferences.

Natural and Cultural Parameters of the Study Sites

The areas of study fall into two humidity zones. The relative humidity for the rainforest, the moist, semideciduous forest, and the Guinea savanna is greater than 60 percent, whereas that for the Sudan savanna is about 40 percent. The rainfall level and distribution throughout the year separate the study area into three groups. The two forest zones, with mean annual rainfalls of 1,700 mm and 1,200 mm for rainforest and for moist, semideciduous forest, respectively, belong to the high-rainfall area. These areas also have a bimodal pattern of rainfall: March–July and September–October are the wet seasons. In the Guinea savanna mean annual rainfall is 1,100 mm, whereas in the Sudan savanna it is 1,000 mm (Table 7.2); both savanna areas have a single rainy season from July to October. The mean maximum temperatures also vary, increasing as one moves from the forest zones into the northern savanna zones. In the rainforest zones, maximum temperatures fall between 29°C and 30°C, whereas in the Guinea and Sudan savannas temperatures are 33.6°C and 34.5°C, respectively. The mean minimum temperatures are 23.4°C and 21.1°C for the forest areas and 22.3°C for the savannas.

Soils in the rainforest and semideciduous forest are largely ferric cresols, acidic in nature (Table 7.2) and mostly sandy clay in texture. Within the savanna areas,

Table 7.2

General ecological and population description of sampled Ghanaian home garden sites

Geographical location (region)	Eastern		Western	Northern		Upper east
District	East Akim	New Juaben	Ahanta West	West Dagomba	Tolon-Kumbung	Bolgatanga
Altitude[a]	600–750 masl	550–600 masl	100–150 masl	500 masl	450–550 masl	700 masl
Average yearly temperature	25° C	25° C	25° C	28° C	28° C	30° C
Mean annual rainfall[b]	1,050 mm	1,050 mm	1,400 mm	1,139 mm	1,139 mm	1,050 mm
Major soil types[c]	Sandy clay	Sandy clay/silty clay	Sandy clay	Sandy clay	Gravelly sandy clay	Silty clay
Latitude	6°00'–0°55'S	6°00'–6°15'S	4°25'–4°75'S	9°15'–9°31'S	9°16'–10°15'S	10°30'–11°00'S
Longitude	0°20'–0°55'W	0°15'–0°25'W	1°50'–2°15'W	0°45'–1°00'W	1°00'–1°15'W	0°30'–1°00'W
Major agricultural products[d]	Plantain, maize, oil palm, citrus	Plantain, maize, oil palm, citrus	Oil palm, cocoa, plantain	Maize, yam, millet	Maize, yam, millet	Millet, sorghum
District population[e]	189,007	139,370	90,567	300,931	135,084	225,864

a. Data from topographical map obtained from the Survey Department.

b. Data from Meteorological Services Department, Ghana.

c. From Soil Map of Ghana, FAO 1990.

d. Data from Policy, Planning, Monitoring and Evaluation (PPPME) Directorate of the Ministry for Food and Agriculture, Accra, Ghana.

e. Data from 2000 Population and Housing Census (Provisional Results), Ghana Statistical Service, August 2000.

soils in the West Dagomba district are similar to those of the forest in class and texture, whereas soils in the other districts in the savannas are of a different type. In the Tolon-Kumbungu district of the Guinea savanna, the soil is classified as dystric plinthosol and is a gravelly sandy clay in texture. In the Bolgatanga district of the Sudan savanna it is classified as a gleyic lixisol, which is silty clay in texture.

The ethnic groups of Ghana are differentially distributed in the various agroecological regions. Not surprisingly, therefore, the ethnicity of home-garden owners differs regionally. The northern region is predominantly Dagomba (83.3 percent), and so are the home owners, whereas the western and central regions are about half Gomoa (50 percent) and one-third Wassa (30 percent), as are the gardeners. The eastern region has more ethnic groups represented, but the Ashanti (26.7 percent) and the Akim (24.4 percent) predominate, followed by the Ekre (15.6 percent). The ethnicity of home-garden owners reflects these numbers. Whether they are dominant ethnic majorities or are minority groups, all of the various cultural groups of Ghana make home gardens. There were no noticeable differences in their cultivation techniques, though they must have different preferences for particular crops.

Within the study area, modal household size is between 6 and 10 persons (Table 7.3), but in the northern and upper east regions a substantial percentage of households had sizes ranging from 11 to 20 members. The larger household size is correlated with Islam, which allows polygamous marriage and places an emphasis on the extended family.

The residential status and land-tenure systems of home gardeners also vary regionally. In the northern and upper east regions, 98.6 percent and 97.2 percent of farmers, respectively, live on and cultivate family land. In the eastern region, the equivalent figure is 87.8 percent even though only about half of the inhabitants are original residents. In this area, however, most gardeners have purchased a par-

Table 7.3

Size of households surveyed in the study areas

Household size (Number of individuals)	Percentage of farmers		
	Northern	Upper east	Eastern
1–5	4.3	21.3	34.3
6–10	33.2	37.9	47.0
11–15	23.0	31.0	12.4
16–20	17.4	6.9	4.2

cel of land on which to build a house and make a garden. The migratory trend in Ghana is from the north, where rainfall is unimodal and unreliable, to the southeast, where rainfall is bimodal and the soils are rich.

Size, Structure, and Species Composition of Home Gardens

Home gardens in Ghana are generally small (0.16–0.59 hectares; Table 7.4), multistoried, and multipurpose and are found in urban, periurban, and rural communities. Urbanization and increasing pressure on the land around the compounds have all contributed to their small size. Owusu and his colleagues (1994) identified 47 tree species and 34 crop species in the home gardens they studied. The tree species present reflected closely the conditions existing in the particular ecosystem where they grew. For example, the baobab (*Adansonia digitata*) was found in home gardens of the northern savanna but not in the forest zone, whereas the oil palm (*Elaeis guineensis*) was found in the forest zone but not in the northern savanna. Over 90 percent of all home-garden fields were made around the compound for convenient accessibility to the food supply.

A substantial proportion of home-garden fields in the northern region (47.8 percent) are fenced to avoid destruction by domestic animals such as goats, sheep, and cattle. In the northern, upper east, and eastern regions, however, more than 50 percent of home gardens are not fenced (Table 7.4). Over 80 percent of home gardeners in all three regions own the land where they garden (Table 7.4), a fact that contributes to the considerable effort they make to maintain the fields in good shape, resulting in a great deal of stability for the system at large.

In both the rainforest and moist, semideciduous forests, home gardens had multistoried structures composed mainly of three stories but sometimes four. The uppermost canopy consisting of trees was a perennial layer made up of such

Table 7.4

Characteristics of home gardens

Description	Percentage of farmers		
	Northern	Upper east	Eastern
Enclosure: not fenced	52.2	74.2	75.5
Location: around compound	93.0	98.5	97.9
Size of garden: 0.1–1.0 hectare	83.7	—	77.6
Land-tenure system: family owned	95.8	87.0	87.8

species as mango (*Mangifera indica*), oil palm (*Elaeis guineensis*), Indian almond (*Terminalia catapa*), and avocado pear (*Persea americana*). Immediately below this layer one finds both annual and perennial species, the most common and important annual being plantain (*Musa* spp.); the perennial species include fruit trees such as citrus, soursop (*Annona muricata*), sweet apple (*Annona squamosa*), pawpaw (*Carica papaya*), and guava (*Psidium guajava*). The third story consists of vegetables, including eggplant (*Solanum* spp.), amaranthus (*Amaranthus* spp.), cocoyam (*Xanthosoma sagittifolium*), root crops, yam (*Dioscorea* spp.), cassava (*Manihot esculenta*), and medicinal plants (e.g., *Solanum torvum, Ocimum gratissimum, O. canum*). The lowest story consisted of species that were 20 cm or less in height; for example, Indian heliotrope (*Heliotropium indicum*), and creeping plants such as sweet potato (*Ipomoea batatas*). The density of plants in these gardens also varied—some were closely spaced and others widely spaced.

Domestic animals such as poultry and/or goats were raised in some home gardens; even cattle were kept in Kukurantumi, Osiem, and Nkronso. An adventuresome home gardener in Kukurantumi also reared snails in his backdoor garden.

The total number of species recorded in the home-garden survey differed for the various agroecological zones in the study. Generally, the total number was higher in the forest than in the savanna, but within the forest zones, most semideciduous forests had a higher total number of species than the rainforest: 104 and 93 species, respectively. These species also belonged to a wide range of families: 36 families in the moist, semideciduous forest gardens and 37 families in the rainforest gardens (Table 7.5). In the savanna, 51 species belonging to 29 families were recorded for Guinea, and 40 species belonging to 28 families for the Sudan, which had the least number of species (Table 7.5). Detailed species lists can be found in forthcoming publications. Species found in home gardens were used for different purposes, among them food and medicine (Table 7.6). Other species were used for hedging, ornamental purposes, and shade.

Table 7.5

Total number of species identified in gardens in the different agroecological zones

	Regions surveyed			
	East	Western and central	Northern	Upper east
Species	104	93	51	40
Families	36	37	29	28

Table 7.6

Total number of species per use category

Use category	Number of species identified
Cereals	4
Legumes	7
Roots and tubers	12
Fruits and nuts	23
Oil crops	3
Spices	8
Medicinal plants	30
Vegetables	18

Gene Flow between Home Gardens and Other Ecosystems

Germplasm found in home gardens comes from different systems, depending on the uses to which the species are put. Food-crop germplasm came from four main sources: other home gardens, farms, the market, and research institutions (Fig. 7.2). Local varieties of oil crops and fruit trees, for example, were introduced via the market (e.g., coconut) or came from the gardens of friends, relatives, or acquaintances (e.g., mango, avocado pear, sour sop, guava) or from plants growing in farmers' fields (e.g., oil palm). Market crops may originate either from other

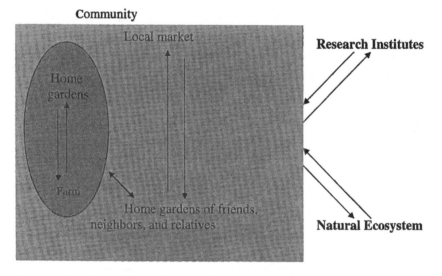

Figure 7.2. Geneflow within the home-garden system

home gardens or from farmers' fields, either locally or from another nearby village or town. Big markets, scattered in different villages, have particular days on which they operate, attracting people from other villages with wares to sell. Thus, a fruit or an oil palm bought at a market on market day may originate from another village, resulting in gene flow that goes beyond the immediate perimeter of village gardens or farms. Home gardens also contain varieties of species, such as citrus and oil palm, that originated in research institutions. A few wild tree species such as *Spondias mombin* and *Chrysophyllum albidum* are introduced from the natural ecosystem when people gather their fruits. Germplasm for medicinal plants and fuel wood comes largely from the natural ecosystem, although some movement of germplasm also takes place between home gardens. *Solanum torvum* and *Ocimum gratissimum* are examples of species whose germplasm moves among home gardens and between home gardens and the natural ecosystem.

Social and Demographic Profile of Farmers

Important social parameters and practices differentiate farmers living in various regions of Ghana for they are by no means a homogeneous lot. Among the home gardeners surveyed gender roles were found to vary significantly by region (Table 7.7). In the northern and upper east regions most farmers were male (88.7 percent and 86.8 percent, respectively), whereas in the eastern region most were female (57.7 percent).

The majority of farmers in the northern (91.4 percent) and upper east regions (83.3 percent) were also full-time farmers, whereas an appreciable number (35.2 percent) of the respondents in the eastern region were only part-time cultivators. This reflects the fact that better employment possibilities in nonfarming activities are found in the east. When possible, farmers prefer to combine a salaried job with part-time work on the land.

Table 7.7
Gender of the home-garden farmers that were sampled

	Percentage of farmers by region		
Gender	Northern	Upper east	Eastern
Males	88.7	86.8	42.3
Females	11.3	13.2	57.7
Total	100.0	100.0	100.0

Table 7.8

Formal education achieved by home gardeners

	Percentage of farmers by region		
Educational status	Northern	Upper east	Eastern
No formal education	84.3	63.6	32.3
Up to 10 years	12.9	31.9	52.0
Above 10 years	2.8	4.5	15.7

The educational status of farmers in the study areas varied widely (Table 7.8). The highest illiteracy rate was found in the northern region, where 84.3 percent of respondents had no formal education at all. The upper east region had an illiteracy rate of 63.6 percent, and the rate was lowest in the eastern region, where it was 32.3 percent. In the northern region, 12.9 percent of respondents had up to 10 years of formal education, followed by 31.9 percent in the upper east region, and 52.0 percent in the eastern region. In the eastern region, 15.7 percent of respondents had more than 10 years of education, whereas in the northern and upper east regions less than 5 percent had comparable education. The higher rates of illiteracy in the north can be attributed to the fact that Islam is the dominant religion, and parents prefer to send their children to Arabic schools. Moreover, increasing demand for farm labor has meant lower rates of enrollment in the schools of the northern and eastern regions. In any case, the fact remains that farming is not an occupation reserved for the illiterate and unschooled but is practiced by educated and uneducated Ghanaians alike.

Methods of land preparation also varied among regions. In the northern region, ploughing the home-garden soils with a tractor (47.9 percent of all fields) is followed by ridging with hoes (28.2 percent), or ploughing with bullocks (23.9 percent). In the upper east and eastern regions, the hoe is the most common implement used (94.1 percent and 83.3 percent, respectively). Tilling with the help of the hoe improves the water retention capacity of the soils, particularly during the dry season.

Fertilizer is used more frequently in the northern region—in the form of compound organic waste and manure—than in the eastern region, where the soils are inherently more fertile. These differences in the use of technology correlate with the variables discussed above. Thus, full-time and educated male farmers in the north tended to use tractors and ploughs more frequently than farmers in other regions and also to employ more inputs.

Marketing and Utilization

In the upper east region, where food security is a major problem, 85.5 percent of households consumed all the produce obtained from their home gardens. The corresponding figures for the northern and the eastern regions were 60.0 percent and 49.0 percent, respectively. The fact that people in the upper east consumed almost all their home-garden produce is not surprising; this region is noted for its high population density and highly fragmented land ownership. Most farmers need to plant the major staples, such as millet and sorghum, in their own gardens because those are the only fields available to most households.

In the northern region, 35.6 percent of households sold between 10 percent and 50 percent of their home-garden produce, consisting mostly of maize, which in this area is both a cash crop and a staple food crop (Table 7.9). In the eastern region, where plantain is the major commercial crop, 11.8 percent of households sold between 20 percent and 50 percent of the product; 27.4 percent sold between 60 percent and 90 percent, and 9.8 percent sold all the plantain they produced. With better management and less theft, plantains grown in home gardens could easily become more marketable than plantains from bush fields.

Most major crops are grown to feed the family. Table 7.10 shows the principal reasons why the cultivation of home gardens is increasing. The provision of food

Table 7.9

Percentage of produce from home gardens sold by farmers in the study areas

	Percentage of farmers by region		
Percentage of produce	Northern	Upper east	Eastern
0	60.0	85.5	49.0
10	4.3	4.8	0.0
20	5.7	0.0	3.9
30	11.4	0.0	0.0
40	12.8	3.2	2.0
50	1.4	4.8	5.9
60	2.0	0.0	0.0
70	2.4	1.7	3.9
80	0.0	0.0	7.8
90	0.0	0.0	15.7
100	0.0	0.0	9.8
Can't tell	0.0	0.0	2.0
Total	100.0	100.0	100.0

Table 7.10

Major reason for the increase in home-garden cultivation within the study areas

	Percentage of farmers mentioning reason		
Reason	Northern	Upper east	Eastern
Convenience	38.0	0.0	12.1
Food and income	47.7	80.0	82.8
Can't tell	14.3	0.0	3.4
Other	0.0	20.0	1.7

and income for the household was a major reason given in all the study areas, as well as the convenience of being located around the home. Nevertheless, some farmers produced certain crops exclusively for the market. In the eastern region, citrus and cocoa are cultivated mainly or exclusively for sale, and some plantain and coconut are also commercialized. In the northern region, groundnuts and tobacco (both 40 percent of respondents) are the two most important cash crops produced and rice is the third (20 percent of respondents).

Gender Roles

Men and women participated differently in home-garden activities. Their activities vary from region to region and between different ethnic groups within the same region according to the culture, history, and contemporary situation of the people concerned. Understanding such role partitioning will help greatly in the generation and transfer of new technologies that accelerate the development process.

In the northern region land preparation, weeding, and the sale of produce are carried out mainly by men. In the eastern region, land preparation is carried out mostly by men, whereas weeding and the sale of produce are carried out by both men and women. In the upper east region, land preparation and weeding are carried out by both, except for the few cases where the produce is sold, in which case it is done by women. In all regions planting is carried out by both genders. These gender differences relate to cultural attitudes and preferences and are in no way biologically or ecologically determined (Tables 7.11–7.13). In the section that follows we will discuss the varietal diversity and management of three important crops. These serve to illustrate some of the social practices and cultural preferences that underlie genetic diversity in the various areas.

Table 7.11

Gender roles in home-gardening activities in the northern region

Task	Percentage of farmers who perform tasks			
	Males	Females	Both	N/A
Land preparation	97.2	1.4	1.4	0
Planting	21.1	4.2	73.3	1.4
Weeding	55.9	6.4	37.7	0.0
Sale of produce	70.5	19.7	2.8	7.0

Table 7.12

Gender roles in home-gardening activities in the eastern region

Task	Percentage of farmers who perform tasks			
	Males	Females	Both	N/A
Land preparation	44.2	15.8	38.9	1.1
Planting	28.1	22.9	49.0	0.0
Weeding	35.4	21.9	39.6	3.1
Harvesting	27.7	20.3	44.5	7.7
Sale of produce	1.1	11.8	43.0	44.1

Table 7.13

Gender roles in home-gardening activities in the upper east region

Task	Percentage of farmers who perform tasks			
	Males	Females	Both	N/A
Land preparation	11.8	2.9	83.8	1.5
Planting	0.0	29.4	70.6	0.0
Weeding	1.4	8.7	89.9	0.0
Harvesting	0.0	10.4	88.1	1.5
Sale of produce	0.0	38.3	5.0	56.7

Major Yam Species Found in Home Gardens

Results of the study of yam varieties show that home gardens in the study areas differed with respect to the most common species of yam grown in them (Table 7.14). In the northern region, *D. rotundata* was the major yam species planted (89.1 percent), followed by *D. alata* (10.9 percent). The eastern region had the highest number of yam species. In the home gardens of the western and central regions, *D. cayenensis, D. alata,* and *D. praehensilis* were the major species encountered. But farmers still favored *D. cayenensis* and *D. alata* over *D. rotundata*. Differences in species cultivated reflect cultural preferences and not ecological conditionas.

In the home gardens of the northern region, the varieties of yam sold—mostly kpono, laboko, and chenchito—were usually staked, so that they would yield one cylindrical tuber. The varieties that were not usually sold were mostly unstaked, allowing the farmer to harvest from a few to many small tubers per mound. Thus, the least uniform and smaller tubers were destined for home use.

Ownership of yams in the home gardens also differed regionally. In the northern, western, and central regions, more men grew yams in their home gardens than women. This may be due to the fact that more men in the north hold title to the land. In the eastern region, slightly more females than males owned gardens with yams growing in them. Thus, as with other crops, yam cultivation is, to some degree, gender specific.

Diversity of Plantains in Home Gardens

We studied plantains in depth only in the eastern, western, and central regions, where they are more common in home gardens and constitute a major part of the diet of the inhabitants. In southern Ghana, plantains grow alongside many other crops in and around towns and villages. More varieties of plantain thrive in the home gardens of the eastern region than in those of the western and central regions; the most common variety is apantu, a false horn plantain, followed by apem, a French plantain (Table 7.15). Not surprisingly, apantu is used to prepare fufu, a staple food of the local people, whereas apem is used to prepare ampesi, another staple food of the people. Apantu is early maturing, whereas apem takes longer to mature; the latter commands a higher price because of the many hands it has (groups of fingers attached at the same point). Abommiensa and borede sebo, all false horn plantains, and nyeretia, a French plantain, were not common in the home gardens studied. Plantain varieties can be differentiated according to bunching and finger characteristics and the color of the pseudostem.

Table 7.14
Dioscorea spp. (yam species) found in home gardens in the study areas

Scientific name	Common name	Northern	Western, central	Eastern
Dioscorea alata	Water yam	10.9	30	28.8
Dioscorea bulbifera	Aerial yam	0	10	2.2
Dioscorea Cayenensis	Yellow yam	0	30	13.3
Dioscorea dumetorum	Bitter yam	0	0	13.3
Dioscorea esculenta	Chinese yam	0	0	2.2
Dioscorea praehensilis	"Kookooase"	0	20	26.7
Dioscorea rotundata	White yam	89.1	10	6.9
Dioscorea sp.	Other yam species	0	0	2.2
Total		100	100	100

Plantain suckers are made widely available through exchange. Farmers exchange varieties readily, thus enriching the diversity of their stands. There are some exceptions, however, such as onniaba, a French plantain that is very tasty, and abommienu, which yields two bunches of plantains at one time; the majority of farmers were unwilling to exchange either of these varieties.

Plantains are put to multiple uses. Besides being used to prepare fufu or am-

Table 7.15
Diversity in plantain varieties in the eastern and western and central regions

Local name of plantain	Percentage by region	
	Western and central	Eastern
Abommiensa	0.0	2.4
Apantu	69.7	38.1
Apem	18.2	21.4
Borede Sebo	0.0	2.4
Borede wuio	0.0	4.8
Essammiensa	0.0	2.4
Eassammienu	3.0	0.0
Jamaica	0.0	2.4
Kwadu brode	6.1	0.0
Nyretia apantu	0.0	4.8
Nyretia	3.0	0.0
Onniaba	0.0	7.1
Osoboaso	0.0	14.3
Total	100.00	100.0

pesi, the fruits are eaten roasted or fried. Other parts of the plant are also utilized. The leaves are used as animal fodder, the flower and roots for medicine, and the pseudostem for fiber. The peel of the fruit is fed to goats and sheep. If burnt, the ashes are mixed with oil to prepare soap. Thus, this is one of the species that is best integrated into the lives of Ghanaian farmers.

Diversity in Pearl Millet

Because millet (*Pennisetum glaucum*) is quite drought resistant, it is cultivated more in the upper east region, where it is of major dietary importance, than in the northern region (Table 7.16). Recall that the upper east region is in the Sudan savanna zone, where rainfall is lower than in the northern region (Guinea savanna zone). Home-garden owners in the northern region planted more sorghum (*Sorghum bicolor*) and maize (*Zea mays*) in their gardens than *Pennisetum glaucum*.

Two varieties of pearl millet, early and late, were identified from the study areas. Early millet takes three months to mature and for this reason is found

A woman in northeastern Ghana drying guinea corn (*Sorghum bicolor*) on the side of her house for next year's home-garden seed

Table 7.16
Millet occurrence in home gardens in
the northern and upper east regions

Region	Percentage
Northern	37
Upper East	63
Total	100.0

mostly in the upper east region, where the rainfall season is shorter than in the northern region. Most farmers in the north grow late millet, which takes four months to mature.

Millet has different uses in the various regions. In the north, the grain is used to make flour, and the stalk and leaves are used for animal fodder. In the upper east region, however, where the principal millet farmers are members of the Frafa ethnic group, this grain is used almost exclusively to make flour for family consumption. Thus, millet cultivation and use is strongly correlated with ecological factors.

A patch of sorghum growing in a home garden in northern Ghana

Conclusions: Home Gardens as
Conservation Units

As a category, home gardens contain the highest population of some under-utilized fruits in Ghana. They are important ex situ conservation sites for several species: *Annona muricata* (soursop), *Annona squamosa* (sweetsop), *Spondias mombin* (jobo), *Psidium guajava* (guava), *Persea americanum* (avocado pear), and *Mangifera indica* (mango). Home gardens are also important for in situ conservation of indigenous varieties of some crops, for example, *Elaeis guineensis* (oil palm), *Cocos nucifera* (coconut), *Pennisteum* spp. (millet), *Sorghum bicolour* (sorghum), and *Dioscorea* spp. (yam). Furthermore, home gardens are important sites for the domestication of wild varieties of species such as wild yam (*Discorea habayere*), bringing them into the local agricultural system. Finally, home gardens serve as entry points for the introduction of new varieties—such as different plantain cultivars—into the broader agricultural system.

The diverse species of cultivated plants found in the Ghanaian home gardens are well-adapted to the various agroecological zones in which they grow. In the forest region (evergreen, moist, semideciduous) of the eastern and western zones, home gardens having at least three stories were planted with annual and perennial fruit trees, vegetables, and creeping plants. In the savanna zone, home gardens are less structurally complex. They contain more cereal crops and leafy vegetables than the forest zone does. They also contain more timber species and fewer fruit trees.

The plant species present in the Ghana gardens also reflect the socioeconomic background of the farmers involved. We have discussed regional differences in household size, the amount of time devoted to farming, the land-tenure situation and cultivation practices, the farmer's educational level, and the gender partitioning of cropping tasks. Again, important regional differences in these parameters emerge. We have indicated some of the cultural factors, including access to land and employment opportunities, family structure, and religious beliefs, that may help to explain these contrasts. We also discussed the various crops that are commercialized in the various regions of Ghana. Whereas most crops are grown to feed the family, a few are grown partially or exclusively for sale. This shows the double function that home gardens perform—to improve the nutritional status of the household and to increase the family budget in this cash-limited section of the developing world.

In order to illustrate some of the factors affecting production, we selected three species (yams, plantain, and pearl millet) for a detailed consideration of their varietal diversity, distribution, and use. Clearly, the crops are grown for different regional uses by different social groups.

To conclude, it is imperative that we understand the salient home-garden production parameters in Ghana from both an ecological and social perspective. The marked degree of variability that exists should serve as a warning to government agents and foreign developers not to ignore regional differences. Doing so will almost certainly lead to the failure of development projects. To take such differences into account at least gives such schemes a chance to succeed.

Acknowledgments

We would like to thank all those who helped to make this study a success. Our special thanks go to the officer in charge and the staff of the Agricultural Research Station at Okumaning (Kade) for the assistance they gave us in connection with the detailed studies of plantains. We are also grateful to Mr. Opoku-Agyeman, of the Plant Genetic Resources Centre, Bunso, for his help in the detailed studies of yams. And we wish to thank Mr. Michael Asiedu, of the Plant Genetic Resources Centre, Bunso, for the analysis of data on the detailed species studies. We greatly appreciate the cooperation of the owners of the home gardens surveyed. Finally, we would like to express our profound gratitude to the International Plant Genetic Resources Institute (IPGRI) and the German government (Deutsche Gesellschaft für technische Zusammenarbeit [GTZ], Deutsche Stiftung für internationale Entwicklung [DSE]) for making this study possible.

References

Abbiw, D. K. 1990. *Useful Plants of Ghana: West African Uses of Wild and Cultivated Plants*. London: Intermediate Technology Publications, and Kew, Richmond Surrey (U.K.): Royal Botanic Gardens.

Asare, E. O., S. K. Oppong, and K. Twum-Ampofo. 1990. Home gardens in humid tropics of Ghana. In K. Landauer and M. Brazil, eds., *Tropical Home Gardens*, pp 80–93. Tokyo: United Nations University Press.

Dickson, K. B., and G. Banneh. 1988. *A New Geography of Ghana*, rev. ed. London: Longman.

Dokosi, O. B. 1969. Some herbs used in the traditional system of healing diseases in Ghana. *Ghana Journal of Science* 9(2): 119–30.

Irvine, F. R. 1930. *Plants of the Gold Coast*. The Gold Coast Government.

Irvine, F. R. 1961. *Woody Plants of Ghana, with Special Reference to Their Uses*. London: Oxford University Press.

Owusu, J. G. K., S. J. Quarshie-Sam, K. A. Nkyi, and S. K. Oppong, eds. 1994. *Indigenous African Food Crops and Useful Plants, Their Preparations for Food and Home Gardens in Ghana*. Tokyo: United Nations University and Paris: Institut National de la Recherche Scientifique (INRA), Natural Resources Survey Series No. B1.

eight

Home-Garden Biodiversity in Two Contrasting Regions of Guatemala

César Azurdia and José Miguel Leiva

Processes of Diversity

The distribution of genetic diversity is not a random occurrence but the result of selective processes that occur naturally and/or are the result of human manipulations. The extreme geographic variation and rich cultural traditions that characterize specific areas of the globe result in spectacular regional patterns of plant diversity. We hope to demonstrate the importance of taking into account spatial and zonal differences when attempting to explain the distribution of plant-genetic resources. Cultural factors alone—in this case ethnic affiliation—do not always explain the entire range of genetic variation in the plant world. Diversity is always the result of natural and cultural forces combined.

As the geographical bridge between the continents, Mesoamerica serves as a corridor linking the flora of North America with that of South America and the Caribbean region. Thus, a large repertoire of plants contains flora originating from these three regions, in addition to many endemic species. In fact, Meso-america is home to a significant number of poorly known but important species—wild and cultivated—that have long been regarded as useful plants by the native populations. Today, these species are succumbing to the degradation of their native habitat and the development of high-tech production systems. Fortunately, however, important species still find a home where traditional agriculture is practiced. By considering them a vital component of their farming system (Azurdia 1981), small farmers are playing an important role in the conservation and development of little-known but useful species. Significantly, these farmers belong to the Mayan, Zapotec, Mixtec, Aztec, and other indigenous groups, long recognized for their cultural achievements. A substantial percentage of the rural population is also "ladino," the name given to the vigorous mestizo descendants of indigenous and Spanish parents. Not surprisingly, the cultural richness of Mesoamerica is also reflected in the high biodiversity of crop plants found here today. Thus, the study of home gardens must include research into the socioeconomic background of farmers and the ecologies where they live. Approximately 18 percent of farm income is dependent on the sale of home-garden products, including basic resources such as firewood, wood, fruits, crops, and medicinal plants (Leiva, Ovando, and Azurdia 2001). Yet even though gardens have always played an important role in the farm economy and distribution, detailed economic studies are few and far between.

Home Gardens of Guatemala

One of the most famous early studies of Guatemalan home gardens was done by Anderson (1967), who described the structure and composition of an orchard garden in the Indian village of Santa Lucía. He found that the agrosystem was carefully designed to prevent soil erosion and colonization of the garden by unwanted weeds, while retaining moisture and making the best possible use of all available space and soil. The orchard garden containing about 25 species is an example of the kind of multiple cropping that closely follows the layout of a natural ecosystem. About half of the species present in the home garden were native. This system also produced different goods all year long, and there were always food and condiments available for use by the household.

A more recent study of home gardens in Guatemala was conducted by Leiva and Lopez (1985) in the Polochic watershed, a part of the Caribbean slope located in the eastern part of the country. Elevations here range from 2,000 meters above sea level in the highest part to close to sea level at the lowest end. Different kinds of home gardens are found in the various ecological strata. As expected, home gardens in cold regions are less diverse in plant composition than home gardens in hot and wet regions. Moreover, 63 percent of species are native to the home gardens of El Estor, Izabal (lowest part), and 29 percent are native to the home gardens of Purulhá (highest part).

The majority of the home gardens produce crops for home consumption, although in both regions there are special ones where commercial species predominate. The best example is the garden dominated by *Chamaedorea*, a *Palmaceae* that produces inflorescens with economic value. In such home gardens, farmers manage the ecosystem to increase production by manipulating the different strata and using additional inputs. An example of a home garden with a commercial objective is in the village of San Agustín Acasaguastlán (Paiz 1994), where tropical trees are the dominant crop. The ecosystem of such orchard gardens closely follows that of the forest itself: tall trees that form the highest level are interspersed with shorter trees, and shrubs, climbers, and herbs fill up the spaces between the trees and the ground level. Garden structure and composition make the best possible use of every available ecological niche.

Our Guatemalan home-garden study concentrated on two main areas: the predominantly ladino semiarid zone in the eastern part of the country and the predominantly indigenous (Q'echi and Pomochi) zone in the subtropical, forested region of Alta Verapaz, in the north of the country. Interestingly, within the semiarid zone, ethnicity made little difference in home-garden characteristics. Important contrasts emerged, however, when we compared home gardens in the semiarid zone with those in the subtropical zone. This underscores the importance of taking regional ecologies into account.

The Semiarid Zone of Guatemala and Its Home Gardens

The area we first studied is between the departments of El Progreso, Zacapa, and Chiquimula (see map, Fig. 8.1). The zone has an approximate surface of 924 km², an estimated population in 1993 of 150,000 inhabitants, and a population density of 162 persons per square kilometer. With an annual rainfall of between 550 mm and 800 mm, an average temperature that varies from 21°C to 27°C, and a potential annual evapotranspiration of between 600 mm and 800 mm, the more appropriate designation for such an area is subtropical very arid forested area. The

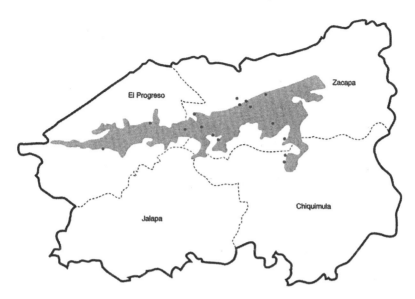

Figure 8.1. Map of the home-garden study sites in the semiarid zone of Guatemala

natural vegetation is made up of thorny shrubs and plants. The region is poor in natural resources and its inhabitants live in extreme poverty.

In 1991, information was obtained from a sample of 46 home gardens distributed in 17 rural communities in El Progreso, Zacapa, and Chiquimula (Table 8.1). Home gardens vary greatly in size, from 90 m² to 2500 m², and are usually square or rectangular. Approximately a third of the surface is covered by infrastructures, such as the dwelling, pigsty, poultry house, and cellar. The rest (65 percent of the area) is covered by plants (see Fig. 8.2 for the correlation between garden surface area and number of species).

The structure, composition, and dynamics of local home gardens vary in relation to the interaction over time of different components, especially environmental and cultural ones. The environment, including the climate, the soil, and the slope of the land, defines the species that can be grown. Home-garden composition is determined mostly by such factors as lack of water for irrigation and scarcity of propagating stocks, or seeds (Fig. 8.3). Home gardens with 16 to 62 species were found in the sample, with an average of 33 species per unit.

Four clearly defined vegetational layers were found in almost all the kitchen gardens we visited: trees (20 percent), shrubs (28 percent), herbs (44 percent), and climbing plants (8 percent). Of a total of 276 species inventoried, almost half are native to the semiarid area of Guatemala and the rest introduced. Table 8.2 gives

Table 8.1

Number of home gardens visited in rural communities during the study of home gardens in the semiarid region of Guatemala

Department	Municipality	Communities	Home gardens visited
Chiquimula	Chiquimula	El Ingeniero	3
		Petapilla	3
El Progreso	San Agustín Acasaguastlán	Cabecera municipal	3
	San Cristobal Acasaguastlán	El Manzanal	3
	Guastatoya	Río Guastatoya	3
Zacapa	Cabañas	Agua Caliente	2
		Cabecera municipal	3
		San Vicente	2
	Río Hondo	Cabecera municipal	3
		Km 129	2
		Lo de Mejía	1
		Nuevo Sunzapote	1
		Pasabien	2
		Santa Cruz	2
	Usumatlán	El Jute	9
	Zacapa	Llano de Calderón	2
		Llano de Piedra	2
		Total	46

the most frequent species encountered in the various strata of the home gardens found here. The native species found in home gardens make up 37 percent of the natural vegetation of the region (Alarcón 1992).

Cultural aspects relating to the use and destination of species, as well as their composition, structure, and management, affect the direction and rate of change that continuously take place in home-gardens systems. Only 13 percent of the families interviewed admitted to earning an income from the sale of products from their home gardens. Nearly half the families stated that the products from their home gardens were for family consumption but did not deny the possibility of selling or exchanging some products occasionally (Fig. 8.4). In fact, those families that admitted selling some of their home-garden products did so to intermediaries who visit the communities in order to obtain seasonal produce, principally fruits: citruses (*Citrus* spp.), hog plums (*Spondias purpurea*), mangos (*Mangifera indica*), coconuts (*Cocos nucifera*), cashews (*Anacardium occidentale*), and the like.

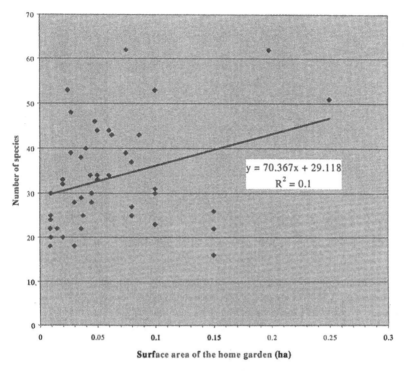

Figure 8.2. Correlation between the surface area of the home garden in the semiarid zone and the number of species found within it

They also obtain vegetables such as chipilín (*Crotalaria longirostrata*), lorocos (*Fernaldia pandurata* and *Fernaldia brachypharynx*), quilete (*Solanum americanum*), and manioc or yuca (*Manihot esculenta*). Products are taken to the most important markets of the region or are shipped directly to Guatemala City to be sold.

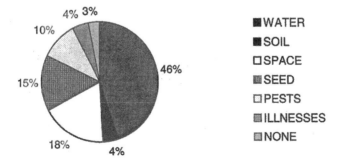

Figure 8.3. Factors that affect the handling and composition of home gardens in the semiarid zone

Table 8.2

Main species in the different strata of home gardens in the semiarid region of Guatemala

Common name	Scientific name	Stratum	Main uses
Aloe	*Aloe vera*	Herbaceous	Medicinal
Cashew	*Anacardium occidentale*	Arboreal	Food
Soursop	*Annona muricata*	Arboreal	Food
Ivy	*Anredera vesicaria*	Trailing	Ornamental
Coral vine, mountain rose	*Antigonon leptopus*	Trailing	Ornamental
Bouganvilia	*Bougainvillea buttiana*	Trailing	Ornamental
Bouganvilia	*Bougainvillea glabra*	Trailing	Ornamental
Chaltecoco	*Caesalpinia velutina*	Arboreal	Firewood, fence posts
Chile, pepper	*Capsicum annuum*	Herbaceous	Food
Bird pepper, chiltepe	*Capsicum annuum* var. *glabriusculum*	Herbaceous	Food
Papaya	*Carica papaya*	Shrub	Food
Goosefoot	*Chenopodium ambrosioides*	Herbaceous	Food, medicinal
Lime	*Citrus aurantiifolia*	Shrub	Food
Orange	*Citrus sinensis*	Shrub	Food
Coconut	Cocos nucifera	Arboreal	Food
Grand cayman	*Cordia dentata*	Arboreal	Firewood, fence posts
Calabash	*Crescentia alata*	Shrub	Medicinal
Crotalaria or chipilín	*Crotalaria longirostrata*	Shrub	Food
Dumbcane	*Dieffenbachia picta*	Herbaceous	Ornamental
Yam	*Dioscorea alata*	Trailing	Food, medicinal
Loroco	*Fernaldia pandurata*	Trailing	Food
Bastard cedar	*Guazuma ulmifolia*	Arboreal	Firewood, fence posts, medicinal
Hibiscus	*Hibiscus rosa-sinensis*	Shrub	Ornamental
Common periwinkle	*Lochnera rosea*	Herbaceous	Ornamental
Loofah, smooth sponge gourd	*Luffa cylindrica*	Trailing	Domestic use
Mandevilla, red riding hood	*Mandevilla* sp.	Trailing	Ornamental
Mango	*Mangifera indica*	Arboreal	Food
Cassava, or manioc, or yuca	*Manihot esculenta*	Shrub	Food
Mint	*Mentha citrata*	Herbaceous	Food, medicinal
Banana	*Musa* spp.	Shrub	Food
Guava	*Psidium guajava*	Shrub	Food
Bowstring hemp	*Sansevieria hyacinthoides*	Herbaceous	Medicinal, ornamental
Black nightshade or quilete	*Solanum americanum*	Herbaceous	Food
Hog plum	*Spondias purpurea*	Arboreal	Food
Tamarind	*Tamarindus indica*	Arboreal	Food
Yellow bells, yellow elder	*Tecoma stans*	Arboreal	Firewood, medicinal
Yard long bean, asparagus bean	*Vigna unguiculata* subsp. *Sesquipedalis*	Herbaceous	Food
Yucca	*Yucca elephantipes*	Shrub	Food

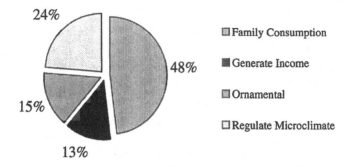

24%

48%

15%

13%

■ Family Consumption

■ Generate Income

■ Ornamental

□ Regulate Microclimate

Figure 8.4. Home-garden functions that depend on the needs of the owner's family

Other Cultural Aspects Associated with the Home Gardens of the Semiarid Zone

Almost all of the families interviewed belong to the ladino (mestizo) group; only 4 percent belong to the indigenous minorities of the region (Fig. 8.5), most of whom live in the semiarid highlands. Nevertheless, no differences between the two groups were apparent in terms of the structure, composition, or management of their home gardens. This may reflect the extent to which the indigenous groups have absorbed latino values and practices. Both groups plant the usual maize, beans, and vegetable crops.

The large majority of the families interviewed live on their own property, and the others rent a lot on someone else's farm. The average family has four members. The medium age for the kitchen garden is 18 years. Although agriculture is still the principal activity of the region (see Fig. 8.6), only 14 percent of the inter-

4%

96%

□ LADINO GROUP

■ INDIGENOUS GROUPS

Figure 8.5. Cultural groups of the semiarid zone in Guatemala

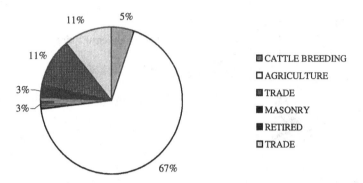

Figure 8.6. Occupation of the family head among the home gardeners of the semiarid zone

viewees own all the land they cultivate. The remaining group rents some additional land for the cultivation of basic grains, tobacco, or melons, or sells their labor.

The management of kitchen gardens for home consumption is simple, being basically limited to cutting down the canopy trees and irrigating and weeding the crops. Other practices, such as the application of fertilizers and pesticides, are carried out to a limited extent in orchards for commercial exploitation. Women are most involved in home-garden care; they look after the cultivation of comestible plants (vegetables, roots, and condiments), plants with medicinal properties, and, of course, ornamentals. Men cultivate fruit trees that provide shade and freshen up the environment around the house. No single criterion explains the distribution of plants in home gardens. Women usually introduce the plants of interest to them near the dwelling, whereas men introduce fruits and crop fruits so as to create a favorable microclimate, particularly during the dry season (Fig. 8.7).

The Alta Verapaz Home Gardens

Within Alta Verapaz Department, in the north of the country, we studied two subregions with diverse ecological conditions but less pronounced cultural differences. The first region, or the northern part, is a humid subtropical hot forest inhabited by the Q'echi indigenous people. The second region is located in the central mountains, where Q'echi and Pocomchí people live in a humid subtropical cold forest. Ladinos are present only in the lowlands. Despite ethnic divergence, the home gardens made by the inhabitants of both regions share many features in common. Nevertheless, subtle differences exist, most of them related to the settlement history of the two subregions.

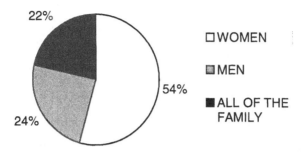

Figure 8.7. Participation of each gender in home-garden care in the semiarid zone

The Alta Verapaz Department (see map, Fig. 8.8) is located in the northern part of the country and covers 8,686 km² (8 percent of the national area). Here, altitudes vary, from 20 m to 1,200 m above sea level. The weather changes according to the region; the lowlands are hot and humid, whereas the mountains are cold and humid. Temperatures range from 14°C to 27°C, and precipitation varies from 2,000 mm to 6,000 mm.

In the study region, home gardens have different names. Q'echi' communities label this agroecosystem *ch'och,* meaning the space that surrounds the house; Pocomchies name it *pat,* meaning house, and ladinos call it a *solar* or *sitio.* Home-garden size also varies in the two Alta Verapaz study areas. In the lowlands, home gardens range from 400 m² to 2,000 m² in size, and in the mountains they range from 3,200 m² to 5,600 m²; the means are 1,000 m² and 1,900 m², respectively. Not surprisingly, the smallest home gardens are in areas of recent colonization, high population density, considerable urban development, and well-developed transport.

Most of the home gardens we surveyed showed five layers: trees, shrubs, herbs, vines, and epiphytes. Such layers vary depending on their uses, on gender preferences, distribution, and time when the home garden was established. Tall trees that form the highest level are interspersed with shorter trees. The tree stratum is composed of species that generally grow in the nearby natural ecosystem (primary and secondary forest), as well as trees deliberately planted by farmers. In the warm region there are more tree species than in the cold region; they serve to regulate shade and humidity within the home garden. Fifty-nine species (23 percent of the species found) were reported from the tree stratum in the cold region, and 84 species (30 percent of the species) from the tree stratum in the warm re-

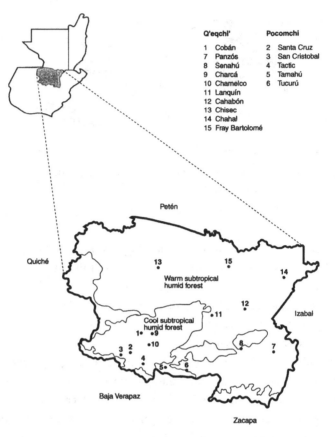

Figure 8.8. Map of the study villages in Alta Verapaz Department of Guatemala

gion. Fruit and woody trees are the most common species in this stratum (Table 8.3). Because trees could represent a potential danger if they fall, they are not planted close to houses, and their growth is regulated by pruning.

Coffee, different kinds of fruits such as bananas, and species that came from the wild are represented at the shrub stratum in both regions (Table 8.4). Shrubs reach no more than 2–5 meters and represent 25 percent and 23 percent of the useful plants found in home gardens of the warm and the cold region, respectively. These species do not show a specific distribution pattern in the home garden, being used as ornamentals, vegetables, and fruits. Such species are kept in the system because they usually generate shade for other species such as coffee or are used to support climbing vines.

Herbs growing in the lower layer belong to both annual species and short-cycle crops (Table 8.4). Most grow spontaneously and are managed by the farmers them-

Table 8.3

Most frequent species that comprise the tree stratum in home gardens of
Alta Verapaz, Guatemala

	Hot zone		Cold zone	
Number	Scientific name	Frequency (%)	Scientific name	Frequency (%)
1	*Gliricidia sepium*	89	*Persea americana*	97
2	*Citrus sinensis*	89	*Citrus sinensis*	90
3	*Bixa orellana*	83	*Prunus persica*	68
4	*Persea americana*	78	*Inga sp.*	65
5	*Inga paterno*	76	*Eriobotrya japonica*	58
6	*Psidium guajava*	74	*Persea schiedeana*	55
7	*Cocos nucifera*	72	*Bixa orellana*	55
8	*Byrsonima crassifolia*	70	*Erythrina berteroana*	52
9	*Citrus aurantiifolia*	67	*Pouteria viridis*	48
10	*Theobroma cacao*	67	*Perymenium grande*	48

selves. Species such as *Solanum americanum, Capsicum annuum* var. *aviculare,* and *Eringium foetidum* are acceptable weeds because they are widely used for food, and for this reason they are listed among the most frequent species in Alta Verapaz home gardens. This stratum has the greatest number of useful species—vegetables, spices, ornamentals, and medicinals—within home gardens. Ninety-five species (34 percent of the species) were reported from the warm region and 117 species (47 percent of the species) from the cold region. Farmers take special care of this stratum; for instance, they sow these plants in the vicinity of the house, they regulate their shade, and they water them when necessary. This stratum showed a predominance of introduced, nonnative species.

The vine stratum is made up of scandent shrubs or herbs belonging to the following families: Cucurbitaceae, Passifloraceae, Fabaceae, Convolvulaceae. Most of these species (Table 8.5) are important as food. In the lowlands, this stratum contains 10 percent of the total species, and in the cold region 6 percent. The epiphytic stratum is composed of the families Orchidaceae, Piperaceae, and Cactaceae. In both regions they make up close to 1 percent of the species population. Most of these species are used as medicines or ornamentals and are planted in the home garden by farmers who bring them in from the nearby forest.

A total of 414 useful plant species comprising 297 genera and 103 families were identified in the Alta Verapaz region. The number of species in home gardens within the warm region ranges from 23 to 81, with a mean of 50 species; in the cold

Table 8.4

Most frequent species that comprise the herbaceous and shrub strata in home gardens of Alta Verapaz, Guatemala

Species Name	Frequency in hot zone (%)	Frequency in cold zone (%)	Stratum
Ananas comosus	65		Herb
Calathea insignis		81	Herb
Capsicum annuum	48	55	Herb
Capsicum annuum var. *glabriusculum*	65		Herb
Carica papaya	33		Shrub
Chamaedorea tepejilote		77	Shrub
Coffea arabica	80	100	Shrub
Colocasia esculenta	54	84	Herb
Dahlia imperialis		94	Herb
Elettaria cardamomum	41		Herb
Eringium foetidum	63	65	Herb
Gladiolus hortolanus		77	Herb
Hamelia patens	35		Shrub
Hibiscus rosa-sinensis	78	48	Shrub
Manihot esculenta	39		Shrub
Musa nana		58	Shrub
Musa paradisiaca	48	55	Shrub
Musa sapientum	85	65	Shrub
Musa spp.		74	Shrub
Ocimum campechianum	37		Herb
Piper auritum	33		Shrub
Saccharum officinarum	65	87	Herb
Solanum americanum	37	87	Herb
Solanum betaceum		68	Shrub
Taetsia fruticosa var. *ferrea*	35	68	Shrub
Xanthosoma violaceum	52	74	Herb
Yucca elephantipes	39	61	Shrub
Zea mays		65	Herb

region the number ranges from 26 to 94, with a mean of 56. In both regions, native species (55 percent) predominate slightly over introduced species (45 percent).

Home gardens are diverse as a result of differences in the agroclimate as well as in the farmers' objectives. A combined cluster analysis using data from home gardens in the warm and cold regions revealed that there are some differences between the two. This can be attributed mainly to ecological factors, with cultural differences being secondary.

The greatest number of species in the Alta Verapaz home gardens are used for

Table 8.5

Most frequent species of climbers in home gardens of Alta Verapaz, Guatemala

	Hot zone		Cold zone	
	Scientific name	Frequency (%)	Scientific name	Frequency (%)
1	*Sechium edule*	52	*Sechium edule*	100
2	*Cucurbita moschata*	39	*Phaseolus coccineus*	87
3	*Ipomoea batatas*	28	*Cucurbita moschata*	68
4	*Phaseolus vulgaris*	22	*Ipomoea batatas*	39
5	*Dioscorea bulbifera*	22	*Rubus* sp.	29
6	*Passiflora* sp.	20	*Phaseolus* sp.	29
7	*Mucuna pruriens*	17	*Phaseolus* sp.	23
8	*Momordica charantia*	13	*Ipomoea* sp.	13
9	*Vigna sesquipedalis*	13	*Asparagus plumosus*	10
10	*Philodendron* sp.	11	*Passiflora ligularis*	10

food. Thus, 126 species (45 percent of the total species in the region) in the warm region and 96 species (38 percent of the total species) in the cold region are edible, but only about 25 species are truly important and commonly grown. The food category is comprised of species that produce mainly fruits and vegetables. Fruits are most important in home gardens in the warm region, whereas vegetables are most important in the cold region. Part of the excess production of both regions is sold at the local markets, thus alleviating the general poverty of the inhabitants.

The people of the Alta Verapaz practice traditional medicine based on extensive knowledge; they do not have easy and free access to Western medicine. For this reason, 26 percent and 33 percent of the species reported from the warm region and cold regions, respectively, were useful medicinal plants. In the study region, cultural richness is the rule. Thus, many species are used in traditional activities such as patronal festivities, religious celebrations, special dishes, and handicrafts.

Q'echi' is the most important ethnic group living in the lowlands, and Pocomchi the most important in the mountains. Ladinos are present only in the lowlands. Most farmers in the lowlands are colonists, compared with the ones in the cold mountains. The most frequent family size is 7–9 members (48 percent and 42 percent of the families in the lowland and mountains, respectively). Within the indigenous household, both genders are involved in home-garden work, but men seem to invest slightly more of their available time in agriculture. Men select the seeds and planting materials for the most economically important species such as

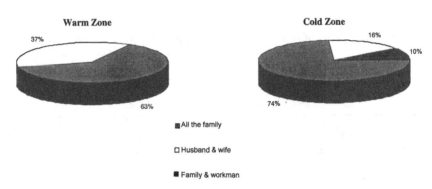

Figure 8.9. The role of family members in the care of home gardens in the Alta Verapaz Department

fruit trees, coffee, and cardamom. Women decide what root crops, vegetables, spices, and medicinal plants should be grown in the garden. All family members, including children, participate in home-garden tasks (Fig. 8.9). The most important management activities that the family performs are tilling, planting, watering, weeding, and harvesting. In the coffee and cardamom commercial growing mountain regions, about one-tenth of the households hire extra labor. Fertilizer and pesticides are used mainly in these gardens. Information on land tenure indicates that in both regions most of the farmers own the land on which they make their home gardens. Additionally, an important percentage of the farmers own another piece of land, called a *parcela,* where they cultivate other kinds of crops.

The length of time that farmers have been living in either region varies. The lowland area was opened to development approximately 35 years ago; for this reason, people who live there have done so for an average of 15 years. Most of the people who live in the central mountains are descendants of families who have lived in the region for generations. It was reported that these families have been living in this region for up to 56 years. Despite the disparity in the time of settlement and differences in the average size of the parcel of land they cultivate, the home gardens of both Alta Verapaz subregions share many characteristics. This is less true when the gardens of the semiarid zone are compared with those of Alta Verapaz.

Comparisons and Conclusions

The two areas of Guatemala where we conducted research, namely, the semiarid zone and the Alta Verapaz region, show startling differences in their ethnic composition and their home-garden characteristics:

The Semiarid Zone	Alta Verapaz
96 percent ladino; 4 percent indigenous	Predominantly indigenous
Size range, 90 m²–2,500 m²	Size range, 1,000 m²–1,900 m²
A total of 276 species; 48 percent native	A total of 414 species; 55 percent native
Four vegetation levels	Five vegetation levels
Household size, 4 persons	Household size, 7–9 persons
Not everyone owns land	Majority owns land, some have an extra parcel
Over half of gardening is done by women	Both genders work on gardens, but men invest slightly more labor

The semiarid zone is populated mainly by ladino families, whereas the Alta Verapaz region is largely populated by indigenous groups. Some home gardens in the semiarid zone are very small indeed, whereas others are quite large; in the Alta Verapaz, home-garden size is more uniform. The total number of plant species is significantly larger, and they are arranged in more levels in Alta Verapaz than in the semiarid zone. Most houshold heads in Alta Verapaz own the land they cultivate, whereas many in the semiarid zone do not and are forced to rent extra parcels. Finally, households are larger and the gender division of labor is more equitable in Alta Verapaz than in the other region.

From this we can see how important it is to take spatial and zonal differences into account when conducting country studies of home gardens. Clearly, a great deal of regional variability exists in the physical parameters surrounding home gardens and in the socioeconomic circumstances characterizing the farmers who cultivate them; this is the rule rather than the exception. These differences must be taken into account when designing countrywide projects aimed at increasing home-garden productivity and conserving their great diversity. In many regions of Mesoamerica home gardens are undergoing drastic change as populations increase and farmers adopt new technologies, new plant species, and novel forms of cultivation.

These agroecosystems serve as refugia for wildlife and regulators of the microclimate. They are repositories for many plant species that remain threatened in their habitat, thus offering a splendid opportunity for their conservation. For these reasons, the study of home gardens is mandatory in all efforts to understand, improve, and support an effective method for the in situ conservation of plant-genetic resources.

Conservation of biodiversity in home gardens has always been an important tradition within the Mesoamerican region. These living gene banks must be seriously taken into account, independent of and also as a complement to, ex situ gene-bank collections. In situ conservation of crop-plant biodiversity is the only assurance we have that valuable genetic traits will be available for the future improvement of important cultivars.

References

Alarcón, R. H. 1992. Caracterización de la comunidad de yaje (*Leucaena duversifolia* Sclecht Bent) en la zona semiárida de El Progreso y Zacapa. Thesis, Facultad de Agronomía, Universidad de San Carlos de Guatemala.

Anderson, E. 1967. *Plants, Man and Life*. Berkeley: University of California Press.

Azurdia, C. 1981. Estudio de las Malezas en Valles Centrales de Oaxaca. MA Thesis, Colegio de Postgraduados, Chapingo, Mexico.

Leiva, J. M., and J. Lopez. 1985. Los sistemas agroforestales de la cuenca del rio Polochic: composición y características. *Tikalia* (Guatemala) 1–2: 47–84.

Leiva, J. M., W. Ovando, and C. Azurdia. 2001. Socioeconomic characterization of home gardens in two communities of Chisec, Alta Verapaz, Guatemala. Faculty of Agronomy and International Plant Genetic Resources Institute, Working Paper.

Paiz, C. M. 1994. Caracterización de las areas irrigadas en la cuenca del rio Hato, San Agustín Acasaguastlan, El Progreso. Thesis, Facultad de Agronomía, Universidad de San Carlos de Guatemala.

nine

Venezuelan *Conucos*
Reversing Threats to a Traditional System

*Consuelo Quiroz, Margaret Gutiérrez M.,
and Trinidad Pérez de Fernández*

The Value of the *Conuco*

Traditional Venezuelan home gardens are known as *conucos* within the local culture. This Arawak word is also used in other Caribbean countries, notably Cuba, Dominican Republic, and Puerto Rico, to denote the multistory association of traditional crop plants grown around rural homesteads. A key feature of the Arawak conuco is the intercropping, in mounds, of root crops (manioc, sweet potato, and tannia) with herbaceous plants (beans and chilies) and fruit trees (guava, papaya, avocado, and banana, introduced early in the Spanish conquest). Venezuelan conucos are part of a system of low external input that relies heavily on organic fertilizers, household labor, and local knowledge.

The conuco produces food for the household in accordance with local habits and needs. This form of cultivation has been essential for the food security of Venezuela's poor rural households, whose members have scarcely benefited from the country's oil-export boom. Unfortunately, economic reliance on oil export revenues has promoted a growing dependence on imported foods, leading to a decline in the production and consumption of local crops. Fortunately, a significant diversity of tropical root crops, fruits, and peppers can still be found in the conucos of small farmers practicing low-input agriculture. This diversity can in the future be used to develop a richer, more balanced diet for the poor.

The research reported in this case study provides a starting point for understanding the processes that promote the maintenance of diversity for key home-garden species. It also identifies factors that promote the stability, variety, and economic value of conucos. We argue that a high value must be placed on conucos as privileged places for the in situ conservation of plant-genetic resources. This point has been made before with reference to home gardens in general, but it deserves to be reinforced using as specific examples the variations that exist within the particular conuco system of Venezuela.

Methods

The structure and function of conucos varies according to the ecozones present in Venezuela. For this study, we selected for closer inspection the central zone (645–1,200 masl) of the Serranía del Interior, near the borders of Aragua and Carabobo states, and three zones at different elevations (0–500 masl; 500–1,500 masl; 1,500–2,400 masl) in the Andean region of the state of Trujillo (see map, Fig. 9.1). Most of the conucos that remain today are found at higher elevations. We surveyed the diversity in 150 conucos across all sites and selected a sample of 36 conucos to represent each of the types with their respective ecozone (Ewel and Madriz 1968). The conucos selected provided data allowing for the identification of key home-garden species that displayed significant genetic diversity. Four criteria were consistently used across the sites to select conucos for intensive study and analysis, namely: (a) the presence of a high number of species per conuco, (b) the creation and cultivation of the conuco for over five years, (c) the consumption of most products by household members, and (d) the willingness of farmers to collaborate with the research project. A complete plant inventory was carried out on the selected sample based on regular weekly visits and interviews and on the participation in the research of the farmer households. The inventory (Table 9.1) contains the local and scientific names of all species, along with their uses.

Key home-garden species were selected from among the total population of useful plants based on the following criteria: (a) the species is present in most home gardens in the zone, (b) it is representative of one of the strata in the home-garden structure, (c) it has significant diversity according to farmers' perceptions

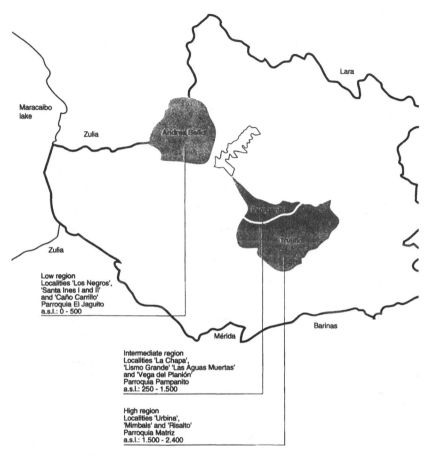

Figure 9.1. Map of three zones at different elevations in the Andean region of the State of Trujillo

and classification, (d) it contributes significantly to the household's food security, and (e) the species is native to the region. The key species that were selected included common bean (*Phaseolus vulgaris*, known locally as caraota) in the lower stratum, papaya (*Carica papaya*) in the middle stratum, and avocado (*Persea americana*) in the upper stratum.

Species Diversity in Conucos: A Typology

Our in-depth study of diversity in the sample of 36 conucos in the Serranía del Interior and in the state of Trujillo revealed the existence of 591 plant species belonging to 362 genera and 101 plant families (Badillo, Schnee, and Benitez de Rojas 1985; Schnee 1973). In order to compare their similarity and to establish a

Table 9.1

An inventory of the species grown in the Venezuelan conucos

Latin Name	Local Name	Uses
Allium cepa	Cebolla	Food
Apium graveolens	Apio España	Food
Allium porrum	Ajo porro	Food
Allium sativum	Ajo	Food
Allium schoenoprassum	Cebollín	Food
Aloe vera	Zábila	Medicinal
Ambrosia artemisiifolia	Altamisa	Medicinal
Ananas comosus	Piña	Food
Anethum graveolens	Eneldo	Medicinal
Annona cherimola	Chirimoya	Food
Annona squamosa	Anón	Food
Annona muricata	Guanábana	Food
Arracacia xanthorrhiza	Apio	Food
Arthemisia absinthium	Ajenjo	Medicinal
Artocarpus altilis	Gran pan	Food
Begonia sp.	Begonias	Ornamental
Beta vulgaris	Remolacha	Food
Bixa orellana	Onoto	Food
Bidens cynapiifolia	Cadillo de perro	Medicinal
Borago officinalis	Borraja	Medicinal
Brassica oleraceae	Repollo	Food
Brassica oleraceae L. var. *Botrytis*	Brócoli	Food
Brassica oleracea L. var. *botrytis*	Coliflor	Food
Cajanus cajan	Guandú or quinchoncho	Food
Calathea alluia	Guapito	Food
Canavalia sp.	Toddy	Food
Canna sp.	Capacho	Ornamental
Capsicum frutescens	Ají	Food
Carica papaya	Lechosa	Food
Cassia racemosa	Cañafistula	Medicinal
Cederla odorata	Cedro	Timber, shade tree
Chrysobalanus icaco	Icaco	Food
Chrysophyllum cainito	Caimito	Food
Cicer arietinum	Garbanzo	Food
Citrus limetta	Lima	Food
Citrus sinensis	Naranja	Food
Citrus reticulata	Mandarina	Food
Cleome spinosa	Paraíso	Medicinal
Clusia minor	Quiripiti	Medicinal
Cocos nucifera	Coco	Food
Coffea sp.	Café	Food
Cordia alliodora	Pardillo	Timber, shade tree

Table 9.1 continued

Latin Name	Local Name	Uses
Crescentia cujete	Taparo	Food
Croton malambo	Palomatías	Medicinal
Cucumis sativus	Pepino	Food
Cucúrbita ficifolia	Zapallo	Food
Cucurbita maxima	Auyama	Food
Cuminum cyminum	Comino	Food
Cymbopogon citratus	Malojillo	Medicinal
Cyperus rotundus	El corocillo	Weed
Daucus carota	Zanahoria	Food
Dioscorea sp.	Ñame	Food
Eriobotrya japónica	El níspero del Japón	
Eryngium foetidum	Cilantro	Food
Eucalyptus robusta	Eucalipto	Medicinal
Ficus carica	Higo	Food
Furcraea humboldtiana	Cocuiza	Food
Geonoma baculifera	Caña de la India	Medicinal
Hibiscus esculentus L.	Dormidera, ñajú, or qimbombó	Medicinal
Hibiscus rosa-sinensis	Cayena	Ornamental
Impatiens sultanii	Coquetas	Ornamental
Inga sp.	Guamos	Food
Ipomoea batatas	Batata	Food
Ipomoea stolonifera	Bejuco de cadena	Medicinal
Jacquinia barbasco	Chirca or barbasco	Medicinal
Kalanchoë pinnata (Lam)	Colombiana	Medicinal
Lactuca sativa	Lechuga	Food
Lepechinia bullata	Orégano Orejón	Medicinal
Lippia sp.	Orégano	Food
Lycopersicum esculetum	Tomate	Food
Malus pumila	Manzana	Food
Malpighia emarginata	Semeruco	Food
Mangifera indica	Mango	Food
Manihot esculenta	Yuca	Food
Manilkara acharas	Níspero	Food
Marantha arundinaceae	Sagú	Food
Matricaria chamomilla	Manzanilla	Medicinal
Melicoccus bijugatus	Mamón	Food
Melissa officinalis L.	Toronjil	Medicinal
Mentha officinalis	Yerba buena	Medicinal
Minthostachys mollis	Orégano acidrado	Medicinal
Momordica charantia	Cundeamor	Weed
Musa AAA distinct varieties	Cambur	Food
Musa AAB distintas variedades	Plátano	Food

Continued on next page

Table 9.1 continued

Latin Name	Local Name	Uses
Musa ornata	Platanillo	Ornamental
Ocimum basilicum	Albahaca	Food
Origanum mejorana	Mejorana	Medicinal
Passiflora sp.	Parchas	Food
Pectis sp.	Comino de cerro	Food
Persea americana	Aguacate	Food
Petroselium sativum	Perejil	Food
Phaseolus vulgaris	Caraota	Food
Pisum sativum	Arvejas	Food
Plantago major	Llantén	Medicinal
Pouteria sp.	Zapote	Food
Prunus persica	Durazno	Food
Psidium guajaba	Guayaba	Food
Pteridium aquilinum	Helecho macho	Weed
Punica granatum	Granada	Food
Rosmarinus officinalis	Romero	Medicinal
Rubus furibundus	Mora	Food
Ruta graveolens	Ruda	Medicinal
Saccharum officinarum	Caña de Azúcar	Food
Sambucus nigra	Sauco	Medicinal
Sambucus peruviana	Sauco-valeriana	Medicinal
Sclerocarpus coffeaecolus	Flor Amarilla	Weed
Sechium edule	Chayota	Food
Solanum tuberosum	Papa	Food
Syzygium jambos	Pomarrosa	Food
Syzygium malcaccense	Pomagás	Food
Syzygium paniculatum	Cereza	Food
Tamarindus indica	Tamarindo	Food
Theobroma cacao	Cacao	Food
Verbesina caracasana	Tarilla	Weed
Vigna unguiculata	Frijol	Food
Vigna sp.	El frijol	Food
Viola sp.	Violetas	Ornamental
Xanthosoma sp.	Guaje u ocumo	Food
Zeamays	Maíz	Food
Zingiber officinale	Jengibre	Medicinal
Zornia perforata	Curía	Medicinal

A home garden in the middle elevations of the Andean zone in Venezuela

typology for conucos rich in agrobiodiversity, we set up a hierarchical ascending classification, with the conucos as the dependent variable. This classification allowed us to distinguish three groups or types of conuco in the Andean zone and a single type for the central zone based on the frequency and commonality of various species. The first type has an average of 30 species in common, with *Capsicum, Carica,* and *Citrus* predominating. The second type has an average of 16 species in common per conuco, with *Capsicum, Carica, Citrus,* and *Bixa orellana* being the most frequent. The third type occurs at higher elevations and also has an average of 16 species in common, but coffee is the most frequent species. The middle elevations contained the gardens with the most numbers of species. Finally, the fourth type of conuco, prevalent in the central zone, has an average of 31 species in common per garden; bananas and plantains, beans, coffee, and annona spp, were the species that occurred most frequently.

From an ecological and conservation perspective, the conucos at middle elevation in both the Andean and the central zone contained the greatest and possibly the most significant diversity. While all the conucos studied are found within the dry tropical forest ecosystem, the premontane zone, at elevations between 600 and 1,700 masl and average annual precipitation between 550 and 1,100 mm, contained 60 percent of the diversity-rich conucos, with an average of 70 species per garden. The number of species per garden declines as one moves to lower elevations, with an average of 52 species per conuco.

A home garden in the locality of La Chapa in the middle elevations of Venezuela

Slope and gradient were important features of the ecosystems containing conucos rich in diversity. In the Andean zone, the majority of the conucos were on hillsides or on small terraces on very steep slopes; only 7.4 percent were located at the base of hills or on level fields. In the central zone, all the conucos studied were situated on hillsides with fairly steep slopes.

Natural ecosystems composed of dense forests are found mainly at the highest elevations covered in this study, to wit 1,600–2,000 masl. Below this range, the environment consists mainly of secondary forests that are subject to considerable human impact and are marked by the presence of coffee farms. In this ecozone conucos are most numerous and contain the richest diversity. In the lowland ecologies, intensive cropping systems, grazing, and other human activities have created a savanna landscape with reduced floristic diversity and home gardens that are poorer in species. At higher elevations, however, conucos certainly provide the niches where traditional cultivars and species that are not found in the cropping systems of the savannas can survive and even flourish.

Socioeconomic Factors

Production from the conucos is largely for household consumption, but nearly all conuco farmers from the central zone and 41 percent of those from the Andean zone also sell some of their produce. Those home gardens that produce exclusively for home consumption tend to be smaller and to occupy less than one hectare. Conucos larger than one hectare provide households with significant income from the sale of home-garden produce.

The location of the conuco in relation to roads and transport is a factor in maintaining agrobiodiversity. In the areas under study, there are basically three types of access roads: unimproved dirt roads, improved dirt roads, and paved roads. Conucos reached by unimproved dirt roads contained 38–65 species per garden. Conucos reached by improved dirt roads contained 33–123 species per garden, while those accessible by paved roads contained 22–82 species per garden. This allows us to infer that moderate ease of access favors the maintenance of high diversity; where access is too difficult, the gardens benefit less from exchange and may have a more limited demand for diversity. In those conucos with access via paved roads, households also have easy access to markets, a fact that may reduce the need to maintain a large number of useful species in the conuco and also correlates with the increased proportion of home-garden produce that is sold. The diversity-rich conucos at middle elevations were also the oldest; some had been established up to 70 years ago. Households with several generations of members tending conucos had the most diversity, and their members were the most knowledgeable in the uses and adaptations that crops and crop varieties could make to the local environment. The age of the persons largely responsible for the management of the conucos was an important factor in the maintenance of diversity. The gardens with the richest diversity were managed by persons over 60 years of age.

House types can also be correlated with the amount of species diversity. One type of house is made of adobe with dirt floors and a zinc roof; the other is a cement house with a zinc roof. The gardens cultivated around the traditional adobe house had on average twice the number of species (59) than the gardens made around cement houses in the central zone. In the Andean zone, however, the type of house was not a significant variable.

The land-tenure situation in which households found themselves was quite different for each of the zones studied. In the Andean zone, most households making home gardens are smallholders having title to their land; in contrast, in the central zone, most household heads rent land. Although differences in tenure did not correlate with differences in the amount of diversity maintained within the respective conucos, the availability of household labor was a key factor affecting the maintenance of diversity within home gardens. Where there was abundant male and female adult and youth labor to manage the home garden, plant diversity was significantly higher.

Households obtain a wide range of incomes from their farms: from the sale of field and home-garden produce, from wages obtained as field laborers, from the sale of livestock, and from trade in elaborated products such as syrups, liquors, and medicinal plants. In addition, some household heads receive cash through remittances sent by family members who are not currently residing within the household. The proportion of cash income that households derive from their home gardens may range from nothing to nearly all. As expected, households that derived a significant portion but not all their income from the sale of home-garden products tended to have the highest diversity in their gardens. Households that derived a major portion of their income from wages paid to members working as day laborers or in permanent employment outside their farms had significantly less diversity in their conucos. Where a cash income was difficult to obtain from farm products because of lack of transport facilities or absence of markets, cash remittances from family members residing off farm allowed resident farmers to work freely and increase the diversity of plants in their home gardens. Households in which conuco farmers did not hire themselves out as day laborers had an average of 53 species per garden whereas households whose members derived a significant income as day laborers had an average of only 24 species per garden. The educational level of the household heads responsible for the conucos was not an important variable. Although 80 percent of the conuco managers were literate, their level of education did not correlate with successful management of diversity. In fact, the conuco with the greatest plant diversity was managed by an illiterate farmer who had a plentiful supply of household labor.

The most detailed measurements of diversity were conducted on those key species that typified the conuco systems of the two zones. Farmers recognized seven distinct types of chilli peppers (*Capsicum* spp.), representing a reservoir of diverse germplasm and knowledge about this species (Benavides and Montaño 1995; *Descriptores para Capsicum* (Capsicum *spp.)* 1995; Villalba 1999); five distinct types of papaya (*Descriptors for Papaya* 1988); and four types of avocado, a classification that was confirmed by agromorphological characterization (Avilán and Rodríguez 1997). Conuco farmers did note the loss of wild avocado types formerly growing alongside the more domesticated varieties. In general, the avocado varieties grown by farmers in their conucos were rustic and well adapted to environmental stresses. They also had organoleptic properties that were highly valued by local consumers. For these reasons they have persisted despite their low yields and lower ratio of flesh to seed. Beans, another key conuco species, were intercropped among the other plants present. The preference was for climbing beans, and the materials maintained were distinct from those being marketed commercially. These bean varieties are handed down from generation to generation and exchanged among households. Farmers indicated, however, that there is a shortage of seed for those bean varieties that are destined for planting in conucos because they have taste and cooking qualities that are highly valued by the household.

Conclusions

The economic changes that have occurred during the last half century have reduced the number of traditional Venezuelan farmers and have placed many pressures on their food cultures, agronomic practices, and economic opportunities. Because conucos make tangible contributions to agrobiodiversity and household food security, it is imperative that we understand their potential role in improving livelihoods in rural areas. Fortunately, Venezuela's national policymakers for biodiversity conservation and genetic resources are increasingly receptive to including conucos as part of an overall national genetic-resources conservation strategy. In the strategies envisaged, the crop-genetic diversity maintained by farmers in their conucos (in situ conservation) would complement ex situ conservation through the system of national genebanks.

The study reported here documents the high level of species diversity that exists within the conucos. An unavoidable and fundamental conclusion is that the conucos maintain distinctive plant-genetic resources with respect to other agricultural systems in the surrounding area. Comparisons of the crop varietal diversity of key species present in the conucos with the varieties being promoted commercially or by development programs show that conucos do maintain distinctive crop types. Furthermore, in several cases the varietal diversity of key conuco species was distinct from those held in ex situ collections of plant-genetic resources. In other cases, such as papaya, where the ex situ collections have been decimated by disease and periodic neglect, the conucos represent a source of germplasm having a wide range of morphological diversity in fruit type and plant architecture.

In order to include conucos as a component of in situ conservation efforts of agrobiodiversity that complement ex situ conservation programs, it is important to identify, as was done in this study, the essential characteristics of the conuco ecology and the salient socioeconomic features of the households that manage them. Conucos found at middle elevations (600–1,400 masl) had the greatest diversity of species, were the most stable over time, and contained more distinctive varieties of key species. Among the ecogeographic factors that correlated positively with the maintenance of diversity in conucos were the age and size of the conuco and the ease or difficulty of access to them. Moreover, the size of the household—particularly the availability of household labor—was crucial for the maintenance of agrobiodiversity. Larger households, where men, women, and children were available to participate in home gardening, had the highest and most significant crop and tree diversity. The necessity of engaging in labor migration for wages reduced the capacity of resident household members to maintain diversity in their conucos. However, the marketing of conuco products did not seem to affect negatively the management of diversity. This is important, as it clears the way to develop strategies that increase household income through the sale of the diversity-rich conuco products. Many of the cultivars grown in conucos differ from those available commercially, especially condiments and medicinal plants, and are appreciated for their superior qualities.

For the key species—namely, beans, avocados, peppers, and papaya—the significant degree of genetic diversity existing in home gardens was not readily available through genebanks or commercial seed sources. Households continue to exchange germplasm for key conuco species, within and in some cases across their ecozones, through barter, friendly exchanges, and local markets.

In Venezuela, the ability to exploit a varied topography and ecology for the deployment of diverse plant-genetic resources has been underestimated. The traditional system, such as the conuco, remains one of the few where the generation and use of plant-genetic diversity is constantly taking place. Cultural changes, such as rapid urbanization and the export/import orientation of the petroleum-based economy, have reduced the conuco planting areas in many major agricultural regions. Nonetheless, this study has attempted to identify the zones, the systems, and the factors that can be targeted to support the maintenance of the conuco as a component of Venezuelan agriculture. It has shown that conucos serve to maintain agrobiodiversity and unique crop germplasm and to provide a vital income to the households that manage them. We have taken a first step in identifying and adding value to the conuco system, arguing that it should be made an integral part of both a Venezuelan national genetic-resources conservation strategy and a development policy for households living in rural areas.

References

Avilán, L., and M. Rodríguez. 1997. Descripción y evaluación de la colección de Aguacates (*Persea* spp.) del Centro Nacional de Investigaciones Agropecuarias. Maracay, Fondo Nacional de Investigaciones Agropecuarias – IICA/CREA. PROCIANDINO/fruthex. (Serie a NPt. 12).

Badillo, V., L. Schnee, and C. Benitez de Rojas. 1985. *Clave de las familias superiores de Venezuela*. Caracas, Venezuela: Espasandes S.r.l. Editores.

Benavides, M., and N. Montaño. 1995. Evaluación agronómica de doce selecciones de ají (*Capsicum chinense* cq.). Venezuela, Agronomía y Agroecología 1 (Oral (1), p. XII. Congreso de Botánica, Ciudad Bolívar, 21–27 Marzo.

Ewel, J., and A. Madriz. 1968. *Zonas de vida de Venezuela. Memoria explicativa sobre el mapa ecológico.* Ministerio de Agricultura y Cría MAC. Venezuela.

Descriptors for Papaya. 1988. Rome, Italy: International Board for Plant Genetic Resources (IBPGR).

Descriptores para Capsicum (Capsicum spp.) 1995. Rome, Italy: International Plant Genetic Resources Institute (IPGRI); Taipei, Taiwán: Centro Asiático para el Desarollo y la Investigación relativos a los Vegetales (AVRDC); and Turrialba, Costa Rica: Centro Agronómico Tropical de Investigación y Enseñanza (CATIE).

Schnee, Ludwick. 1973. *Plantas Comunes de Venezuela.* Universidad Central de Venezuela, Facultad de Agronomía. Maracay, Venezuela: Ediciones de la Biblioteca.

Villalba, J. C. 1999. Cultivares de ají (*Capsicum* spp.) en conucos indígenas en los alrededores de Puerto Ayacucho, Estado Amazonas. *Memorias del Instituto de Biología Experimental* 2:57–60.

ten

Casamance, Senegal: Home Gardens in an Urban Setting

Olga F. Linares

Widespread agreement now exists that urban and peri-urban farming improves the quality of life for people living in the fast-growing and crowded cities of the developing world (United Nations Development Program 1996), and it does so in many important ways. City farming increases food security by providing a year-round supply of healthy and easily accessible food for the household. It can add significantly to the family budget by providing crops to be sold in the market. It opens up employment possibilities in contexts where jobs in industry, commerce, and government are few and far between. It offers pleasant gathering places for adults and children in their moments of leisure.

In addition to the direct benefits it brings to the resident population, urban farming has major indirect benefits to make. Among these are the improvement of the city's sanitary conditions through new waste-management alternatives and reducing pollution (Smith 1999). Farmers also enhance the ecology of the city and increase biodiversity by converting empty lots and other unused spaces into green orchards planted with fruit trees and other vegetation that attract beneficial birds and insects. Finally, grounds that are cultivated provide well-surveyed spaces where people can be safe from marauding gangs and antisocial individuals. Doubtless, then, urban farming greatly benefits city dwellers by offering many alternatives for obtaining a more secure livelihood.

Unfortunately, however, much more information exists on the economic and ecological benefits that urban agriculture provides than on the social mechanisms and management strategies that farmers actually employ to grow crops successfully. For this reason, I have focused in this chapter on how farmers acquire cultivable land in the city, how they plant their home gardens, what they plant in them, and what uses the gardens serve—all important components of urban agriculture. In circumstances where constraints on land, water, and labor are severe, as is especially the case in urban settings, farmers are called upon to exercise their considerable ingenuity and expertise to make ends meet, or perhaps even to make a profit (United Nations Development Program 1996: 211–31). For comparative purposes, it is also important to place home gardening in the context of other agricultural endeavors engaged in by city dwellers within the city limits and beyond. Often farming is only one of several possible activities that urban people are involved in, and so it also seems necessary to discuss other livelihood strategies open to them. Estimating correctly the time and effort required to grow crops at home in the face of other competing interests and alternative demands provides a more complete picture of the farmer as an economic agent wisely managing the land, labor, and other resources of the household.

Ziguinchor, a Town in Lower Casamance

The Lower Casamance region is located in the southwestern corner of Senegal wedged between the Gambia and Guinea-Bissau. In contrast to the northern sector of the country, the climate is tropical; its seven-month rainy season nourishes a luxuriant original vegetation composed of sub-Guinean species. The Jola, who number more than 350,000, form the bulk of the farming population (Linares 1992). Ziguinchor, the administrative center of the region, is a city of more than 125,000 inhabitants, 35 percent of whom are Jola. It is a fast-growing city, as thousands of new immigrants, in their majority Jola farmers coming from rural areas, migrate to its sprawling neighborhoods or *quartiers* in search of salaried jobs (Bruneau 1979). Old quarters, such as Santhiaba and Boucotte, have grown and expanded, and new ones, for example, Peryssac, Kandé, and Colobanne, have sprung up. Even so, the nonurbanized area is perhaps three times the size of the built-up area. Population densities range from 150 persons per hectare in the older quarters to 35–40 persons per hectare in the newer quarters. By a great majority, the people do not have legal title to the parcels of land where they have built their houses (Linares 1996). There are few industries in town: SONACOS (or Société Nationale de Commercialisation des Oléagineux du Sénégal), the groundnut-processing plant, is the largest employer, but there are also grouped enterprises (SODIZI) such as a lime factory, a center for vocational training, a printing press, and the like. Together with the administration, which has a few posts open every year, the aforementioned enterprises employ only a few hundred workers, many of them only seasonally. Hence unemployment is high, and many recent immigrants must turn to peri-urban farming to survive.

Getting Access to Land

Ziguinchor is surrounded by lowlands covered with rice fields, which the inhabitants cultivate under several forms of tenure arrangements (Hesseling 1986). Beyond these depressions lie the slightly raised plateaus where the dominant crops are millet and groundnuts, or peanuts. The original inhabitants of the town, the Bainouk, are in the business of renting land to more recent immigrants. They sometimes lend the land to someone under the proviso that at the end of the rains he must prepare the land so that the owner's wife can make an *etool*, or garden, during the dry season. There are many instances of exploitation, as when the Bainouk owner waits until the field is well prepared and then takes it back or when the owner of a field rents it to two different people. If a Jola who has rented a *biit*, or rice field, to grow rice during the rainy season wants to use the land as an etool, to grow sweet potatoes during the dry season, he must pay again. The going rate in 1994 was 5,000 CFA francs ($10.00) for a parcel measuring 20 m².

There are other ways to get access to cultivable land on the periphery of town besides renting from the Bainou. Land may be rented from other Jola, or it may be borrowed from friends and relatives. The examples provided later give a sense of the multiplicity of tenure arrangements that are possible.

It is often more difficult to find permanent empty spaces near a dwelling to make a home garden than to rent rice fields on the outskirts of town. Frequently, the lots where people construct their homes are small, and they have rarely been allotted by the administration, so they are untitled. The pattern of using common property or administrative land is opportunistic and requires much ingenuity.

Maize growing in a Ziguinchor home garden during the rainy season

Often, for example, the town authorities decide to build a large road through one of the townships, and so they bulldoze a 29m strip of land that, of course, remains unfinished. These would-be roads get dry and dusty during the dry season and fill with puddles of water, mud, and dangerous mosquitoes during the rainy season. Those who live next to the road grow millet and other grains and vegetables alongside the road, leaving a small bicycle path in the center. One often sees one side of the road being cultivated by one person, the other side by his neighbor living on the opposite side of the road. Another place where people make temporary home gardens is in lots under construction. The owner of the house being built adds a few bricks each year in order to show his relatives that he is constructing a home and has no cash available to lend them. The rest of the time the lot lies idle, and people grow their crops in the midst of the nascent structures. All these arrangements are temporary, of course, but they can last for a long time. Meanwhile, by planting crops alongside abandoned roads, in ditches, and around half-built houses, farmers improve the sanitation of the town.

Those more fortunate individuals who have backyards of sufficient size plant more permanent crops such as fruit trees. They still grow maize and millet in their home gardens during the rainy season and vegetables, both native and non-native varieties, during the dry season using well irrigation. The case studies given below provide a glimpse into the various kinds of home gardens that are grown.

A woman harvests maize from her Ziguinchor home garden

Home Gardens in Context

For several years now we have been conducting a study of urban agriculture among Jola immigrants from rural areas to the town of Ziguinchor (Linares 1996). The purpose of the research is to evaluate the role of farming in the context of the total economic life of migrants. The available sample consists of several hundred individual cases. Of these, about half make home gardens of one type or another ranging from small, simple plantings of maize or millet around the house to carefully managed gardens planted with staples for household consumption during the rainy season and with vegetables for sale during the dry season. Among the vegetables planted are hardy African species such as jaxatu in Wolof (*Solanum aethiopicum*, a kind of bitter eggplant used extensively for seasoning), bissap (*Hibiscus sabdariffa*, a sorrel whose leaves are consumed as a vegetable), okra (*Abelmoschus esculentus*, traditionally used in soups), native yam (*Discorea* spp.), and several species of peppers. Other vegetables are of New World or Asian origin: sweet potatoes, tomatoes, onions, groundnuts, cassava, eggplant, zucchini, and so forth. After foreigners, mainly Europeans, began to flock to the hotels of Ziguinchor and Cap Skirring, such products as carrots, lettuce, and many pulses were added to the list of crops grown. Other garden variants are orchards planted with fruit trees. If grown around the house, orchards will definitely be counted as home gardens. Some garden variants cannot be strictly classified as home gardens because they are not built within the boundaries of the household, but they will be addressed here because they are an important part of the farming strategy of Jola farmers. Among these are fruit tree orchards made on fields that are owned, rented, or borrowed in surrounding suburbs or nearby towns. These are often important sources of cash. Another recent common form of gardening consists of planting sweet potatoes, beans, cabbage, and the like on rice fields after these have been harvested. This is a very good use of the moisture that remains in the fields during the dry season.

Contrary to the usual assumption, the households of those who have migrated to cities often become larger rather than smaller. And this is because urban residents must take under their roof a number of boarders: for example, younger relatives and children of friends who are attending school or young men who are undergoing training in one of many standard occupations, such as carpentry, metalworking, baking, truck driving, and so on. Older relatives, too, who are ill and under medical care in one of the town hospitals come to stay, often for long periods of time. In the last decades, a war between Jola separatists and government forces has left hundreds homeless in the countryside. Abandoning their villages and fields, these refugees have come to Ziguinchor to live with relatives and friends.

Now it is one of the real virtues of urban farming that it provides all household members, including visitors, an opportunity to contribute their labor to fill the needs of the resident family. Thus, every able-bodied person is expected to work during their spare moments in one or more of the fields of the household head. They include school children after hours and during weekends, young apprentices when they are off work, and even the elderly who clean vegetables and take them to market, select seeds for future planting, and survey young children while their mothers are away working in the biit.

Home Gardens: Some Case Studies

The cases presented here do not pretend to represent a random sample of the population or their economic performance. On the contrary, they have been carefully chosen to illustrate the gamut of cultivation practices that come under the rubric of home gardens that urban migrant farmers in Ziguinchor engage in. To place the examples in proper sociological perspective and to convey the range of economic activities within which home gardens are embedded, I will provide background information on the farmer and his or her family. Bear in mind that individuals, as well as the agricultural activities they conduct, have histories—their diverse trajectories reflect the different sets of opportunities and limitations that farmers face each passing year. No two years are the same; not only are weather conditions different but also the social and economic order under which farmers must operate is always changing. Every year farmers must renegotiate usage of land, engage extra field hands, obtain new seed, and, if possible, buy fertilizer and pesticides.

Gardens Away from Home

The examples given below describe the efforts of Ziguinchor dwellers to cultivate gardens away from home. Although not strictly classifiable as home gardens, they are listed here because they provide a good contrast to the cultivation practices that take place in backyard contexts and adjacent empty lots.

Case 1: Ibou Koli was born in 1961 in the village of Diatang, 44 km north of Ziguinchor by road. He came to Ziguinchor in 1974 to be trained as a carpenter and stayed with matrilateral kin in Jisukpapaye, one of the quarters in town. He worked in his trade for some years without much success. Meanwhile, he went back every year to Diatang to cultivate the rice fields of his widowed mother, but after 1981 he stopped because of the drought. He then started cultivating a biit in Ziguinchor that he rented from an old Bainouk lady for the price of 3,500 CFA francs each season. He cultivates the biit during the rainy season with his wife and with help from women hired to transplant at the daily wage of 500 CFA each. The rice that is harvested feeds his family for three to five months. During the dry season (*contre saison*), Ibou and his wife convert the biit into a sweet potato patch associated with tomatoes, jaxatu, peppers, and onions. These crops are sold in the central market by his wife, who has a permanent stall there. The sale of these products, especially the sweet potatoes, is so profitable that it pays for the rent of the biit and for the labor. It provides enough income to feed a household of four young wards, three small children, and three adults. Ibou has stopped doing carpentry because his field garden is more profitable.

Case 2: Bakary Diedhiou (i.e., Jeju) was born in 1920 in the village of Suèl, 4 km to the northeast of Diatang. After a stay in Marsassoum, a community 50 km northeast of Ziguinchor, he came to Ziguinchor to learn carpentry. His wife, Aissatou Coly, also from Suèl, had for a long time worked with a Frenchman by the name of Henry, who was then director of the Chamber of Commerce of Ziguinchor. He had purchased a big parcel of land in one of the quarters of Ziguinchor, where Bakary and Aissatou also came to live. When Henry died, he left the property to the couple, who found themselves with a large terrain, half of which they converted into an etool, planted with fruit trees, millet, groundnuts, and other crops such as pineapples. The other half, which they cultivated as a biit during the rainy season was converted into a sweet potato garden (another kind of etool) during the off season. The sweet potato garden was so extensive that they had to hire extra labor.

Case 3: Gnima (Ñima) Coly is a widow. She was born in Diatang but lived for a number of years first in Marsassoum, then in Adéana, 40 km east of Ziguinchor, where her husband eventually died. Feeling alone, Gnima came to Ziguinchor to stay with an acquaintance from Adéana until she was able to move into her own home, which she built in the quarter of Leone on a lot given to her by her brother-in-law. She began cultivating in rented rice fields but stopped because the owners kept taking them back each time she had a good harvest. Now she cultivates in borrowed fields in Djifangor, a scant 4 km from where she lives, with the help of hired hands. In 1994 she paid 18,000 CFA to have fields transplanted and 4,000 CFA to have them harvested. Her family consumes 210 kg of rice every month, so the rice harvested from these fields only lasts three months. But every year, during the off season, Gnima also makes a vegetable garden in one of the biit. She grows sorrel, jaxatu, gombo, bissap, lettuce, tomatoes, and cabbage, which her daughter sells in the market. With the proceeds from the sale of vegetables, the modest amount of rice she grows, and the occasional cash that her daughter's son, an electrician, gives her, Gnima can feed her large family. The household consists of Gnima, a grandson in school, her daughter and her son, as well as six teenagers in school, and three others at home.

To summarize, two male household heads came to Ziguinchor to work in a skilled occupation but they no longer do so. All three migrants cultivate rice fields during the rainy season and make vegetable and sweet potato gardens in the same fields during the dry season using the residual moisture. The etool are usually managed by the wives, who also sell the produce. Because the rice fields they own, rent, or borrow are some distance from their own homes, the etool they make do not strictly qualify as home gardens, but they are an important garden variant that is becoming more popular every year.

Home Gardens in Town

Home gardens may range from desultory plantings around the house to carefully managed parcels planted with diverse crops for home consumption and sale. The case studies given below illustrate the diverse histories of Jola immigrants to Ziguinchor who went about getting access to cultivable land and how their home gardens fit in with the other agricultural practices engaged in by the household members. It also provides some information on the food needs of the household and the role that farming plays in the family budget.

Case 1: Alassane Badji came to Ziguinchor in 1960 as a clerk for a Frenchman in an import-export business that has since closed. In Ziguinchor, Alassanne married Anna and they raised a family. For the last four years, he and his wife have grown sweet potatoes during the dry season in a biit lent to them by a woman friend of Anna, who in turn rents it from a Bainouk to cultivate rice during the rainy season. During the dry season they also make an etool alongside the adjacent road, in land destined to enlarge the road. The couple cultivates one side of the strip, and their neighbors the other side. They grow millet for home use and string beans, cabbage, jaxatu, bissap, and other vegetables for sale in the market. After these crops are harvested, the land is cleared of all vegetation. In his backyard, Alassane has made a sweet potato nursery, which he has fenced to protect it from animals. With the proceeds from the sale of the sweet potatoes and the vegetables, Alassane and Anna can feed a family consisting of them both, an adult daughter with her child, two more adults and a child in school, or a total of five adults and two children. They all work in the home garden

Case 2: Fatou Bodjan was born in Suèl. She came to Ziguinchor with her husband, a policeman, who is now stationed in faraway Tivaouane. She cultivates a biit in Mandina, a village about 5 km outside of town, which requires a three-hour walk to reach. She rents the biit for 5,000 CFA, and with the rest of the money her husband sends her, she also hires a tractor for 3,500 CFA to prepare the land. In addition Fatou cultivates a garden in Djibelor, which her husband bought five years ago from a Bainouk. In it Fatou grows mangoes, lemons, and cashews, all for sale; she also plants some groundnuts and squash. At home in Ziguinchor, Fatou has made a home garden that she planted with fruit trees, namely, bananas, mangoes, palm trees, and papaya. The family sits in the shade of the garden during the heat of the day. A portion of the etool is planted with millet every rainy season. With the cash her husband sends her and what she earns from produce sales, plus the millet she harvests, Fatou maintains a family of two sons, a brother's wife, three sons of her husband's brother, and one son of her own brother. She is fortunate that her sister-in-law and all the boys help her with agricultural work.

Case 3: Lamine Diedhou (Jeju), who is about 61 years old, came to Ziguinchor as a young man. He worked as a pharmacist most of his life, retiring only last year. For many years, Lamine has cultivated two rented biit in Mpak, about 18 km by road straight south of the city. These rice fields are prepared by a tractor from PIDAC (Projet Intérimaire de Developpement de la Casamance), a government service, but he and the men he hires must furrow and ridge the field with the *kajandu*, the special fulcrum shovel used by the Jola to prepare the land. In a bad year he harvests only 280 bundles of rice, the equivalent of 490 kg of milled rice, enough for four or five months, but in a good year he can harvest twice that much. Nonetheless, Lamine is not quite self-sufficient in rice. The family consumes 6 kg of rice at lunch and dinner, and so after his own stores are finished, Lamine must buy 150–200 kg of rice every month. Mariama, one of his wives, also cultivates an etool that she plants with diverse vegetables including eggplant, jaxatu, onions, cabbage, tomatoes, and lettuce. With the money she earns selling vegetables she buys cooking utensils and clothes for her and the children. Lamine and Mariama's household is very large because they have several relatives living with them. Household members include Lamine and his two wives, a married son, his wife and children, plus eleven teenagers, all in school. They all contribute labor to the home-garden enterprise.

Case 4: Sunfietu Djallo, an elderly woman born in St. Louis, one of Senegal's important cities located north of Dakar, was married to a Jola from Kagnarou, a village 40 km north of Ziguinchor. He came to Ziguinchor long ago to work as the governor's driver; he died in 1989. She does not cultivate a biit, but she does plant a very large etool on land they bought in Kandialang, about 4 km from town. In the back of her house she has also made a home garden that she plants with squash, groundnuts, and millet during the rainy season. The house is also surrounded with fruit tress, mainly lemons, mangoes, and guavas. Two large guavas sell for 25 CFA and one big mango for 100 CFA. In her home garden Sunfietu raises small plants that she takes to the Kandialang etool. With what they make from both gardens she and her divorced daughter can pay for help with the etool and also buy the 50 kg of rice they consume monthly.

Case 5: Lamine Djiba was born in 1947 in Talloum and came to Ziguinchor in 1969 as an employee of the French commercial enterprise Peiryssac. He bought some land in the quarter Jisukpapaye. After Peyrissac went bankrupt, Lamine worked in another enterprise, Morel and Prom, from 1973 to 1979, and then in the groundnut-processing plant as an official crop weigher. At the end of the groundnut season he works as a guard at the local agricultural station. From his arrival in Ziguinchor, Lamine has cultivated a garden every year. He cultivated millet in Birkamanao and rice in a biit in Bouyouyou, about 10 km south of the city, which he rented for 15,000 CFA from a Jola Bayotte. To help one of his wives transplant, Lamine paid a society of women the sum of 3,500 CFA. Lamine cultivates millet all around his house. With his other wife, they also make a home garden which she plants with sweet potatoes, manioc, lettuce, tomatoes, and taro. He also makes a home nursery for young mango trees, which he sends to his young brother in his native village of Talloum so that he can make an orchard. With what he earns from his jobs and what he gets from his etool, Lamine is able to provide for his family, which consists of him and his two wives, two young male relatives and five teenagers in school.

These few examples demonstrate that even though they are not the household's only agricultural pursuit, home gardens make an important contribution to community life and family welfare. Individuals like Alassane who cultivate vegetables along abandoned roads prevent stagnant water from collecting and mosquitoes from breeding in puddles. Alassane, Fatou, Lamine Diedhou's wife, Sunfietu, and others add trees and bushes to otherwise empty land, thus attracting birds and fruit-eating bats and creating shady spots for family and friends to spend their hours of leisure in complete safety. Home gardens engage the labor of otherwise unoccupied lodgers and visiting family members. Most important, home-garden products contribute healthy food for the family, including fruits, vegetables, sweet potatoes, and millet. Whatever surplus is produced is sold in the market, usually by the wife. Although some home gardeners, such as Fatou and Lamine Djiba, receive some form of income, the money they earn from home-garden produce sales is a welcome addition to their modest budgets.

Management Practices

A typical example will convey some idea about how home gardens are actually managed and by whom. It is important to keep in mind that in Jola culture agriculture is a shared pursuit. Despite the fact that the gender division of labor varies regionally, both men and women everywhere engage in agriculture. The same is true for home-garden cultivation.

Kasi Koli was born in 1959 in Katinong, a village more than 56 km to the northwest of Ziguinchor. He migrated in 1978 to learn to be a baker. For a while he worked in a bakery but left it to become a laborer with the groundnut oil refinery, working on a six-month contract. During the rainy season Kasi cultivates a biit in association with Karafa, an elderly widow with matrilateral ties in Katinong who lives next door. Kasi prepares the fields that Karafa rents or borrows, and the society of women from Katinong transplants in them. The first biit is not far from where they live in Ziguinchor. Karafa rents this land from a *métisse* for 5,000 CFA. The second biit is in an old quarter of Ziguinchor called Gourot; Karafa borrows these fields from an old friend of her husband. Hence Karafa, with Kasi's help, cultivates rice in real intraurban spaces. They also tend another biit farther away, in a quarter called Leone.

Together with his wife Howa, Kasi also cultivates a home garden behind his house on a sizeable parcel of land destined to enlarge the road. The garden is fenced against animals. They plant maize and sweet potatoes during the rainy season, strictly for home use. These crops are not fertilized. Once they are harvested at the beginning of the dry season, Kasi turns over the soil with the kajandu and spreads 20 kg of fertilizer on the etool. This consists of small pellets made from what is left after the oil is extracted from the groundnuts, to which ammonia and other products are added. The pellets are sold at 60–80 CFA per kilogram. Howa then plants the garden with a variety of vegetables: kunega, or gumbo, cabbage, eggplant, lettuce, and tomatoes. The nonnative vegetables are grown from seed packets imported from Europe. All throughout the dry season the plants are watered by Kasi and Howa in the morning and afternoon with water they draw from a well that is right in the midst of the garden. In 1992 the etool was a big success. Howa made 35,000 CFA by selling the vegetables in the market. In 1993, however, the etool failed because Howa had to go back to Katinong to help Kasi's sick mother harvest her rice. Three times while she was away, chickens ate the seeds that Kasi planted. When Howa returned, they made a nursery of tomatoes and cabbage in a large pan and then transplanted the seedlings. But it was already January and the sun was too strong; it dried the soil and no amount of watering helped. In the years that followed Kasi and Howa went on cultivating their etool, usually with considerable success. When I last visited them in February 2000, they had not prepared their etool because the fencing made from woven dried palm fronds (called *karinten*) that they needed to protect their plants from their neigh-

Kasi showing the extent of his fenced home garden, which lies in back of a dirt road in Ziguinchor, Casamance

bor's sheep, goats, and chickens had increased in price. But they were saving their money to buy more fencing the following year and again plant a flourishing etool that feeds both of them and their four children and still produces enough vegetables for sale at a significant profit.

To summarize, Kasi, the household head, does a great deal of farming in addition to holding a part-time job as a laborer. He cultivates rice in outfields and makes a home garden in an adjacent parcel. As with most families, both genders work in the garden, planting basic grains for family consumption during the rainy season and nonnative vegetables for marketing in the off season. It is important to point out, however, that the couple is unable to make a garden every year because they lack the means to buy fencing or are short of labor. Thus, contrary to general assumptions, urban home gardens are not always stable or even successful. A multitude of factors, including incursion by animals, lack of irrigation water, insecurity of tenure, and even theft, can greatly affect home-garden productivity.

Conclusions

These case studies argue for the need to regard home gardening in urban contexts as an important livelihood option for migrant families coming into town from the

Kasi and Howa irrigating their dry-season vegetables with water from a well

surrounding countryside. Home gardens serve a social function, bridging the gap
between rural contexts and urban life, facilitating the movement of people back
and forth between these poles. Contrary to common opinion, people who migrate to the city do not stop farming altogether. More often than not, they establish orchards and home gardens because salaried jobs are hard to come by and
almost never pay well enough for household heads to feed and clothe their de-
pendents, pay school fees and taxes, or meet the many other expenses incurred by
an extended family. The extra cash that wives make selling home-garden produce
in the market goes a long way toward meeting these obligations. And, in addition,
some women earn extra money by selling palmwine, making soap, or transport-
ing fish.

In their home gardens members of the household cultivate indigenous African
vegetables whose nutritional value compares favorably and even exceeds nonnative vegetables such as eggplant and tomato (Seck 1997:47). Some species are
highly polymorphic; jaxatu, for example, has at least four subspecies or groups.
Similarly, gombo has at least seven recognized species, and bissap also has a number of varieties not yet fully described. Although we do not know how many landraces of these indigenous vegetables actually grow in Jola home gardens, farmers
insist that they are always looking for new and better varieties. Given the Jola custom of continually trading seeds and seedlings to improve their stock, it is very

likely that they grow several species of traditional African vegetables. Certainly, with respect to nonnative vegetables, the Jola are always buying packets of imported tomato seeds, for example, or acquiring new cabbage plantings from a neighbor.

The parcels of land that immigrants cultivate as *biit*, or forest plot, are either borrowed or rented. Few immigrants own this type of land in the peri-urban zone. Individuals who are willing to lend land are usually relatives or close friends of the users. How far into the future Jola will be able to continue using, renting, borrowing, or buying land remains to be seen. Ziguinchor is a fast-growing town, and much of the land in the peri-urban zone is being developed for individual housing or for municipal projects.

Because few Jola have security of tenure for the land they cultivate and because their household crops are subject to many vicissitudes, home gardens are not always the stable, dependable systems that are described for rural areas. But, for the moment at least, it makes good sense for rural Jola migrants to continue what they do best—farm where they can, in intraurban spaces or at some distance from home. Doing so allows them to survive in the city while educating their children and improving their future livelihood options.

References

Bruneau, J.-C. 1979. *Ziguinchor en Casamance: la croissance urbaine dans les pays tropicaux*. Travaux et documents de géographie tropicale 36. Bordeaux: Centre d'études de géographie tropicale.

Hesseling, G. 1986. Le droit foncier dans une situation semi-urbaine: le cas de Ziguinchor. In B. Crousse, E. Le Bris, and E. Le Roy, eds., *Espaces disputés en Afrique Noire: pratiques foncières locales*, pp. 113–32. Paris: Karthala.

Linares, O. F. 1992. *Power, Prayer and Production: The Jola of Casamance, Senegal*. Cambridge: Cambridge University Press.

Linares, O. F. 1996. Cultivating biological and cultural diversity: Urban farming in Casamance, Senegal. *Africa* 66(1): 104–21.

Seck, A. 1997. Conservation and utilization of germplasm of traditional African vegetables in Senegal. In L. Guarino, ed., *Traditional African Vegetables*, pp. 46–51. Rome: International Plant Genetic Resource Institute.

Smith, O. B., ed. 1999. *Agriculture Urbaine en Afrique de l'Ouest*. Ottawa, Canada: Centre de recherches pour le développement international, and Wageningen, The Netherlands: Centre technique de coopération agricole et rurale.

United Nations Development Program. 1996. *Urban Agriculture: Food, Jobs, and Sustainable Cities*. Publication Series for Habitat II, Vol. 1. New York: United Nations Development Program.

Part 3

Managing and Conserving Genetic Diversity in Key Crops

eleven

A Case Study of Key Species in Southern Vietnam

Farmer Classification and Management of Agrobiodiversity in Home Gardens

Monika Gessler and Urs Hodel

Plants that are used for medicine, food, and agroforestry are found in Vietnamese home gardens distributed across the varied ecosystems in the country (Gessler, Hodel, and Eyzaguirre 1998). In order to assess their potential contribution to agrobiodiversity it is important to determine if the cultivars found within home gardens represent a distinctive assemblage of plants and the portion of the total genetic diversity for a species they represent. It is equally important to understand how people manage these genetic resources in ways that ensure their maintenance and availability over time. Comparative, multidisciplinary research across ecologies and cultures combined with the analysis of economic and institutional factors can shed light on trends and dynamic processes in the management and maintenance of plant diversity.

In this chapter we review data from a sample of 100 home gardens that were surveyed during intensive field studies carried out in 1996 and 1997 in the Mekong Delta, the lowlands, midlands, and highlands of the southern provinces of Lam Dong, Dong Nai, Binh Duong, Long An, and Cantho in Vietnam (see map,

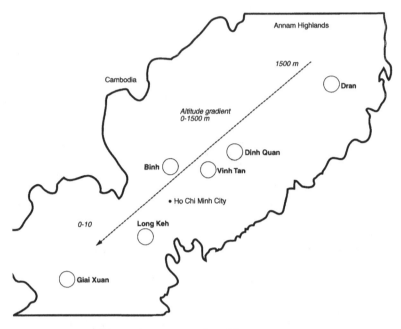

Figure 11.1. Map of the study sites in southern Vietnam

Fig. 11.1). The home gardens were managed by households from several ethnic groups, among them the dominant Kinh group and the Nùng, Chil, Châu Ma, and Khmer ethnic minorities (see Gessler et al. 1997). We considered many key factors, including ecological variation and the socioeconomic status, cultural identity, and traditions of the farmers involved. The results suggest some important elements relating to the management practices and plant uses that are associated with the high levels of species and varietal diversity.

Local Classification Systems and the Perception and Management of Diversity

In home-garden production household members determine the kinds of plants and varieties to be used, the best planting time for them, the proper sites, and the labor necessary for their care. Farmers' decisions are not linear; rather, farmers consider many factors simultaneously and make decisions intuitively. Both on-farm and off-farm factors determine farmers' selection of crops and varieties. On-farm factors include skills, available land, land tenure, available planting material, capital, credit, family labor, and biophysical characteristics such as climate, soil, landscape, and irrigation possibilities. Off-farm factors that might influence the decision of what to plant are market access, including the role of middlemen, and the presence of local or regional industries. Other off-farm factors are policies, traditional customs, and support services, such as transport, cooperatives, and agricultural extension services.

The folk taxonomy and selection criteria that farmers use when planting and managing species and crop varieties constitute important ethnobotanical indicators of plant-genetic diversity. This kind of information about local cultivars can be revealing; it, therefore, is increasingly being included in the passport data on plant-genetic resources held in genebanks (Eyzaguirre 1995). Moreover, the study of local knowledge and classification systems provides insight into the traits and characteristics of crop varieties that farmers consider important (Van Dorp et al. 1993). According to Boster (1984) and Brush, Carney, and Huaman (1981), a farmer's evaluation of the different varieties, as well as decisions about which to grow and which to exchange with others, is conducted with reference to generic names used in the local classification system. The perceptions encoded in the folk taxonomy are most often based on the morphological or organoleptic characteristics of the varieties in question (e.g., color, relative size, shape, taste, or smell). Evaluation is also based on cultural associations with certain objects or a place of real or presumed origin or on how a variety was introduced (Boster 1984; Berlin 1992; Martin 1995).

Often, when crops have a high cultural value and are used for many different purposes, they have a high diversity of variety names (Boster 1984; Schneider, Widyastuti, and Djazuli 1993). Having many names for local varieties is indeed a significant indicator of genetic diversity in a crop (Eyzaguirre 2000). Folk taxonomic richness may be a way of differentiating plants in terms of their distinct properties, ecological adaptations, or ritual functions (Heider 1969). Different names often result from the varying perceptions that farmers of different cultures, or even of a different gender, hold when classifying the same varieties. Thus, women and men may look at different aspects of a variety and thus give them different specific names. With reference to a taro variety that has numerous, big leaves and yellow corms and cormels, for example, men who are more concerned with the leaves might give it a name that relates to this feature, whereas women who are more interested in the color of the tubers will choose another name accordingly. The household's or individual's perception of plant and variety diversity does not necessarily coincide with genetic diversity. Nonetheless, such perceptions are important in order to understand how diversity is maintained and managed in home gardens.

The perception of diversity within key species was restricted to crops grown in home gardens or fields. Farmers rarely provided information about varieties observed in uncultivated land or forest, except for taro, sweet potato, wild eggplant, and jackfruit. Varieties occurring in uncultivated land were only mentioned if they were grown in the home gardens or fields as well. The large number of different names, and the inconsistencies underlying individual descriptions for varieties, do not allow us to give a definite number of morphologically distinct varieties. Nonetheless, they indicate a strong interest among farmers in the distinctive properties and the range of variation within their crops. (A complete catalog of species cultivated and maintained in home gardens is available in Gessler et al. 1997, Annex II.)

The key home-garden species considered were identified based on their frequency, distribution, and the way they are reflected in the multilayered structure of the home gardens, comprising fruit trees, bushes, herbs, and roots and tubers. The ethnobotanical analysis considered four types of information: (a) the local phenotypic and genotypic variation of the crop, (b) the local perception of diversity, (c) the indigenous knowledge related to the varieties, and (d) the social aspects of garden management and variety selection.

Managing Diversity within Key Home-Garden Species

In general, farmers from the sites we surveyed recognized more varieties than they actually planted in their gardens. For this reason, ethnobotanical information includes the total folk-taxonomic knowledge of a farmer and is not restricted to those varieties that he or she plants. Although it was not always possible to corroborate with direct field observations and descriptors the information obtained from the farmers, an ethnobotanical approach allowed us to obtain a wider impression of the diversity in the various agroecologies than would have been possible if we had included only material from the home gardens. By including the wider ecosystem, we could gain a better understanding of how farmers perceived their environment, including neighboring gardens, the uncultivated land, and natural areas such as forests. In the section that follows, we will discuss the history, classification, and use of some key species in Vietnam. These are by no means all the key species used but only an illustrative sample of the classification system and the distribution and uses to which these crops are put. Table 11.1 shows the average number of varieties grown in the home garden for each key species and the average number of varieties that are known by the farmers.

1. *Sweet potato* (Ipomoea batatas)

Sweet potato was introduced into Vietnam some centuries ago and now ranks among the most important root crop in terms of cultivated area, especially in the

Table 11.1

Grown (G) and known (K) number of varieties for selected key species

Site	Kaki		Longan		Jackfruit		Sweet potato		Cassava		Taro		Eggplant		Bitter gourd		Chayote	
	G	K	G	K	G	K	G	K	G	K	G	K	G	K	G	K	G	K
Dran	3.1	4.9	1.0	1.0	2.1	2.5	2.0	2.9	1.9	2.4	2.5	3.8	2.4	5.4	1.3	2.3	1.2	1.9
Dinh Quan			1.0	1.0	1.9	2.6	1.8	2.1	1.3	1.5	2.2	2.8	1.7	2.0	1.7	2.0		
Vinh Tan			1.3	2.7	2.1	2.5	1.9	2.3	1.6	3.1	3.0	3.5	1.9	3.1				
Binh Chuan			1.4	1.9	1.6	2.3	1.7	2.6	1.3	2.6	1.4	2.6	1.3	2.3	1.0	1.3		
Giai Xuan			1.1	1.9	1.4	3.6	1.6	3.6	1.6	2.5	3.1	4.1	1.1	2.0	1.0	1.5		
Long Khe			1.0	1.3	1.0	1.2	1.0	1.3	1.3	1.7	2.5	4.1	1.3	2.9	1.2	1.8		
Average	0.5	0.8	1.1	1.6	1.7	2.5	1.7	2.5	1.5	2.3	2.4	3.5	1.6	2.9	1.0	1.5	0.2	0.3

Table 11.2

The distribution of sweet potato (*Ipomea batatas*) over the individual sites compared with water spinach (*Ipomea aquatica*) and *Ipomoea mauritiana*

Site	Number of households	*Ipomoea batatas* Percent of households	Total area (m²)	*Ipomoea aquatica* Percent of households	Total area (m²)	*Ipomoea mauritiana* Percent of households	Total area (m²)
Dran	14	75	526	–	–	–	–
Dinh Quan	20	90	536	60	94	–	–
Vinh Tan	11	75	185	42	138	–	–
Binh Chuan	18	56	355	44	264	6	10
Long Khe	17	24	24	71	130	5	1
Giai Xuan	20	60	162	90	474	–	–
Average		63	1,788	53	1,100		

north of the country (Ho and collaborators 1994). It was found in all the home-garden sites surveyed (Table 11.2). The roots of sweet potato are not widely used as human food in South Vietnam, as they are in other Southeast Asian countries. In many parts of the south, sweet potato is mainly grown as pig fodder. It is considered a low-status, poor people's food plant. Thus, the number of varieties now found in individual gardens is not as great as the number reported by Schneider, Widyastuti, and Djazuli (1993) from Irian Jaya, where sweet potato is highly valued as food by the local inhabitants.

Some sweet potato varieties are becoming rare. A few older varieties can now be found only in particular home gardens, never in crop fields. Owing to the decreasing importance of sweet potato as human food, it is likely that varieties lacking the hardiness, high biomass, and starch characteristics that make it good fodder for pigs will disappear. The Hung Loc Agricultural Research Center in Dong Nai Province keeps a collection of almost 9,000 different accessions of sweet potato, although only 116 are indigenous accessions from the south. Like other tuber or root plants, sweet potato occurs less frequently in the Mekong Delta (see Table 11.2).

The local classification of sweet potato varieties is complex. *Khoai lang* is the Vietnamese folk-generic term for sweet potato (*Ipomoea batatas*). To describe different varieties within the species, suffixes are added after *khoai lang*. Most often they are morphological descriptions of certain features, for example, khoai lang vo ðo ruôt tràng, sweet potato tuber skin red, tuber flesh white. From the 153 collected records, fifty-two different names for sweet potato varieties emerged:

morphological characteristics	67%
folk genera, such as *Cucurbita maxima* or *Ipomoea aquatica*	12%
place of origin	6%
long history of the variety	6%
qualities possessed by certain items, such as duck foot–shaped leaves or honey-sweet tuber flesh	4%
name of the person who introduced the variety	2%
culinary characteristics, such as starchy tubers	2%
maturation time until harvest	1%

Analogies with other species often replace abstract adjectives such as color. *Khoai lang bi* refers to the deep orange color of the pumpkin (*Cucurbita maxima*), which the root flesh of this sweet potato variety resembles. Names of origin refer mainly to the place where the variety was first observed, for example, khoai lang ðà lat. However, a name can also indicate the kind of habitat the variety originally came from, for example, khoai lang cu lân nui, meaning mountain sweet potato. Several different names may be used to describe the same variety.

The highest number of names for sweet potato varieties (21) was found in Vinh Tan, the lowest in Long Khe (2). In the initial phase of the survey, female and male farmers of a household were interviewed separately. The outcome was very interesting. In one household, both members indicated two different varieties in the garden but gave them different names (Table 11.3). The names given by the woman related to the color of root skin and flesh, whereas the names given by the man related to the shape of the leaves. This practice, which is repeated with other crops and other sites, shows that names reflect the personal use or the experience that each gender has with a certain part of the plant. In the household mentioned, the woman was responsible for planting and harvesting sweet potato roots; thus, she knows the exact color of the starchy roots. The man, who was not involved in the management of this plant, knows only its external appearance, such as the shape of the leaves.

Knowledge about sweet potato varieties and their uses differs greatly within a community. Different farmers often described identical varieties in different or even conflicting ways. Conflicting information was found to exist not only across different households but also within the same household; individuals seem to per-

Table 11.3

Diversity of sweet potato variety names in the same household

	Local variety name	English translation	Gender
Variety 1	Khoai lang vo đo, ruôt tràng	sweet potato, skin red, flesh white	F
	Khoai lang lá tron	sweet potato, leaves round	M
Variety 2	Khoai lang vo tràng, ruôt tràng	sweet potato, skin white, flesh white	F
	Khoai lang lá khia	sweet potato, leaves like duck feet	M

ceive differently the visible characteristics for identifying identical varieties. Color did not appear to be important in some contexts; thus the green of the vines might be described as being white or yellow. When farmers describe different varieties of sweet potato, they often use morphological characteristics for tubers, leaves, and vines (Table 11.4). Tubers were mentioned in 139 of the 153 records, leaves in 93 records, and vines in 47 of the total records. The color of the tuber skin was used to describe varieties slightly more often than the color of the tuber flesh. The color of the tuber was more important than its shape. Among the morphological characteristics of the leaf, its shape was more often mentioned than its

Table 11.4

Frequency for the most important morphological characteristics cited for sweet potatoes

	R	1Rf	1Rs	3R	L	1L	3L	H	1H	3H
R	139									
1Rf	–	90								
1Rs	–	68	98							
3R	–	14	13	24						
L	79	65	52	16	93					
1L	42	31	25	6	–	51				
3L	52	48	40	8	–	22	61			
H	41	28	27	10	35	21	25	47		
1H	30	20	22	8	26	15	18	–	34	
3H	2	2	1	0	1	0	0	–	–	11

Note: R = tuber; 1Rs = color of tuber skin; 1Rf = color of tuber flesh; 3R = shape of tuber; L = leaf; 1L = color of leaf; 3L = shape of leaf; H = vine; 1H = color of vine; 3H = shape of vine.

Table 11.5

Most common criteria and combinations of different criteria among
153 records of sweet potatoes

Most frequent criteria	Number of records	Frequency (%)
1Rs	21	14
1Rs, 1Rf, 3L	17	11
1Rs, 1Rf	11	7
1Rs, 1Rf, 1L	7	5
1Rs, 1Rf, 1L, 3L, 1H	7	5
Others	86	58

Note: 1Rs = color of tuber skin; 1Rf = color of tuber flesh; 1L = color of leaf; 3L = shape of leaf;
1H = color of vine.

color. The vine was only occasionally used to distinguish varieties, and its color was considered to be more important than its shape. In short, the criterion most often and most exclusively used to distinguish the different varieties (see Table 11.5) was the color of the tuber skin, followed by the combination of color of tuber skin and flesh, together with the shape of the leaves, and finally the combination of color of tuber skin and flesh alone.

Sweet potato leaves are widely consumed boiled or steamed as a leafy green vegetable. While the leaves are a nutritious component of the human diet, they are also an important source of fodder. The roots are nowadays mostly used to feed livestock. Sweet potatoes are often planted close to the pig stalls. Two traditional varieties, khoai lang tàu bí and khoai lang ông cô, are both grown exclusively in Binh Chuan; they have been ignored by most other farmers. Khoai lang ông cô does not have very big roots and is reported to be starchy and less sweet. *Khoai lang tau bi* was described as having an aromatic and sweet flesh.

2. *Longan* (Dimocarpus longan)

Longan trees were found in home gardens of all the sites surveyed; they are highly valued, and farmers like to have at least one longan tree in their gardens. In some parts of the Mekong Delta farmers grow high-quality longan in large stands within their orchards. Variety selection depends on the quality of the soil and the availability of seedlings. Seedlings of high-quality, commercially preferred varieties are expensive and difficult to get and have pronounced water and soil fertility requirements.

Longan fruit trees are most popular in Binh Chuan, where they are grown in

Table 11.6

Distribution of *Dimocarpus longan*

Location	Average number and range of different varieties per garden	Average number of trees per garden	Total of different varieties per site	Frequency of occurrence per site (%)
All sites	1.0 (0–3)	3.5	6	45.6
Dran	0.5 (0–2)	0.3	1	25.0
Dinh Quan	0.5 (0–2)	0.3	4	25.0
VinhThan	0.8 (0–3)	13.5	3	33.3
Binh Chuan	1.8 (0–3)	4.6	3	83.3
Long Khe	0.9 (0–2)	1.5	3	47.1
Giai Xuan	1.2 (0–3)	4.6	4	55.0

83 percent of the home gardens (Table 11.6). The largest parcels planted with longan are found in Vinh Tan; some contained up to a hundred trees. In the surveyed home gardens longan was planted mainly for home consumption. Only a few households in Binh Chuan and Giai Xuan had enough surplus after the harvest to sell in the market. Longan trees in full production are seldom more than twenty years old.

Experts from the Long Dinh Fruit Research Center classify the different longan varieties grown in southern Vietnam into three groups comprising *Dimocarpus longan, D. longan malesianus,* and *D. longan obtusus.* The folk term for all longan varieties is nhán. During our survey we found eleven different varietal names for nhán; nine of these varieties can be classified under one of the three aforementioned groups. Most names, such as black pepper seed or dragon eye seed, make analogies based on the morphological characteristics of the seed. Names may also refer to the place of origin.

All varieties included within the nhán long group (*Dimocarpus longan [Lour]*) can be recognized by the broken skin of their seeds. The white split on the big, black, round seed is said to look like the split pupil in a dragon's eye. The fruits are big with a yellow to light yellow skin. The fruit flesh is watery and sweet. Varieties of this group were mentioned in both sites of the Mekong Delta, in Binh Chuan, and in Vinh Tan.

Varieties within the nhán tiêu da bó group (*Dimocarpus longan malesianus*) were described as having small fruits with small black seeds, hence the name black pepper seeds. The fruit skin was described as dark yellow or brown, like the skin of cows, and the leaves were said to be thin and long. Varieties of this group were found in all of the sites except in the highlands. Nhán ðia phuong (*D. longan*

Table 11.7

Most common criteria used by farmers to distinguish
longan varieties

Criteria	Number of records	Frequency (%)
1Fs	7	8
3L	5	6
2F	4	5
2S, 2F	4	5
2S, 1Fs, 3L	4	5
2S, 2F, 2L	4	5
2F, 3L	4	5
Others	52	61
Total	84	

Note: 1Fs = color of fruit skin; 2F = size of fruit; 2S = size of seed; 2L = size of leaf;
3L = shape of leaves.

obtusus) varieties were found in Binh Chuan and in the two Mekong Delta sites. These varieties are local; they grow in places with sandy soil, where high-quality varieties of the nhán tiêu da bó group do not grow well. The leaves of these varieties can be easily distinguished from others by the curled nature of the leaf margin and the smooth hairs beneath. The fruits are small to medium sized, with a yellow or dark yellow fruit skin.

Farmers distinguish longan varieties based on the following criteria in decreasing order of importance: size of seeds (36 scores), size of fruits (26 scores), color of the fruit skin (23 scores), shape of the leaves (23 scores), size of the leaves (21 scores), and thickness of the fruit flesh (15 scores). The list of the most common single criterion and combinations of different criteria is given in Table 11.7.

3. Eggplant (Solanum sp.)

In Vietnam, the term eggplant is used for *Solanum melongena,* but it includes other species such as *Solanum undatum* and *Solanum procumbens.* Eggplant species were found in all of the surveyed sites (Table 11.8). The highest diversity was found in Dran, where ethnic minorities collect wild eggplant varieties from the forest and plant them in their home gardens. In all the sites, eggplant can be grown throughout the year on all irrigated soil types.

The folk term for similar eggplant species is *ca,* the same word used to describe other prominent members of the Solanaceae family such as *Lycopersicon esculen-*

Table 11.8

Distribution of eggplant species across the sites

Location	Average number and range of different varieties per garden	Average number of plants per garden	Total of different varieties	Frequency of occurrence (%) across gardens per site
All sites	0.5 (0–5)	27	8	46.6
Dran	0.9 (0–3)	4	5	68.8
Dinh Quan	0.4 (0–1)	98	3	45.0
Vinh Than	0.8 (0–4)	3	6	50.0
Binh Chuan	0.3 (0–2)	24	2	28.0
Giai Xuan	0.4 (0–1)	10	2	40.0
Long Khe	0.7 (0–3)	3	5	52.9

tum (ca tomat). During our survey we encountered 44 different local names for eggplant. Within the group *Solanum melongena* alone, we found 15 different names; ten of these 15 describe violet varieties, three describe green varieties, and two describe white varieties (see Table 11.9). Most names describe a specific shape or the color of the fruit skin. Shape and size were sometimes substantially different. Cà dái dê, or goat testicle eggplant, a term that was used exclusively in Vinh Tan, Dran, and Dinh Quan (midland and highland sites), refers to the curved shape of the fruit. The term cà phoi tìm is used in Giai Xuan to describe the lung-shaped fruit, which is bigger than that of cà dái dê and straighter in shape. In Binh Chuan, the color of the violet, lung-shaped eggplant fruit was sometimes described as brown.

Solanum undatum, or cà phaó, was found in all of the sites except Giai Xuan. Cà phaó, which can be translated as "bullet eggplant," has round fruits 2–5 cm in diameter and is usually white. However, in Vinh Tan, where cà phaó was found in almost all the surveyed households, varieties were often distinguished further by additional attributes, including the size of the fruit or the color or pattern of the fruit skin. Varieties can be white, violet, white with green stripes, white with violet stripes, and green with white stripes. One respondent may include all such detailed descriptions and distinctions. The high diversity of names for this species (9), as well as the different morphologies in fruit color and size, might indicate the occurrence of different genotypes. A closer look at the genetic level through isoenzyme analysis would settle this point.

Cà ðia, or dishlike eggplant, and cà bát, bowllike eggplant, are probably the

Table 11.9

Different names of varieties within eggplant *Solanum melongena*

Variety name	English translation	Number of records	Locality
Violet colored			
Cà dái dê	Goat testicle	11	A, B, D
Cà dái dê tìm	Violet goat testicle	1	B
Cà dái tìm	Long violet	5	A, F
Cà nâu	Brown	2	C
Cà phoi soc	Lung shaped, colored stripes	2	E
Cà phoi tìm	Lung shaped, violet	6	E
Cà tìm	Violet	9	A, D, E, F
Cà tìm dài	Violet, long	1	C
Cà tìm len	Violet, big	1	C
Cà tìm nho	Violet, small	1	C
White colored			
Cà tràng	White	4	D, E, F
Cà dái tràng	Long white	2	F
Green colored			
Cà phoi xanh	Lung shaped, green	4	E
Cà dái dê xanh	Green goat testicle	2	B
Cà xanh	Green	2	E, F

same or closely related varieties. Both have white fruit that are broader than long, measuring 5 × 8 cm on average. They were found in all the sites except Binh Chuan and Giai Xuan. The taxonomic classification of this group is unclear. Some Vietnamese scientists classify them under *Solanum melongena* subsp. *esculenta*. However, because of the morphological characteristics of the leaves and the fruits, we would rather group them under *Solanum undatum*. Table 11.10 lists the total area cultivated in eggplants across all home gardens.

Farmers distinguish eggplant varieties on the basis of fruit and leaf morphology but only occasionally on the color of the blossom. The color of the fruit skin was mentioned by 83 respondents as being an important criterion. In fact, the most commonly used single criterion is the color of the fruit skin or the shape of the fruit, or a combination of these two criteria (see Table 11.11).

Solanum undatum (cà phaó) is easy to cultivate and is grown for home use as well as for sale in the market. The fruits can be cooked by boiling or frying and are commonly used to prepare salty pickles. *Solanum melongena* has a better market value than *Solanum undatum* and therefore is grown extensively in places such as Dran, Binh Chuan, and Giai Xuan. It is usually boiled in a soup or fried in oil.

Table 11.10
Cultivated area of eggplant through all surveyed home gardens

Latin name	Vietnamese name	Average area per site (m²)	Percent of gardens	Total area (m²)
S. melongena esculentum	Cà tim, cà ởe	13.7	14.6	498
	Cà xanh	2.3	8.7	197
	Cà dia trang	2.0	1.0	12
S. undatum	Cà phao tim	12.2	12.6	73
	Cà phao trang, cà tron tay	6.7	12.6	1,965
S. thruppii	Cà gai	0.7	2.9	4
S. virginianum	Cà trái-vàng	0.3	1.0	2
S. procumbens	Cà còi = cà bò quánh	0.2	1.0	1

4. Banana (Musa paradisiaca)

Banana is planted throughout the country; it has been a traditional crop for millennia. Because Vietnam is rich in banana diversity and has many local varieties present, including wild types, it is considered to be a global center for the genetic diversity of the species. Sixteen different varieties of banana were found in the home gardens surveyed. Across all sites, banana plants average 36 per home garden with a median of 17 plants, confirming the existence of virtual banana orchards within home gardens (Table 11.12). The variety chuôi la ba was represented by 100 plants in one home garden in the Dran site, chuôi hot by 100 plants

Table 11.11
Most common criteria and combinations of different criteria among 130 records to distinguish eggplant varieties

Criteria	Number of records	Frequency (%)
1Fs	33	25
3F	23	18
1Fs and 3F	19	15
1Fs and 2F	8	6
2F	8	6
1Fs and 2F and 3F	5	4
1Fs and 3F and 1L	5	4
Others	21	16
Total	130	100

Note: 1Fs = color of fruit skin; 2F = Size of fruit; 3F = Shape of fruit; 1L = color of leaves.

Table 11.12

Distribution of banana varieties

Site	Average number and range of different varieties per garden	Average number of banana clusters per garden	Total of different varieties per site	Frequency in gardens (%)
All sites	2.4 (0–5)	36	15	94
Dran	1.8 (0–5)	40	7	94
Dinh Quan	2.3 (0–4)	30	7	85
VinhThan	2.8 (0–5)	31	8	92
Binh Chuan	2.6 (0–5)	24	8	94
Long Khe	2.0 (1–4)	35	6	100
Giai Xuan	3.3 (1–5)	54	8	100

in Song Be, and chuôi già by 200 and 100 plants in Dran and Giai Xuan (Cantho), respectively. Chuôi xiem was represented by over 100 plants in two home gardens in the Giai Xuan site (Cantho) and by 200 plants in a home garden in Long Khe.

In 1995, banana production in Vietnam reached 1.28 million tons, or 2 percent of world production and 0.4 percent of the world export market. However, present cultivation techniques are outdated; most banana orchards have not been established properly, and plants are dispersed and uneven in maturation times, making harvesting costly and fruit quality poor.

The edible banana varieties that are widely disseminated are almost always a combination of the two original species, namely, *Musa balbisiana* and *Musa acuminata*, which is called *Musa paradisiaca*, a variety group derived from the diploid and triploid *Musa acuminata* and *Musa balbisiana* types. Its distribution across the sites is given in Table 11.13. Banana is possibly the most consistently named group of local plants with high diversity within species. The folk taxonomy coincides with classification based on formal agromorphological characterization. Differences in types also coincide with the different growing environments.

Banana plants from the group AA (*Diploidea Acuminata*) are suited to alluvial soils and are therefore most often found in the Dinh Quan and Vinh Than sites, where it averages 12 and 8 plants, respectively, per home garden. This banana is also widespread in Giai Xuan, where 70 percent of the home gardens surveyed contain at least a few plants of this variety. In this group, *chuôi cau trang* is very popular and is marketed everywhere in the country, making its relative value high. The ripe fruit is bright yellow, is good tasting and has excellent smell. According to farmers, this is the most fragrant of all bananas. In the south of Vietnam, *chuôi bôm*, from the same group, is very common. Its fruit is suitable for drying.

Table 11.13

Distribution of *Musa* varieties as frequency of occurrence in % of home gardens and average number (N) of clusters per site

Musa spp.	Group	Vietnamese name	Dran (%)	Dran (N)	Dinh Quan (%)	Dinh Quan (N)	Vinh Tan (%)	Vinh Tan (N)	Binh Chuan (%)	Binh Chuan (N)	Giai Xuan (%)	Giai Xuan (N)	Long Khe (%)	Long Khe (N)	All (%)	All (N)
All varieties		Chuối	94	39.6	85	29.6	92	31.3	94	24.2	100	54.8	100	35.4	94.2	36.3
paradisiaca	ABB	Chuối xiêm, Chuối su	6	0.6	60	8.7	75	14.2	50	3.4	75	28.8	71	19.4	56.3	12.8
acuminata	AAA	Chuối già	6	12.5	55	8.4	33	5.3	61	4.4	80	11.7	29	1.6	46.6	7.5
balbisiana	BB	Chuối-hôt			5	0.3	8	0.4	67	12.1	30	2.1	59	10.4	29.1	4.3
acuminata	AA	Chuối bom	25	1.3	65	8.5	67	5.0	6	0.2	70	6.5	24	2.3	29.1	2.8
acuminata	AA	Chuối cau	6	1.3	25	2.9	25	1.6	11	0.4	10	0.4	6	1.2	25.2	2.56
paradisiaca	ABB	Chuối la ba	75	20.3											13.6	3.2
acuminata	AA	Chuối com	31	1.6					28	1.7	5	0.5	12	0.6	12.6	0.7
paradisiaca	ABB	Chuối đong								0.0	40	3.7			7.8	0.7
paradisiaca	U	Chuối tra bôt			5	0.2	42	3.1	6	0.4					6.8	0.5
paradisiaca	U	Chuối moc	31	2.2											4.9	0.3
paradisiaca	AAB	Chuối mât							28	1.6					4.9	0.3
acuminata	AA	Chuối tiêu			10	0.8	17	1.4							3.9	0.3
balbisiana	BBB	Chuối sap									20	1.2			3.9	0.2
paradisiaca	AAB	Chuối tá qua									5	0.2			1.0	0.03
sanguinea	*	Chuối do, choui kiêng do					8	0.4							1.0	0.05
nana	*	Chuối già lun, chuối duii			5	0.1									1.0	0.01
chiliocarpa	*	Chuối tram-nai														
coccinea	*	Chuối sen														

Note: AA = Diploidea Acuminata; AAA = Triploidea Acuminata; ABB = Acuminata-Diploidea Balbisiana; AAB = Diploidea Acuminata-Balbisiana; BB = Diploidea Balbisiana; * = unique species.

The group of *chuôi gia* bananas (AAA, *Triploidea Acuminata*) is suited to all kinds of soil and yields well. Because of its good characteristics and a fruit size reaching export standards, bananas from this group are planted more often than the others.

The *chuôi xiem* bananas (ABB, *Acuminata–Diploidea Balbisiana*) are not bound to a particular soil type but are better adapted to the lowlands, being widespread in the Mekong Delta. They are less abundant in the midlands of Vinh Than but are still distributed in over 70 percent of all the sites. The variety *chuôi la ba*, which is of uncertain group provenience, replaces *chuôi xiem* completely in the highlands site.

The AAB varieties (Diploidea Acuminata–Balbisiana), especially *chuôi xiem trang*, are very popular because they are used in traditional ceremonies. Their value is nearly three times that of the *gia* (AAA) group. The light-yellow, medium-sized fruits are not exported.

Conclusions

We have focused on the selection and classification as well as the management and use of selected edible key crop species in Vietnam belonging to the categories fruits, roots/tubers, and vegetables. These species are widely distributed in home gardens and have particular nutritional and economic importance. For some species, we touched upon their history of introduction, whereas for all of them we mentioned the local classification system, or folk taxonomy, and the uses to which they are put. Our purpose was to elucidate the dynamics behind the home-garden management practices that contribute to the maintenance and even increase plant diversity.

Not surprisingly, farmers could give a more detailed description of varieties planted in their own garden than of varieties observed in other places. When the descriptions of identically named varieties in one site are compared, considerable inconsistencies emerge. This is so even if we look only at descriptions by farmers who actually grow a particular variety in their garden. The most frequent discrepancy concerns description of the color of certain plant parts, such as the fruit, petiole, or stem. This might be explained by the fact that Vietnamese farmers, especially old ones, do not know many words for different colors. Thus, they often describe orange as yellow, red, or, more accurately, as dark yellow or light red. Nevertheless, many Vietnamese variety names refer to the color of a specific part of the plant or they make an analogy to another species or to an object that is well known for a specific color. Usually, farmers could describe more accurately the parts of a plant that were used or marketed most frequently, such as the fruits or the roots. It was often difficult to get useful descriptions of the shape or color of other less important plant parts such as the leaves. Most farmers use only a few morphological criteria to distinguish the two or three local varieties growing in their home gardens. The names are usually composed of a primary element, such as nhán for longan, plus a secondary name for further description, for example, nhán tiêu da bó, meaning longan with black pepper seeds (small black seeds). Varying degrees of consistency underscore the classification and naming of local varieties. For some species such as sweet potato, it was difficult to find uniformity, sometimes even within the same household, in distinguishing characters and assigning names. In contrast, for banana and longan, there was a high consistency across communities and ecosystems in the distinctive characters and names that were applied. This may have to do with the variation in uses, and even market demand, for the species.

The perceptions and cognitive dimensions encoded in the names used by farmers reveal a great deal about a particular plant, including its appearance, or morphology, and provenience. But "meaning is also derived from a plant's cultural context; how it is used and perceived in a community" (Martin 1995: 207). It is thus important to keep in mind that folk taxonomies are first and foremost social and cultural constructs; they enable people to manage the genetic resources in their systems to keep the traits they desire. They indicate which plants are culturally important and how diverse they are. A folk taxonomy is also a cultural system facilitating the recall and transmission of crucial knowledge pertaining to the range of use and variation within species. Rather than being regarded as hard and fast classificatory systems dealing with genetic diversity, folk taxonomies are best used to identify the characters and uses of plants that farmers value most. Local systems of classification and management enable us to understand why and how farmers keep the diversity they value in their gardens. The survival and genetic diversity of many plant species and varieties thus depend on the local systems of biological knowledge that communities have developed in order to manage them.

References

Berlin, B. 1992. *Ethnobiological Classification: Principles of Categorization of Plants and Animals in Traditional Societies.* Princeton New Jersey: Princeton University Press.

Boster, J. S. 1984. Classification, Cultivation, and Selection of Aguaruna Cultivars of *Manihot esculenta* (Euphorbiaceae). *Advances in Economic Botany* 1: 34–47.

Brush, S. B., H. J. Carney, and Z. Huaman. 1981. Dynamics of andean potato agriculture. *Economic Botany* 35 (1): 70–88.

Eyzaguirre, P. 1995. Revising IPGRI's collecting forms to include ethnobotanical information. *News and Notes: Plant Genetic Resources Newsletter,* no. 103, p. 45.

Eyzaguirre, P. 2000. Ethnobotanical indicators for assessing the distribution and maintenance of genetic diversity: Example of taro in Yunnan, China. In D. Zhu, P. Eyzaguirre, M. Zhou, and L. Sears, eds., *Ethnobotany and Genetic Diversity of Asian Taro: Focus on China,* pp. 46–50. Beijing: Chinese Society of Horticultural Sciences, and Rome: International Plant Genetic Resources Institute (IPGRI).

Gessler, M., U. Hodel, and P. Eyzaguirre. 1998. Home gardens and agrobiodiversity: Current state of knowledge with reference to relevant literatures. Discussion paper. Rome: International Plant Genetic Resources Institute (IPGRI).Heider, K. G. 1969. Sweet potato notes and lexical queries. *Kroeber Anthropological Society Papers* 41: 78–86.

Ho, T. V., and collaborators. 1994. Root and tuber crop genetic resources in Vietnam. In *Proceedings of the International Workshop on Plant Genetic Resources,* pp. 167–173. Ministry of Agriculture, Forestry, and Fisheries (MAFF) Research Council, Japan, March 15–17.

Gessler, M., U. Hodel, H. H. Cai, V. V. Thoan, N. V. Ha, N. X. Thu, and T. Ba. 1997. *In Situ Conservation of Plant Genetic Resources in Home Gardens of Southern Vietnam.* Serdang, Malaysia: International Plant Genetic Resources Institute (IPGRI), Asia, Pacific, Oceania (APO).

Martin, G. J. 1995. *Ethnobotany: A Methods Manual.* London: Chapman & Hall.

Schneider, J., C. A. Widyastuti, and M. Djazuli. 1993. Sweet potato in the Baliem valley area, Irian Jaya. A report on collection and study of sweet potato germplasm. April-May. Bogor, Indonesia: International Potato Center.

Van Dorp, M., T. Rulkens, S. Masyitah, H. Fahri, and Idris. 1993. Collecting landraces of soyabean, maize, cassava and sweet potato in Indonesia and studying the associated local knowledge. Food and Agricultural Organization of the United Nations (FAO) and Rome: International Board for Plant Genetic Resources (IBPGR) *Plant Genetic Resources Newsletter* 93: 45–48.

twelve

The Diversity of Taro and Sponge Gourd in Home Gardens of Nepal and Vietnam

*Bhuwon Sthapit, Ram Bahadur Rana,
Nguyen Ngoc Hue, and Deepak Rijal*

The Problem

The farming systems of Nepal and Vietnam are complex and diverse, reflecting the risk-averse production strategies that farming households employ. These mixed agricultural production systems are affected by a combination of factors: altitude, rainfall, soil types, and other physical parameters. Within the various agroecosystems climate may change from tropical to alpine over short distances, particularly in Nepal. The effect of these variable conditions can be considerable, governing not only the range of crops that may be grown but also all other farming practices as well. Thus, climatic and physiographic differences, as well as the prevalence of diverse traditional management practices, have contributed to the wealth of agrobiodiversity that characterizes Nepal and Vietnam (Partap and Sthapit 1998; Hodel and Gessler 1999).

234

Home gardens are an important component of the integrated mixed farming systems of Nepal and Vietnam. In order to understand their potential contribution to the conservation of crop-genetic resources, we focus on the crops, varieties, and useful characteristics (crop traits) that are best kept in home gardens. Key to this analysis is the documentation of the amount and distribution of diversity with respect to richness, evenness, and distinctiveness for some species and cultivars. By focusing on two common crops, taro (*Colocasia* spp. and *Xanthosoma* spp.) and sponge gourd (*Luffa* spp.), we hope to illustrate the ways in which farmers maintain distinct populations of these cultivars in their home gardens. The question is how do they accomplish this when households grow only a few plants of each species. What will be the fate of taro and sponge-gourd diversity if home-garden systems disappear? Answers to these questions can provide insights into the present status and future prospects of home gardens as in situ conservation systems in Nepal and Vietnam. A better understanding of the role these two crops play in the diverse agroecosystems allows us to chart the future course of conservation of genetic diversity in these two countries. The comparison between taro, which is clonally propagated and is found both in home gardens and in larger crop fields, and sponge gourd, which is cross-pollinated and seldom grown outside the home garden, is thus useful for illustrating the role that home gardens play in traditional germplasm management systems.

General Aspects of Home Gardens: Contrasts and Comparisons

The people of Nepal and Vietnam rely for the most part on agriculture for their livelihood. Farming is largely subsistence-oriented and is characterized by three components, namely, crops, livestock, and forestry. In both countries, home gardens play an important multidimensional role. Salient differences, nevertheless, underlie the home gardens of both countries. In Nepal, the home garden is traditionally known as *ghar-bari*, whereas in Vietnam it is locally known as *vuon nha*. The types of home gardens that are made, and their composition, vary regionally within each country (see Shrestha et al. 2002; Trinh et al. 2001). Vegetable crops and fodder trees generally dominate home gardens in Nepal, where livestock is an integrated component of the farming system. In contrast, Vietnamese home gardens typically contain many fruit trees and a rich diversity of traditional leafy vegetables, aromatic herbs, spices, and medicinal plants. Here, pigs and poultry are sheltered around the homesteads, where they forage on the by-products of home gardens and kitchens and fish are kept nearby. In contrast, within Nepal, large ruminants such as cattle, buffalo, and goats are kept near the homesteads as the main source of proteins and fertilizers. Fodder trees and forage species are, therefore, important components of home gardens here. Crops are planted to take advantage of specific conditions. For example, climbers are grown near roofs or close to tall trees that serve as support. About 80 percent of rural households still use firewood as the main source of energy; therefore, trees whose leaves can be used as fodder, their trunks as firewood, and their fruit as food are generally preferred. In addition to differences in ecology, distinct food cultures and cultural beliefs account for the different animals, crops, and varieties that are found in Nepal versus Vietnam (Gurung and Vaidya 1998).

Despite these differences, a unified typology of home gardens can be applied to both Nepal and Vietnam depending on the importance placed on the specific species grown: (a) crop-based home gardens; (b) vegetable-based home gardens; (c) fruit-based home gardens; (d) agroforestry-based home gardens; and (e) home gardens planted for religious use. In both countries also, farmers are predominantly smallholders tending an average holding in Nepal of less than 1 ha of cultivated land. In Vietnam, home gardens range from 0.14 to 0.75 ha in size and account for 26 percent to 43 percent of the total cultivated area (Trinh et al. 2001).

The products of home gardens are basically for home consumption; they meet a multiplicity of household needs (Table 12.1). However, in neither country does household production meet all nutrient requirements of the family. Data on food availability suggest that Nepal produces only around 30 percent of its fruit and vegetable requirements and only breaks even with respect to cereals. More than 70 percent of the women and children suffer from anemia, while 65 percent of pregnant women and more than 10 percent of schoolchildren suffer from night blindness (Ministry of Health 1998). The evidence is very similar in Vietnam, particularly among minority ethnic groups, where many people are affected by vitamin, iron, and iodine deficiencies. As a result of the shortfalls farmers practice a range of coping strategies, including collecting wild and uncultivated foods during the deficit months and diversifying crop species in home gardens.

In Situ Conservation of Taro and Sponge Gourd

A strategy to conserve on-farm crop-genetic diversity must be consistent with the livelihood needs of rural households. Based on these household needs and on the biological and socioeconomic factors that surround them, farmers make decisions on what traditional crop varieties to maintain (Jarvis, Sthapit, and Sears 2000). An important direction within this global research is the emphasis on agroecosystem niches and microenvironments that people create specifically to increase the total diversity. By comparing the management of genetic resources in two countries with respect to similar crops, we explore the ways in which households create and manage diversity. Home gardens thus provide havens and breeding grounds for genetically diverse crop repertoires.

The role that home gardens play in on-farm conservation is dependent to some extent on the breeding system of the crop species involved (whether clonal or self- or cross-pollinated), their method of propagation, and the traditional germplasm management system functioning at the household and community levels. There are three distinct channels for obtaining planting materials within a traditional seed system (including clonal planting): (a) seed flows, whereby farmers obtain seed or planting materials of a given variety from the community or from outside sources; (b) human selection of varieties to put in their fields or home gardens, as well as selection of seed for storage; and (c) natural selection of crops and varieties, which enhances their local adaptations. The exchange of seed among farmers results in genetic materials being introduced into local crops. In this activity, as well as in the selection of crops, both women and men play a significant role and both make an important contribution to the farming system at large, but each gender tends to have its own network for the exchange of genetic materials and information (Subedi et al. 2001). Figure 12.1 illustrates the farmer's system of managing plant-genetic resources for household needs in an integrated and dynamic way. When the varieties being used perform below average, or when new opportunities emerge in response to market forces, the farming family looks for new seeds and planting materials.

Taro (*Colocasia esculenta* (L.) Schott)

Although taro is grown from the lowland Red River Delta and Mekong Delta in Vietnam to the high mountains of Nepal, it is a particularly important home-garden crop in the upland hills of Nepal and Vietnam. In both countries, this tropical root crop has a long history associated with the peoples' food cultures and traditions. Valued as a leafy vegetable, it is grown for the multiple uses that the leaves, petioles, stems, corms, and cormels have. Taro (*Colocasia esculenta*) is an important basic element in the household food security of both countries. Tannia (*Xanthosoma sagittifolium*), a more recent introduction from tropical America, is increasingly grown in Vietnam in place of taro, but true *Colocasia* is still the predominant species. Taro is propagated by clones and is found both in home gardens and in the larger agroecosystem. By way of contrast, sponge gourd is cross-pollinated and is exclusively confined to home gardens in a small population size

Table 12.1

Purpose of Home Gardens in Nepal and Vietnam

Purpose	Examples from Nepal	Examples from Vietnam
Livelihoods	• A year-round supply of fresh food is available. • Maize grown in home gardens is harvested and eaten green to supplement the declining stock of the old harvest. • Waste products are recycled for milk and meat production.	• Corm of taro, yam, cassava, potato, and sweet potato are supplemented with staple cereals to prolong their availability in the family. • Waste products are recycled for fish and pork production.
Nutrition	• Many seasonal uncultivated vegetables also supplement the staple food, e.g., jaluka, a wild taro. • Pumpkin (*Cucurbita moschata*) is used for its tender shoot, flower, and fruits; chayote (*Sechium edule*) is used for its tender shoot, fruits, and yamlike roots. • A number of perennial vegetables such as winter beans, tree tomatoes, chillies, etc., provide a regular supply of micronutrients.	• Many aromatic spices and leafy vegetables are harvested from gardens in Vietnam as a salad prior to meals. • The leaf, petiole, corm, and cormels of taro (*Colocasia esculenta*) are rich in Vitamin A. • Home gardens also provide *Ocimum* spp., which are rich in micronutrients values.
Food quality	• A year-round supply of vegetables and fruits treated with fewer chemicals is available for family members in periurban areas.	• Easy access to fresh leafy green vegetables, spices, and herbs allow Vietnamese to eat raw vegetables.
Multiuse from tree (fodder, food, firewood, and timber)	• Nepalese people use various products of trees for food; for example, leaf buds such as kavro (*Ficus lacor*) and siplican (*Crataeva religiosa*) are used for pickling; fruit of katahar (Artocarpus heterophyllus) are used for vegetable; fruit of badahar for fodder (*Artocarpus lakoocha*); and kaphal (*Myrica esculenta*) for fruits.	• Starfruit (*Averrhoa carambola*) is used to prepare sweet and sour fish soup; fig fruit (*Ficus* spp.) is used as green salad; hue, a leafy plant, is used to wrap traditional sticky rice with mung bean and meat inside.
Spices and medicinal plants	• A number of spices such as chilli, ginger, turmeric, cinnamon, garlic, shallot, onion, fenugreek, coriander, and timur (*Xanthoxylum armatum*), among others, are often found in Nepalese home gardens. • Tulasi (*Ocimum sanctum*), babari (*Ocimum basilicum*), marathi, pudina (*Mentha spicate*), ginger, timur, and bojo (*Acorus calamus*) are commonly used to cure colds, coughs, and stomach disorders.	• Specific herbs and spices are grown in Vietnamese home gardens to prepare diverse kinds of foods; for example, sa (*Cymbopogon citratus*), rieng (*Alpinia officinarum*), and mo long (Paederia lanuginosa), needed to cook dog meat, are grown near the kitchen. • Hoang nuh trang (*Ocimum gratisimum*), sacred basil (*Ocimum tenuiflorum*), and some varieties of taro are used for medicinal values.
Green manure and pesticide use	• Asuro (*Adhatoda visica*), titepati (*Artemisia vulgaris*), khirro (*Sapium insinge*), and ankhitare (*Walsura trijuga*) are common green manure crops in Nepal planted on the boundaries of home gardens as live fences; some of them have pesticide value.	

Table 12.1 continued

Purpose	Examples from Nepal	Examples from Vietnam
Cultural use	• Oal, drumstick, lapha sag, and patuwa sag (leafy vegetables) are delicacies of terai people. • Newars, a dominant ethnic group in the Kathmandu Valley, specifically maintain cholecha (*Allium* spp.), black soybean, garlic, shallot, chamsur (*Lepidium sativum*), and red turnip in their home gardens because these plants are commonly used in cultural ceremonies and feasts.	• Hill tribes of Dao' ethnic people consider young bamboo shoots, plain and fermented, as delicacies. • During Tet festival Vietnamese need red fruit (*Momordica cochinchinensis*) to color sticky rice cakes eaten during the festival.
Religious use	• Tulasi (*Ocimum sanctum*) is regarded as a sacred plant, an incarnation of the god Vishnu. • Many home gardeners in terai keep bel (*Aegle marmelos*) for its leaves, which are given as a special offering to the god Shiva. • Many households, especially in urban areas, keep pipal (*Ficus religiosa*), which is regarded as an incarnation of Vishnu, for their daily worship.	• A few fruits such as pomello (*Citrus grandis*), pears (*Pyrus pyrifolia*), green banana (*Musa* spp.), and oranges (*Citrus* spp) are essential for offering to God. • Betel leaf vine (*Piper betle*) is another species maintained in front of the house for use at marriage celebrations.
Farmer's trial and multiplication plot	• Rana bagaincha (palace gardens) are the classical example of the introduction of new plant species in home gardens.	• Most farmers test new varieties of sweet potatoes, chillies, cassava, and fruits in home gardens.
Home for unique plant species and varieties	• Nepalese home gardeners maintain unique types of biodiversity for social prestige or as a hobby; e.g., madale kankro, a large cucumber specially used for making pickles; basaune ghiraula, an aromatic sponge gourd; coconut; and jire khursani, a small hot chilli.	• Flowering taro is used as medicine.
Improving environment	• Some species are maintained for aesthetic value, e.g., ashoka (*Saraca indica*), neem, kadam (*Anthocephalus kadamba*), gulmohar (*Delonix regia*), rudraksha (*Elaeocarpus ganitrus*), and a number of ornamental plant species. • Ashoka, neem, and tulasi are believed to repel insects from the homestead.	• Shade trees are a more common feature in the homesteads of South Vietnam. • In peri-urban areas, the aesthetic value of orchids and ornamental plants is higher than it is in rural home gardens. • Sponge gourd vines are managed on the bamboo mats just in front of the house for shade during hot weather.
Symbol of social status and pride	• Rana palace gardens in and around the Kathmandu Valley and the large home gardens and bagaincha (fruit orchards) of jamindar (landlords) were purposely designed to reflect the owner's status through their size and diversity.	• Retired people take pride in their home gardens as a means to conserve unique diversity and to exhibit to others, for example, in Hue City, Ho Chi Minh City.

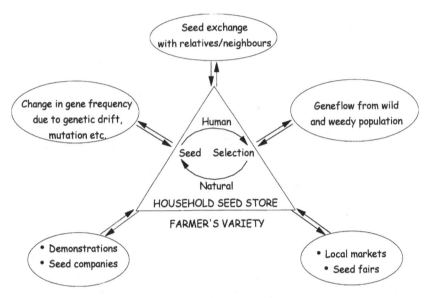

Figure 12.1. Informal seed supply systems in traditional farming systems

(Table 12.2). The taro species and cultivars of Vietnam are adapted to aquatic conditions, as well as to rainfed uplands, both in open fields and home gardens. Nepalese taro species are grown mainly as a monocrop or occasionally as a mixed crop interspaced with maize and various combinations of legumes and spices. Taro is cultivated in a wide range of ecologies, from open fields under a slash-and-burn regime to shady home gardens in the cool high mountains of Jumla (2,300 masl). Farmers also harvest a few wild aquatic taro varieties that are especially valued for their young leaves and petioles, used to prepare special condiments in the local cuisine, such as masura (dried vegetable nuggets used for curry).

Diversity and Distribution of Taro in Nepal and Vietnam

In Nepal, the middle-hill ecosystems harbor greater taro diversity than do low-altitude and high-altitude sites (Rana et al. 2000a, b). Out of 206 households sampled in the Nepalese village of Begnas (600–1,400 masl), located in the middle-hill ecosystem, over 70 percent ($n = 146$) cultivated taro in their home gardens and/or in the large agroecosystem (Table 12.3). On average, farmers grew 2.33 ± 0.31 taro varieties in this village, whereas at other sites farmers grew just one variety at the community level. The maximum number of taro varieties maintained by each household in the Begnas community was reported to be eight (Rana et al. 2000b). The number of taro cultivars that small farmers can name is one ethno-

Table 12.2

Comparative characteristics of taro and sponge gourds in Nepalese and Vietnamese farming systems

Characteristics	Taro	Sponge gourds
Ecological diversity	Low to high mountains (10–3,000 masl)	Low to middle hills (10–1,500 masl)
Agroecosytems	Home gardens, wild and large agro-ecosystem, mixed cropping	Predominantly home gardens
Diversity richness	Middle hills (500–1,000 masl)	Middle hills (700–1,300 masl)
Number of plants per household or area	Few plants to 250 m² in Nepal; few plants to 5 ha in Vietnam	One to five plants per home garden
Source of diversity	Informal seed system; no modern variety available	Informal seed system; few modern varieties available
Breeding system	Clonal	Cross pollinated
Method of propagation	Various parts of plant used as planting materials, e.g., suckers, cormels, corms, eyes, seeds, etc.	Seed (one fruit is enough for an entire village)
Use patterns	All plant parts are used in the wide range of local cuisine; different plant parts are used in different recipes and products. In Vietnam, taro leaves are seldom used by humans, whereas taro corms are rarely used for soup with pork and other meat.	In Nepal, fruits are used for vegetable curry with dried meat, whereas in Vietnam it is used in soup
Direct and indirect value	Perennial food source, rich in Vitamins A and C, associated food culture, medicinal value; some cultivars have market demand	Associated with local food culture, rich nutrition, long fruiting period

botanical indicator of the diversity that they can maintain. Local names help farmers manage genetic resources at the community level, from production to marketing. A total of 24 taro varieties were named by farmers from Begnas, where slightly less than 1000 farming households live. Isozyme analysis of 15 named cultivars selected at random showed that farmers are generally consistent when naming cultivars and that these cultivars do possess a considerable genetic variation among them (Bajracharya et al. 2001).

Although varietal richness of taro is greatest in Begnas Kaski at an elevation of 600–1,400 m (Table 12.3), some rare cold-tolerant cultivars are also grown in the extremely high mountain ecosystem (e.g., Jumla, at 2,300 m). The well-adapted high-altitude varieties from Jumla are reported to have no acridity. Farmers at higher elevations still rely almost exclusively on taro cultivars they have developed

Table 12.3

Household characteristics of taro and sponge gourd growers in ecosites, Nepal, 1999

Parameters	Kachorwa[a] (80–90 masl)	Begnas[b] (600–1,400 masl)	Talium[c] (2,240–3,000 masl)
Total number of households	914	941	759
Number of households sampled	202	206	180
Average family size per household	6.5 ± 0.2	6.5 ± 0.2	6.0 ± 0.2
Average food sufficiency over number of months	7.4 ± 0.3	8.3 ± 0.3	7.5 ± 0.3
Average cultivable farm size in ha (*khet, bari, lekh*)[d]	0.74 ± 0.1 (187)	0.65 (195)	0.33 (179)
Number of land holdings (cultivable farm only)	4.0 ± 0.2	5.2 ± 0.3	18.9 ± 0.9
Percent of households growing taro in home garden (n = 206)		71	
Percent of households growing sponge gourds in home garden (n = 206)		93.3	
Average square meters per household under taro	NA	94.5 ± 7.2 (96)	NA
Total number of taro landraces	3	24	1
Total number of sponge gourds	16	13	NA
Average number of taro cultivars per household	< 1	2.33 ± 0.13 (146)[e]	< 1
Number of sponge gourd plants per household	NA	2–4 plants	5–40
Number of taro plants per household or area	Few plants to 500 m²	Few plants to 250 m²	Few plants to 10 m²

a. Kachorwa lies in the terai region of Nepal. It has high production potential environment characterized by relatively good access to new technologies and inputs, road and market access.

b. Begnas lies in mid hills with intermediate level of access to technologies and inputs, and good road and market linkages.

c. Talium lies in high hills with limited access to new technologies and inputs, no road network and imperfect market conditions.

d. *Khet* is bounded and irrigated or rainfed land, where puddled rice mainly is grown. *Bari* is unbounded and unirrigated upland. *Lekh* is high subalpine climatic zone.

e. Figure in parentheses indicates number of responding households. Since taro is cultivated in home garden scale and varieties were mixed with other crops it was not possible to record exact area under different landraces. Only 96 households responded about area planted. Some landraces are grown on large scale, whereas others are maintained at the scale of a few plants per household.

and the germplasm they maintain. In middle-hill conditions, taro varieties are grown in both home gardens and the larger agroecosystem, intercropped with various cereals, spices, and legumes. In the terai plain area of Nepal, a limited number of taro cultivars are found, including ujarka (white), lalka (red), and katch (itchy leaf), which is fed to animals to bring them into heat.

Among the 24 taro cultivars identified in the farmers' fields located within the Begnas ecosite, only 5 or 6 landraces are widely grown, and these have distinct characteristics that differentiate them. In order to understand the reasons why farmers maintain a large number of taro landraces, we examined the extent and distribution of taro diversity in the village (Table 12.4). Hattipau, khari, khujure rato, and rato pindalu were common taro cultivars grown in large surfaces by 56 percent of the sample households. In situ conservation of such cultivars may not require special conservation efforts. Taro types having a good market demand, multiple uses, and good productivity tend to fall into this category. Other taro cultivars such as dudhe karkalo, kalo karkalo, lahure karkalo, rato mukhe, and rato panchmukhe pindalu are grown by 26 percent of the households but in small

Table 12.4

Extent and distribution of taro cultivars in the Begnas village of Nepal

	Widespread	Local
Common	• Hattipau • Khari • Khujure rato • Rato pindalu	• Chaure • Danthe pindalu • Kalo pindula • Seto pindalu
Rare	• Dudhe karkalo • Kalo karkalo • Lahure karkalo • Ratomukhe pindalu • Rato panchmukhe pindalu	• Chattre/Juke • Kaat • Gante • Khujure kalo • Khujure seto • Rato • Rato danthe • Rato khari • Rato lamo • Satmukhe • Seto karkalo • Seto lahure • Thado • Thado ratomukhe

Source: Rijal et al. 2001.

areas; often, no more than a few plants are found in and around the home garden. From a conservation perspective it is better for many households to grow taro varieties in numerous small home-garden plots than for a few farmers to grow a few cultivars in large areas. A survey of the Begnas site showed that a total of 15 taro cultivars were distributed in a small area, often represented by only a few plants and managed by a few households.

The following traits may explain why some cultivars are grown by only a few households and then in small areas. First, some varieties such as kalo karkalo, lahure, and dudhe karkalo perform badly once they are removed from home gardens and grown in open fields. Second, some taro cultivars are preferred by households belonging to different ethnic groups. For example, kaat is reported to be good for dal (black gram pulse soup), as it dissolves easily; its use reflects specific ethnic preference for thick dal soup. Gante has a higher protein content in the corm (7 percent) and is thus a useful nutrient source for a vegetarian people. Third, various agroecosystems, niches, and production practices (monocropping, mixed cropping, home gardens, and slash and burn) may be better suited for different kinds of taro landraces.

The choice of a particular cultivar may also depend on its compatibility with companion crops. For example, thagne is adapted to upland mixed-cropping systems and can be grown in association with ginger, beans, sesame, yams, sweet potatoes, and pigeon peas. Jaluka, a wild form, is adapted to wet and semiaquatic conditions and is commonly found along streams and canals in open fields. Finally, the use of some cultivars is so limited or specific that there is no need to grow more than a few plants. For example, dudhe karkalo is highly valued for its petiole, which has a low level of acridity and is thus excellent for preparing pickles; however, the other parts of the plant are not used. A few plants of this cultivar are enough to meet the needs of the household. Moreover, the preferred growing conditions found in home gardens may be so niche-specific that increasing the area under cultivation is not possible. For example, kalo karkalo, a taro cultivar used for its petioles and corms, is adapted to fertile soils near compost pits; it is a perennial and can be grown in the shade. Such conditions are limited to home gardens (Rijal et al. 2001).

The survey also revealed that cultivars such as chaure and danthe pindalu are grown in large areas by a few households and are therefore locally common (Table 12.4). They are not usually found in home gardens, however, perhaps because they need more conservation attention since only a few farmers know how to grow them. These cultivars are thus endangered; they are exposed to the erosion of both local knowledge and genetic resources if their custodians decide not to plant them. Few households or group members exchange materials and information about them with outsiders (Subedi et al. 2001). Nevertheless, the exchange of knowledge about taro cultivars grown close to the house in home gardens is probably greater, facilitating their conservation. In general, the rare taro cultivars are grown in home gardens and not in the fields.

In Vietnam, the number of taro cultivars ranged from 3 in the villages of Quang Mao and Dai An to 15 in the village of Tat at the site of Dabac (600–1,200 masl; see Table 12.5). Farmers used local names consistently, which gives us a measure of the diversity existing at the village level. The index of diversity for taro cultivars among six villages gave the following results: the index for the Dabac site (D′ = 0.92–0.93) was followed by Donglac village at the Nghiahung site (D′ = 0.88), then by Yen Minh village at Nho Quan (D′ = 0.85). Tra Cu, a village in the Mekong Delta, had a relatively poor diversity (D′ = 0.5) compared with the other sites (Table 12.5). The average surface area under taro cultivation ranged from 760 m² to 17,617 m² in the study sites (Hue et al. 2001). Some cultivars were found in home gardens only, whereas other types were found in both home gardens and the larger ecosystems.

The general pattern of taro diversity in Vietnam is for two to four local cultivars to be grown by many households in large fields. In areas of high agricultural potential such as Yen Minh, farmers grow popular commercial varieties, including khoai so trang, khoai so doc trang, khoai so dia phuong, and khoai so, in sizeable fields. As a consequence of the market preference that exists in Hanoi for specific taro varieties with uniform qualities, other local taro cultivars used for

Table 12.5

Comparative richness and evenness of taro varietal diversity in different ecozones of Vietnam

Geographic region	Macro site name	Village	Number of cultivars	Area per cultivar (m²)	D′a
Lowland	Nghiahung	Dong Lac	11	571	0.88
		Kien Thanh	4	190	0.75
Midland	Nhoquan	Yen Minh	11	1,602	0.85
		Quang Mao	4	288	0.66
Mountain	Dabac	Cang	10	16	0.92
		Tat	15	725	0.93
Mekong Delta	Tracu	Dai An	3	NA	0.50

Source: Hue et al. 2001.

a. Genotypic diversity (D′) measured by Simpson (1949) index (D′ = 1 − $\Sigma pi2$).

subsistence have been neglected. But in households of ethnically diverse villages such as Tat, Cang, and Dong Lac, one often finds that up to nine local cultivars are still being planted in small plots by a few households (Hue et al. 2001). The rare types, such as khoai mung, khoai tia nep, mon tin among others, are confined to home-garden ecosystems or to niches within larger fields. Farmers cultivate such rare types for various reasons. For example, khoai mung, grown in Dong Lac village, is said to be good for making vegetable soup and preparing pickles. Khoai tia nep is used to prepare a sweet soup. Khoai ngua doc tim is preferred as food for pigs. Mon tim, a variety found only in the home gardens of Nhoquan, is used as medicine for constipation. Similarly, in the Dabac sites, phuoc mong is grown in small patches and is used by the household as a vegetable or to make pickles; here, also, a few plants of bon hom are maintained as medicine for headaches. Such local knowledge is limited to a few households and is therefore in danger of disappearing.

The preceding discussion has demonstrated that rural households in both countries manage significant taro diversity. The analysis also considered the distribution of this diversity. In general, home gardens are particularly privileged places for the maintainance of rare varieties. Varieties that are distributed among a larger number of home gardens are more likely to have the associated knowledge necessary for their maintenance, even if the total population size for a single variety is small. Another important factor in maintaining taro diversity is that this subsistence crop can be put to multiple uses. Several taro cultivars are selected to yield throughout the year, as well as to satisfy local tastes and food habits. The few examples we have from Nepal showed that farmers prefer specific varieties in their local cuisines (Rijal et al. 2001); this accounts for the high degree of taro biodiversity (Table 12.6). Similar trends were observed in Vietnam (Hue et al. 2001).

Home Gardens and Diversity in Sponge Gourds (*Luffa cylindrica* L. Roem)

Sponge gourd is a traditional vegetable crop of Nepal and Vietnam that is commonly found in home gardens. It is grown in the summer, when vegetables are scarce because most arable land is planted with either rice or maize. The crop is grown in lowlands as well as high hills, but varietal diversity is greatest in home gardens at low to middle altitudes (10 masl in the Mekong Delta of Vietnam to 1,200 masl in Nepal). Sponge gourd is a cross-pollinated crop, with insects being the main pollinators. The plant has indeterminate trailing growth vines that need climbing support for better production. Therefore, sponge-gourd plants are grown

Table 12.6

Participatory evaluation of local taro varieties based on their uses in Nepal

Uses/value	Translation	Considered best varieties
Masaura	Taro nugget, used as vegetable	Khujure rato, hattipau
Khasaura	Dried taro leaf, used as vegetable	Khajure rato
Gava	Boiled tender leaf of taro and dried, used as vegetable	Khujure khari, thaune khari
Achar	Pickle (uncooked)	Dudhe karkalo
Achar	Pickle	Kalo karkalo, lahure karkalo
Khaja	Midday snack (boiled)	Kalo karkalo, lahure karkalo
Tandre	Threadlike split of petiole, dried and used as vegetable	Khari, khujure thaune
Koreso	Sliced and dried corm powder	Hattipau, thaune khari
Paise karkalo	Coin-shaped dried petiole, used as vegetable	Khari, khujure
Pindalu tarkari	Corm, used for vegetable curry	Hattipau, kat, khari rato, Khujure, Bermeli
Dal pindalu	With legume soup	Hattipau
Gava hariyo	Green leaf vegetable	Khujure, khari, thaune
Siuro	Green tender flower tips	Khajure, hattipau, thangne

Source: PRA by authors, 1999

around animal sheds, so that the trailing vines can spread over the roof, or on nearby tall trees. In Vietnam, a net structure made of bamboo is placed on the top of fish ponds or on houses to support the vines. This practice is quite common in southern Vietnam, as it provides shade for people and animals during hot weather. The plant produces fruit from the nodes, and the tender fruits are used as a vegetable or added to soup. A single vine of sponge gourd has the potential to produce a large number of fruits over a period ranging from three to six months.

Farmers maintain numerous sponge-gourd cultivars for the many advantages they offer. In Nepal, 91 percent of the households surveyed in the sites of Bara and Kaski cultivated sponge gourds; four to ten plants were being grown by each household (Rana et al. 2000a, b). Short-duration sponge gourds are also occasionally grown as a commercial crop in larger fields in Nepal and Vietnam. But when sponge gourd is grown for the market, there is an increasing tendency to cultivate modern varieties. In such cases, farmers must depend on the market for seeds. In home-garden cultivation, however, the seed comes from fruits that are left to mature after the harvest.

Varietal diversity, measured in terms of the cultivars that farmers could name, was found to be highest (16) in Bara, at 80–90 m elevation, followed by Kaski (13), at 600–1,400 m (Rana et al. 2000a, b). In the majority of the cases, fewer than three landraces were reported to be grown by a household, and none of them were of foreign origin. A total of 23 landraces were grown in Begnas village, six of which were widely grown by many farmers. Of these, hariyo chhoto (green short) and hariyo lamo (green long) were grown by 59 percent–69 percent of the households surveyed, many of which maintain numerous vines. The early fruiting habit of hariyo chhoto is highly preferred because it prolongs the fruiting period due to the slow formation of sponginess. Hariyo lamo bears long fruit with a good yield. Seto chhoto (white short) is less spongy and cooks quickly, but the vine produces few fruits and the harvest cannot be prolonged.

In the Bara site, lamka ujarka (long white) and lamka hariyarka (long green) are widespread sponge gourds, whereas chitkavara is a rare type (Yadav et al. 2001). Basmati golphulia (aromatic swollen chick) is a locally common cultivar. In order to assess agromorphological diversity, a total of 36 accessions of sponge gourd from the Bara ecosite were studied during 1998/99, using International Plant Genetic Resources Institute's descriptors and farmers' descriptors. Variability in quantitative traits was found to exist in all the landraces. Variability was observed in lamka hariyarka for traits such as leaf length, leaf width, internode, and petiole length. However, no variation was observed in growth habit and degree of fruit fiberness. Chitkavara had the highest fresh fruit weight (300 g), followed by lamka hariyarka. Only the basmatiya landrace had any aroma, and only to a moderate degree. Principal component analysis grouped the studied accessions into five clusters. The first principal component accounted for 43.9 percent of the total variation in nine characters. Cluster 1 had the maximum number of accessions (14), followed by cluster 2 (12). Variety names given by the farmers were related to sponge-gourd use and morphological characteristics; these were found to be useful in managing the resources of the community.

A single mature fruit of sponge gourd will produce enough seed for an entire community. Moreover, one or two plants will produce enough vegetables to feed a small family for two to three months. Consequently, farmers need to maintain only a few vines. A small number of early fruit may be set aside for seed, to avoid being contaminated by other sponge-gourd cultivars later on. It is believed that insect pollinators are the main source of geneflow within adjacent households comprising a single sponge-gourd population. The crops and varieties that farmers grow will continue to evolve, guided by natural selection as well as by selection pressures imposed by the farmers themselves. Such selection processes provide the opportunity for continuous crop adaptation. Further research is needed in order to understand how and why a farmer maintains four to five distinct varieties of this cross-pollinated crop in a home garden. But the fact remains that they are able to identify and value distinct varieties of sponge gourds and hence grow several of them within a single garden. More information is still needed, however, on the informal seed system and on how farmers protect cultivars against gene-flow in order to maintain the desired varieties and traits.

The Search for New Taro Variability

The owners of home gardens themselves maintain the planting materials of taro that they need (Rana, Joshi, and Lohar 1998; Shrestha 1998). Our survey of 96 households showed that 89 percent of the farmers saved planting materials and that 83 percent of them replaced the clones after three years (Baniya et al. 2001). Germplasm brought from outside the household was most often obtained through exchange with neighbors (23 percent) and relatives (8 percent). Our own observations, and those made in previous limited studies (Rana, Joshi, and Lohar 1998; Baniya et al. 2001), suggest that farmers continuously experimented with new seed and plant stocks. About 93 percent of the farmers selected planting materials after the harvest, although a few farmers did so before the harvest. Interestingly, farmers select different plant parts for different varieties of taro and they store diverse taro cultivars in different ways (Baniya et al. 2001).

Farmers continually search for new taro variability within or outside their community. They also take their preferred cultivars with them when they migrate. Thus, in the home gardens of the Chitwan District of Nepal, taro diversity is much richer than in any other inner terai region because the rate of migration from the hills is particularly high. Other genetic resources are either inherited or introduced from local markets and seed fairs, or they regenerate spontaneously. In Nepal, one or two plants of *Xanthosoma* are grown around compost pits, to provide the household with petioles for making pickles. Varieties of *Colocasia* are planted in dry and open places within the home gardens. The *Colocasia* and *Xanthosoma* taros are very easy to propagate naturally. Many varieties are conserved at times of barter, as purchases from local markets, and through Maghesakranti, the Hindu festival during winter season (mid January), when neighbors exchange planting materials and enjoy eating taro and yams. In Nepal, taros may be stored in different ways, but most often they are stored in an open place. Although taro diversity is high within the garden, systems of exchange, or the introduction of new germplasm, is minimal in both Vietnam and Nepal. Farmers from Vietnam, and also from the Pacific Islands, harvest taro corms for home consumption, and suckers are immediately replanted in situ. Such practices do not exist in Nepal, increasing the risk of genetic loss for the local system, but making the system more open to new sources of diversity from the outside.

In Vietnam, lowland farmers obtain seed for commercial or small-scale plantings of *Colocasia*. Two other genera, namely, *Xanthosoma* spp. and *Alocasia* spp., are also grown in shade in home gardens. Types of *Alocasia* are not cultivated for their edible roots but for their leaves and petioles, which are widely used as a vegetable; the rhizomes are used for medicine (Hodel et al. 1999). *Alocasia odora* (Vietnamese: bac hà) and *Alocasia macrorrhiza* (Vietnamese: ray) are the only species of this genus that were found in home gardens. Bac hà is widely distributed, being cultivated in all of the surveyed sites; 60 percent of all home gardens contain bac hà. It is usually found close to the water well and the house. The leaves are characteristically directed upward and have large, prominent veins. The consumption of bac hà is restricted to the petioles that are cut and then added to pigbone noodle soup or the sour fish soup called lau, the most common dish prepared from this plant. The species ray is rarely found in home gardens; its frequency in surveyed households was 9.7 percent. It is much larger in size than bac hà. Its root, which emerges from the soil, is not usually eaten but is used to prepare medicines against stomach disorders and allergies. Bac hà (*Alocasia odora*) is consistently distributed over all the various sites, whereas taro varieties (*Colocasia esculenta*) with edible corms, such as môn sáp and môn cao, are preferred in the Mekong Delta. Tannia (*Xanthosoma sagittifolium*) is more frequently found in the midlands and highlands. It is grown for its petioles, which are used as a vegetable and to feed the pigs. Nonetheless, within the species *Colocasia esculenta* there exists a much wider range of names and different morphotypes than in the other edible aroids, thus indicating its prominent place within the traditional food culture of Vietnamese communities. Some taro varieties do not produce corms but have many thin roots and shoots. They usually grow wild, close to or in ponds or irrigation canals, and are found in all of the surveyed sites. Often, these varieties are not used at all, or their use is purely restricted to the edible shoots. The petioles are green up to the top, but the leaves have a small red to purple spot on the surface of the leaf where it is attached to the petiole. From farmers' descriptions and personal observations we conclude that môn nuóc and môn nguá are the same variety.

Farmers give eight different names to taros with edible roots; these refer by analogy to a certain object or materials, such as a human skull or wax. All the different varieties have very similar leaf shapes and therefore can be distinguished only by the color of the petioles and the shape and size of the corms. Khoai môn so, a variety widely found at all sites, characteristically yields many small cormels around the main corm. People eat these cormels, whereas the leaves and petioles are given to pigs. In the midlands and highlands, môn so has green and violet peti-

Table 12.7

Farmer methods of propagation of clonally grown taro diversity in three sites of Northern Vietnam, 2000

Method of propagation	Cultivars	Agroecosystem[a]	Distribution pattern[b]
a) Cormel and sucker	Khoai lui doc xanh	Lowland	Widespread
	Khoai lui doc tia	Lowland	Widespread
	Mac phuoc mong	Upland	Widespread
	Khoai sap	Upland	Widespread
	Khoai mung tia	Upland	Widespread
	Mon tia	Lowland, home garden	Widespread
a) Young suckers	Nuoc tia	Moist area around well	Widespread
	Nuoc xanh	Moist area around well	Widespread
	Khoai ngot	Lowland, home garden	Widespread
	Bac ha	Home garden	Narrow
	Tam dao xanh	Upland, home garden	Narrow
b) Stolon	Man hua vai	Upland	Widespread
	Khoai nuong	Upland	Widespread
	Khoai doi	Lowland	Widespread
c) Head of corm	Kao pua	Upland	Narrow
	Mon	Upland	Widespread
	Mat qui	Upland	Widespread
d) Eyes of corm	Hau doang	Upland	Widespread
	Phuoc oi	Upland	Widespread
e) Seed and suckers	Kay nha	Home garden and upland	Widespread

a. Lowland refers broadly to lowlying fields of Red River Delta and Mekong Delta below 50 masl and upland represents broadly fields situated above 50m in mid to high mountain areas.

b. Widespread distribution refers to cultivars found in other provinces of Vietnam and narrow distribution refers to cultivars specific to certain village or comune.

oles that serve as distinguishing marks. Among the 215 recorded characterizations of taro by Vietnamese farmers, petiole or leaf color was most frequently used to distinguish varieties. The color of the root flesh or the shape or size of the root was less commonly used. Surprisingly, the shape of the leaves—which is a major criterion to distinguish the *Colocasia* and the *Xanthosoma* group—is not an important means of distinguishing between varieties or species.

Methods for propagating clonally grown taro are diverse. Table 12.7 illustrates the various methods of propagation employed in three North Vietnamese sites.

Evaluation and Selection

Farmers continuously select, experiment with, and evaluate new varieties and seeds. Crop diversity in the home garden is influenced by the population structure of the community and the ecology under which the farming community manages diversity. It is also influenced by the skill farmers display in selecting for certain traits. Women farmers select the best corm or cormels for seed and store them separately. Some taro cultivars produce flowers and seeds, and their selection may add new diversity. Farmers may also choose to grow a particular species or variety in a certain ecological niche. Food preferences and the religious beliefs of farmers may also influence the selection process (Gurung and Vaidya 1998).

In Nepal, the context and number of taro landraces maintained by a household was significantly influenced by wealth ($p < 0.01$): resource-rich households keep more diversity in their home gardens than resource-poor households. The amount of taro diversity was also positively influenced ($p < 0.05$) by whether the household cultivated upland parcels (Rana et al. 2000b, c). Resourceful farmers tended to play a key role in the exchange of information and materials within and between communities; in general, they were more knowledgeable than poorer farmers about plant-genetic resources and that is why they were defined as nodal farmers. These nodal farmers are crucial points in social networks that promote geneflow; they could be mobilized and linked into a network to serve as a community germplasm bank (Subedi et al. 2001). Consequently, nodal farmers could play a significant part in the conservation of home-garden species such as taro.

In the case of sponge gourds, individual households may be less important as units of conservation because, first, the small population size of sponge gourds is small since farmers plant few vines; second, sponge gourd is a cross-pollinated plant with a high proportion of male flowers; third, farmers keep early fruits to maintain specific populations; and, fourth, one fruit can yield enough seed for the entire community. For both crops, household members maintain their own networks for the flow of genetic materials and their associated knowledge, all of which help in conservation efforts (Subedi et al. 2001).

Conclusions

Taro and sponge gourds are not priority crops in national agricultural research and development strategies in either Nepal or Vietnam. While this is understandable given their overall economic importance nationally, they are nutritious crops that contribute to household income and health. Home gardens remain the key system for maintaining and developing germplasm for both these neglected and underutilized crops. In the case of taro, which is grown in both crop fields and home gardens, the home garden is where the rare types with important uses and adaptive traits are conserved. For sponge gourd, a crop that is not a major field crop, nor likely to be, home gardens are the primary area of both production and germplasm conservation.

Acknowledgments

We are grateful to Pablo Eyzaguirre, Jessica Watson, and P. K. Shrestha for comments on this paper. Technical and field assistance of NMDG members from the Nepal Agricultural Research Council, LI-BIRD, Vietnamese Agricultural Sciences Institute, and the many farming communities involved in on-farm conservation is gratefully acknowledged.

References

Bajracharya, J., D. K. Rijal, B. R. Sthapit, and D. Jarvis. 2001. Genetic diversity of farmers-named taro cultivars (*Colocasis esculenta* L. Schott) of Kaski, Nepal. Paper presented at the First National Workshop on Strengthening the Scientific Basis of *in situ* Conservation of Agricultural Biodiversity on-Farm, 24–26 April, 2001, Lumle, Kaski, Nepal.

Baniya, B. K., A. Subedi, R. B. Rana, R. K. Tiwari, and P. Chaudhary. 2001. Planting material management of taro in Kaski Districts of Nepal. Paper presented at the First National Workshop on Strengthening the Scientific Basis of *in situ* Conservation of Agricultural Biodiversity on-Farm, 24–26 April, 2001, Lumle, Kaski, Nepal.

Gurung, J. B., and A. Vaidya. 1998. The benefits of agrobiodiversity of the wide range of food cultures in Nepal. In T. Partap and B. R. Sthapit, eds., *Managing Agrobiodiversity: Farmers' Changing Perspectives and Institutional Responses in the Hindu Kush–Himalayan Region*, pp. 55–62. Kathmandu: International Centre for Integrated Mountain Development (ICIMOD) and Rome: International Plant Genetic Resources Institute (IPGRI).

Hodel, U., and M. Gessler. 1999. *In Situ Conservation of Plant Genetic Resources in Home Gardens of Southern Vietnam*. Rome: International Plant Genetic Resources Institute (IPGRI).

Hodel, U., M. Gessler, H. H. Cai, V. V. Thoan, N. V. Ha, N. X. Thu, and T. Ba. 1999. *In Situ Conservation of Plant Genetic Resources in Home Gardens of Southern Vietnam*. Rome: International Plant Genetic Resources Institute (IPGRI).

Hue, N. N., N. P. Ha, L. N. Trinh, N. N. De, B. R. Sthapit, and D. Jarvis. 2001. Taro diversity in contrasting environments of Vietnam: The extent and distribution of taro varietal diversity and use pattern. *Tropical Agriculture* (to be submitted).

Jarvis, D., B. Sthapit, and L. Sears. 2000. Conserving agricultural biodiversity *in situ*: a scientific basis for sustainable agriculture. *Proceedings of a Workshop*, International Plant Genetic Resources Institute (IPGRI), 5–12 July 1999, Pokhara, Nepal.

Ministry of Health. 1998. Nepal micronutrient status survey. Ministry of Health, His Majesty's Government of Nepal and UNICEF/WHO/MI: New Era Limited.

Partap, T., and B. R. Sthapit, eds. 1998. *Managing Agrobiodiversity: Farmers' Changing Perspectives and Institutional Responses in the Hindu Kush–Himalayan Region.* Kathmandu: International Centre for Integrated Mountain Development (ICIMOD) and Rome: International Plant Genetic Resources Institute (IPGRI).

Rana, R. B., P. Chaudhary, D. Gauchan, S. P. Khatiwada, B. R. Sthapit, A. Subedi, M. P. Upadhyay, and D. I. Jarvis. 2000a. *In situ* crop conservation: findings of agro-ecological, crop diversity and socio-economic baseline surveys of Kochorwa eco-site, Bara, Nepal. *NP Working Paper* no. 1/2000. Nepal: Nepal Agricultural Research Council (NARC) and Local initiatives for Biodiversity Research and Development, (LI-BIRD), and Rome: International Plant Genetic Resources Institute.(IPGRI)

Rana, R. B., K. D. Joshi, and D. P. Lohar. 1998. On-farm conservation of indigenous vegetables by strengthening community based seed banking in Seti River Valley, Pokhara, Nepal. *LI-BIRD Technical Paper* No. 3. Pokhara Nepal: Local Initiatives for Biodiversity Research and Development (LI-BIRD).

Rana, R. B., D. K. Rijal, D. Gauchan, B. R. Sthapit, A. Subedi, M. P. Upadhyay, Y. R. Pandey, and D. I. Jarvis. 2000b. *In situ* crop conservation: Findings of agroecological, crop diversity, and socioeconomic baseline surveys of Begnas ecosite, Kaski, Nepal. *NP Working Paper* no. 2/2000. Nepal: Nepal Agricultural Research Council (NARC) and Local initiatives for Biodiversity Research and Development (LI-BIRD), and Rome: International Plant Genetic Resources Institute (IPGRI).

Rana, R. B., P. K. Shrestha, D. K. Rijal, A. Subedi, and B. R. Sthapit. 2000c. Understanding farmers' knowledge systems and decision-making: participatory techniques for rapid biodiversity assessment and intensive data plots in Nepal. In E. Friis-Hansen and B. R. Sthapit, eds., *Participatory Approaches to the Conservation and Use of Plant Genetic Resources*, pp. 117–126. Rome: International Plant Genetic Resource Institute (IPGRI).

Rijal, D. K., R. B. Rana, B. R. Sthapit, and D. I. Jarvis. 2001. The use of taro local varieties in contrasting production systems in Nepal: extent and distribution of taro varieties. Paper presented at the First National Workshop on Strengthening the Scientific Basis of *in Situ* Conservation of Agricultural Biodiversity on-Farm, 24–26 April, 2001, Lumle, Kaski, Nepal.

Shrestha, P. K. 1998. Gene, gender and generation: Role of traditional seed supply systems in on-farm biodiversity conservation in Nepal. In T. Partap and B. R. Sthapit, eds., *Managing Agrobiodiversity: Farmers' Changing Perspectives and Institutional Responses in the Hindu Kush–Himalayan Region*, pp. 143–52. Kathmandu: International Centre for Integrated Mountain Development (ICIMOD) and Rome: International Plant Genetic Resources Institute (IPGRI).

Shrestha, P., R. Gautam, R. B. Rana, and B. Sthapit. 2002. Home gardens in Nepal: Status and scope for research and development. In J. W. Watson and P. B. Eyzaguirre, eds., *Home Gardens and in situ Conservation of Plant Genetic Resources in Farming Systems*, pp. 105–24. Witzenhausen, Germany: University of Kassel and International Centre of Advanced Training, and Rome: International Plant Genetic Resources Institute (IPGRI).

Simpson, E. H. 1949. Measurement of diversity. *Nature* 163: 688.

Subedi, A., P. Chaudhary, B. K. Baniya, R. B. Rana, D. K. Rijal, R. K. Tiwari, and B. R. Sthapit. 2001. Who maintains crop genetic diversity and how? Implications for on-farm conservation and participatory plant breeding. Paper presented at the First National Workshop on Strengthening the Scientific Basis of *In situ* Conservation of Agricultural Biodiversity on-Farm, 24–26 April, 2001, Lumle, Kaski, Nepal.

Trinh, L. N., J. W. Watson, N. N. Hue, N. N. De, N. V. Minh, P. Chu, B. R. Sthapit, and P. B. Ezyaguirre. 2001. Agrobiodiversity conservation and development in Vietnamese home gardens. *Agriculture Ecosystems and Environment* 2033: 1–28.

Yadav, R. B., P. Chaudhary, S. P. Khatiwada, J. Bajracharya, R. K. Yadav, M. P. Upadhaya, B. R. Sthapit, and A. K. Gautam. 2001. Agromorphological diversity of sponge gourds (*Luffa cylindrica* L.) ecosite, Bara, Nepal. Paper presented at the First National Workshop on Strengthening the Scientific Basis of *In situ* Conservation of Agricultural Biodiversity on-Farm, 24–26 April 2001, Lumle, Kaski, Nepal.

thirteen

The Conservation and Evolution of Landraces of Peanuts and Peppers

David E. Williams

From the perspective of crop-genetic resources perhaps the most significant characteristic of all home gardens is their immediate proximity to the farmers' dwellings, allowing intensive interaction between the plants and their human caretakers. Species composition of home gardens is determined primarily by the desire for convenient access to frequently used plants but also by the special environmental or management requirements of some plants, as well as numerous, less obvious cultural, traditional, and ceremonial reasons. Women farmers exert a predominating influence on the composition and management of most home gardens in the neotropics. They spend significantly greater amounts of time working in and around the house, including the home garden, than other family members. Consequently, the primary responsibility and labor for home gardens in the Americas is often provided by the women of the household.

While appearing more or less self-contained, the home garden is in fact an important element of the larger agroecosystem. This larger agricultural system includes the farmers' regular subsistence and commercial plantations, those of her relatives and neighbors, species from the surrounding natural vegetation, and even material from distant regions acquired via seed exchange and market access. The home garden can include elements from all levels of the larger agroecosystem. As an integral part of the traditional agroecosystem, the home garden satisfies needs that the regular field cropping component cannot fulfill.

Some of the characteristics of home gardens and the means of their maintenance have an important function in the local management of plant-genetic resources. The traditional management that peanut (*Arachis hypogaea*) and pepper (*Capsicum* spp.) landraces receive in neotropical home gardens continues to be a key factor in the evolution, diversification, and conservation of landraces of these two species.

The Home-Garden Microcosm

The home garden is a microcosm, not only in the sense of its particular biotic and abiotic character but also because of the dynamic human intervention that governs its floristic composition. In addition to its function as a garden and orchard, the home garden is a multipurpose area that might typically include, among other things, an animal pen, a manure pile, a garbage dump, a compost heap, a trash-burning pit, and a latrine. The sum of all of this activity produces a continuously disturbed environment where the soil is enriched and irrigation water is available. The result is a heterogeneous microcosm where favorable growing conditions can be found or created for a wide diversity of useful plants.

For the most part, species composition, frequency, and distribution of useful plants in the home garden are the deliberate consequence of the owner's individual preferences and needs. But useful plants can also become established in the home garden through accidental, unintentional, or fortuitous introduction. Tomatoes and cucurbits are notorious volunteers in garbage piles and trash heaps and are frequently tolerated, if not encouraged, when they appear. The occasional use of the home garden as an informal latrine is another vector of fortuitous introduction, whereby seeds, particularly those of solanaceous species such as tomato, peppers, and *Physalis,* sometimes germinate in the freshly manured soil after having passed through the human digestive tract (Davis and Bye 1982). Sympatric wild, ruderal, and agrestic crop relatives often volunteer in home gardens and may establish themselves in close proximity to their cultivated kin where introgressive hybridization can take place (Anderson 1952). These spontaneously occurring crop relatives may be eliminated, tolerated, protected, or even encouraged depending upon their usefulness to the farmer (Williams 1985; Jarvis and Hodgkin 1999).

A Locus of Intensified Human-Plant Interactions

The ready accessibility that is the defining characteristic of the home garden allows a much more intensive interaction between farmers and plants than is possible with crops growing in a field. In the home garden, the farmer's attention is usually concentrated on one or a few individuals of a given species or variety, and special care can be provided to ensure the survival, selection, and propagation of favored types. It is not uncommon for innovative farmers to use their home garden as an experimental plot for evaluating or multiplying new species or varieties.

Informal experimentation is frequently observed amongst innovative Amerindian farmers and is an important element in traditional farming systems. Such farmers respond to an innate curiosity regarding new crops and varieties and are keen to detect and propagate variants in the hope of discovering something interesting or useful. Home gardens are used to evaluate materials obtained as gifts from friends and relatives, through trade, or brought back from travels to other areas. They may also serve the purpose of a demonstration garden, to display an interesting plant or variety to friends and provide them with propagules should they be interested in adopting it. In the protected and controlled environment of the home garden, rare or delicate plants can be afforded special care and protection. Seed of open pollinated crops, such as maize, can be safely multiplied in the relative isolation of the home garden to avoid pollen contamination from other varieties.

When different varieties of the same crop are planted in close proximity within the home garden, they can readily cross-pollinate with one another, or even with a nearby weedy relative. Interesting segregates of subsequent hybrid generations can be readily detected and propagated by the observant farmer. Over time, this practice of detecting and selecting new recombinants constitutes an ongoing process that enhances and perpetuates crop-genetic diversity. The sustained intensity of human selection that takes place there has prompted several authors to recognize home gardens as loci for plant domestication and diversification (e.g., Anderson 1948, 1952; Kimber 1978).

It is often stated, and generally accepted, that subsistence farmers manipulate broad inter- and intra-specific crop diversity as a deliberate strategy to reduce risks under unpredictable growing conditions and to satisfy the requirements of special environments and uses. While it may well be a valid explanation underlying the practice, this reasoning may lie below the threshold of consciousness of the farmers themselves, whose interest in agrobiodiversity is culturally conditioned and reinforced by custom. In many cases it would appear that native farmers are simply cultivating diversity for diversity's sake. Whatever the reason, the fact remains that native farmers demonstrate a profound affinity for crop-genetic diversity, and the home garden is one of the main places where they actively foster and nurture it.

Peanuts and Peppers in Neotropical Home Gardens

Examples involving peanuts (*Arachis hypogaea*) and peppers (*Capsicum* spp.) illustrate some of the different functions that home gardens play in traditional farming systems and in the conservation of crop diversity. In the traditional farming systems studied, peppers are predominantly home-garden crops and are only occasionally planted as a field crop. In contrast, peanuts are primarily sown as a field crop but are also planted in home gardens to a lesser extent and for special purposes such as seed multiplication. While the examples are taken from specific Amazonian and Mesoamerican agroecosystems, most of the same mechanisms, motives, and evolutionary consequences are echoed in other crops, and in other home gardens, throughout the American tropics and beyond.

Peanuts and the Playa Agricultural System

Along the western headwaters of the Amazon River, native farmers employ a traditional farming system that exploits seasonally exposed alluvial soils, yet also depends upon upland swidden plots and home gardens. Known as *playa* agriculture, this is an intensive double-cropping system in which riverine sandbars (playas) and upland plots are alternately planted according to the season, with part of the harvest from one being used soon thereafter as seed for sowing on the other. In the playa agricultural system, early producing varieties of peanuts (*Arachis hypogaea* ssp. *fastigiata*) and other short cycle crops are sown on the new-formed sandbars soon after they become exposed by the falling river level at the end of the rainy season. No felling of trees, clearing of vegetation, or soil preparation is required; the seeds are sown directly into holes made in the moist sand with a planting stick. When sufficient seed and suitable playas are available, two people can sow several hectares of peanuts in a short time.

In a Tacana Indian village in northern Bolivia, six distinct landraces of peanut

Varieties of peanuts being planted by the Tacana Indians of Bolivia using
the playa system

were being cultivated under this system (Williams 1996). Women farmers played
a clearly dominant role in the decision-making concerning the planting and harvesting of the crop. The seeds of two landraces are customarily planted in a single
hole, a practice that favors geneflow when the plants flower. Little additional care
is required until the peanuts are ready to be harvested. The earliness of the varieties planted means that they can be harvested after 3 or 4 months, before the beginning of the rainy season when river levels rise again, submerging the sandbars.
Harvesting is accomplished by simply uprooting the plants from the loose, sandy
soil, with the mature peanuts still attached. The women then carefully remove
the pods from the plants, discarding any that are diseased, malformed, or immature, thereby exerting a fruit-by-fruit selection pressure. The freshly harvested
peanuts are carried to the village still in their pods, where they are spread out on
mats to dry for several days before they can be stored, traded, sold, or consumed.
The peanut seed is stored in the pods, in woven bags or baskets suspended from
the house rafters. In the warm, humid Amazonian climate, the viability of seed
stored in this way is short-lived. Moreover, the seed stored in the house is also susceptible to damage from insects and fungi, as well as depredation by rodents, mis-
chievous children, and even the farmer herself, who may be obliged to use the
seed to feed her family if other food becomes scarce.

Harvesting the peanut plants

To offset the risks inherent in storing peanut seed in the house, a second crop is planted in the heavier upland soils, often in the home garden, during the rainy season when the playas are submerged. This upland planting is usually smaller, and its primary purpose is to provide fresh seed for the next season's sandbar planting. This seed crop is often planted together with other home-garden crops such as maize, tomatoes, and sweet potatoes. In contrast to the customary mixing of landraces when sowing on the playa, in the home garden the seeds of the different landraces are planted separately so that the farmer can control the amount of seed of each she will have available for the next playa planting. Because the peanut varieties used are fast-maturing and do not have seed dormancy, the freshly harvested seed from the home-garden plot will be available in time for sowing on the sandbars that reappear soon after the rainy season ends.

For both the playa and the home-garden plots, the farmers meticulously select their seed for size, shape, seed-coat color, and freedom from disease and insect damage upon harvesting, and again before planting. This double-cropping system subjects the crop to two sexual generations and four events of human selection per year. Therefore, aside from helping guarantee a supply of fresh, vigorous seed, this farming system effectively intensifies the human-plant interaction by providing the farmer with more opportunities to detect, select, and propagate interesting new sources of diversity. The sources of diversity themselves are also enhanced by this system, for the number of events are doubled when sexual recombination, mutation, and intervarietal geneflow may occur.

Unusual intervarietal hybrids or segregant materials are regularly discovered by observant farmers during the growing cycle or seed-selection process. When an interesting new type is detected, or when a small amount of rare seed is obtained elsewhere, the farmer will typically plant the novel germplasm in her home garden, where she can protect, increase, and evaluate it. This is a conscious experimental process through which new varieties are developed and adopted by native farmers.

Peppers, the Quintessential Home-Garden Crop

A visitor to nearly any home garden in the American tropics is practically assured of encountering at least one of the five domesticated species of hot peppers: *Capsicum annuum, C. baccatum, C. chinense, C. frutescen,* or *C. pubescens* (Pickersgill 1969). The spectacular range of shapes, sizes, colors, textures, flavors, and piquancy expressed in the fruits of these plants is exploited to produce countless local and traditional dishes throughout the Americas (Andrews 1984). This is particularly true in indigenous and rural communities where *Capsicum* peppers also make a valuable nutritional contribution to the diet.

Whereas peppers are commonly grown as annual crops in the higher latitudes, in the frost-free tropics the plants become perennial. In a tropical home garden, a typical pepper plant soon becomes a woody bush that may produce abundant fruit more or less continuously for three to ten or even more years, depending upon the species and environment. Peppers are an almost ubiquitous element of neotropical home gardens, and it is not at all uncommon to find one or two representatives of several different pepper varieties, perhaps even different species, being cultivated in a single garden. Moreover, it is very possible that the observant visitor will also encounter a wild form of one those cultivated peppers that appeared spontaneously in the home garden, where it is tolerated and its highly pungent fruits are harvested. If one looks even more closely, intermediate forms resulting from hybridization between the wild and cultivated types may also be found, receiving varying intensities of management depending upon the needs and preferences of the farmer.

The degree of use and genetic diversity of pepper landraces in the Americas bears a strong positive correlation with the presence of indigenous population and culture. Quichua Indian farmers living along the Napo River in eastern

Ecuador typically cultivate several varieties of peppers in their home gardens. The peppers are planted in close proximity to one another and in the immediate vicinity of the house, within easy access from the kitchen. The management of these peppers falls clearly within the domain of the woman of the house, who plants, tends, harvests, and prepares them and who knows the name and distinct qualities of each. Seeds are obtained from family, neighbors, and markets through gifts, exchange, and purchase. The peppers from the immediate vicinity belong to the species *Capsicum chinense* and show a broad range of morphological variation. However, other pepper species and varieties are acquired from markets or other distant sources and planted in the Quichua home gardens, often experimentally to test their adaptation to the local Amazonian conditions. If they survive, they may be retained, allowing opportunities for cross-pollination with the local varieties to occur between the closely situated individuals.

As in many tropical regions, typical Amazonian home gardens appear to the outsider to be unstructured, somewhat messy affairs. The apparent lack of order is partially due to the fact that many of the useful plants—peppers being a good example—are often self-sown plants born from a seed discarded in a trash or dung heap or transported there by a bird or other vector. Rather than attempt to transplant a volunteer seedling to a predetermined plot in the garden, when the farmer detects a self-sown pepper plant she often prefers to protect and tend the plant in the place where it germinated. The cultivation of volunteer seedlings of uncertain origin is a common means by which intervarietal or even interspecific hybrid peppers are propagated. If upon maturity these volunteers are deemed undesirable, they can be easily eliminated, but if they appear useful or otherwise interesting, they may be cultivated and further disseminated. In the Quichua farming system, peppers are cultivated primarily for home consumption and are rarely grown in commercial plantations. However, an abundant home-garden pepper harvest is sometimes taken with other cash crops to a local market for sale or barter.

In Mexico's Yucatan Peninsula, home gardens play a slightly different role in traditional pepper production, evolution, and conservation. The habanero pepper (*C. chinense*) is a popular local landrace grown by traditional Maya in their home gardens, as well as in larger slash-and-burn plantations for commercial production. The Maya also grow several other local pepper landraces pertaining to the species *C. annuum* in their home gardens as well as in larger commercial plots. In addition to these domesticated varieties, a small-fruited, highly piquant wild pepper, corresponding to the species *C. annuum* var. *aviculare*, occurs spontaneously and abundantly in the home gardens as well as around the edges of the slash-and-burn plantations (Latournerie et al. 2001). While not cultivated in plantations, this wild pepper is widely tolerated; it is harvested and consumed from the home gardens, where it is frequently allowed to grow in close proximity to domesticated landraces of the species *C. annuum* and *C. chinense*. The physical proximity of the different but closely related taxa in the home garden gives rise to intermediate forms, including interspecific hybridization with the habanero peppers (*C. chinense*).

It is interesting to note that the Maya farmers in Yucatan prefer to use commercial seed for their commercial plantations, rather than seed they could easily produce themselves. One of the reasons farmers give for preferring commercially produced seed is that the uniformity of the peppers harvested brings a better market price than the heterogeneous harvest produced by their own seed. It can be postulated that the heterogeneity the farmers observe from their own seed crop is due to introgressive hybridization with the ubiquitous wild pepper population. Such heterogeneity is readily observed in many home gardens where the plants in the farmer's pepper patch appear very much like a hybrid swarm. Pepper uniformity is not a priority for home consumption; in fact, the diversity of peppers fostered in Maya home gardens can be selected and manipulated according to the farmers' agronomic needs and culinary preferences. It is not clear the full extent to which Maya farmers' perceive and exploit this source of pepper genetic diversity.

Conclusions

From the standpoint of crop-genetic resources, home gardens constitute a microcosm within which an intensified, dynamic, and sustained interaction takes place between farmers and useful plants. This interaction constitutes part of an ongoing coevolutionary process between humans and plants that may be described as plant domestication, crop improvement, and in situ conservation of genetic resources. The home garden forms an integral part of the larger agroecosystem, within which it serves an important complementary role. A careful examination of a traditional home garden often reveals unique processes, crops, and crop varieties that are not duplicated elsewhere in the agroecosystem to which it belongs.

Results of recent studies support earlier contentions that home gardens are loci for plant domestication and crop evolution, as well as units for the conservation of local landraces. The cultural and biological elements of the evolutionary processes that take place in home gardens should be taken into account when devising strategies that promote home gardens as both conservation and production units.

Acknowledgments

The author wishes to thank Luigi Guarino, Pablo Eyzaguirre, and Cary Fowler for their helpful discussions, suggestions, and corrections on earlier drafts of this chapter.

References

Anderson, E. 1948. Hybridization of the habitat. *Evolution* 2: 1–9.

Anderson, E. 1952. *Plants, Man, and Life.* Boston: Little Brown.

Andrews, J. 1984. *Peppers: The Domesticated Capsicums.* Austin: University of Texas Press.

Davis, T., and R. A. Bye, Jr. 1982. Ethnobotany and progressive domestication of *Jaltomata* (Solanaceae) in Mexico and Central America. *Economic Botany* 36(2): 225–41.

Jarvis, D. I., and T. Hodgkin. 1999. Wild relatives and crop cultivars: Detecting natural introgression and farmer selection of new genetic combinations in agroecosystems. *Molecular Ecology* 8 (12 Supp): 159–73.

Kimber, C. 1978. A folk context for plant domestication; or the dooryard garden revisited. *Anthropological Journal of Canada* 16: 2–11.

Latournerie, L., J. L. Chavez, M. Perez, C. F. Hernandez, R. Martinez, L. M. Arias, G. Castanon. 2001. Exploración de la diversidad morfológica de chiles regionales en Yaxcaba, Yucatán, Mexico. *Agronomía Mesoamericana* 12 (1): 41–48.

Pickersgill, B. 1969. The domestication of the chili peppers. In P. J. Ucko and G. W. Dimbleby, eds., *The Domestication and Exploitation of Plants and Animals*, pp. 443–50. Chicago: Aldine Publishing.

Williams, D. E. 1985. *Tres Arvenses Solanáceas Comestibles y su Proceso de Domesticación en el Estado de Tlaxcala, México.* MSc. Thesis. Colegio de Postgraduados, Chapingo, Mexico.

Williams, D. E. 1996. Aboriginal farming system provides clues to peanut evolution. In B. Pickersgill and J. M. Lock, eds., *Legumes of Economic Importance*, pp. 11–17. Advances in Legume Systematics 8. Kew, U.K.: Royal Botanic Gardens.

fourteen

Characterization in Situ of the Variability of Sapote or Mamey in Cuban Home Gardens

T. Shagarodsky, L. Castiñeiras, V. Fuentes, and R. Cristóbal

Salient Features

Sapote (*Pouteria sapota* [Jacq]) is a large tropical fruit tree propagated from seed that grows up to 30 meters tall on average and is a typical mid- to upper-story tree of the humid neotropics. It thrives in heavy, well-watered soils and is thus common in Cuban home gardens known as *conucos* (Castiñeiras et al. 2000). Because it is still being brought under cultivation in home gardens, there is still wide variation in sapote types. Some sapotes are wild, representing remnants of useful forest vegetation that is preserved when people establish homesteads in the forest zones, while others are clearly the product of human selection over time.

Sapote is originally from Central America, and wild populations of sapote are found from the south of Mexico to the northern part of South America (León 1987). Wild sapote is distributed from sea level up to 1,000 meters above sea level, but trees found above that altitude do not bear fruit. Sapote seeds are recalcitrant, meaning that they do not remain viable for very long after they drop and are exposed. This favors their reseeding naturally around the base of existing trees. Germination is much more likely, however, if the husk is removed, as it is when the fruit is eaten by monkeys, birds, or humans. The sapote fruit, also known as red mamey, is highly valued in Cuba because of its excellent flavor; it is eaten as a fresh fruit and is also used to make fruit drinks, ice creams, and jams. In Central America, El Salvador, Costa Rica, and Nicaragua, respectively, export 40,000, 27,000, and 11,000 metric tons of sapote yearly, thus indicating its growing importance (Gazel Filho et al. 1999). Moreover, its popularity is increasing in the United States due, in large part, to the food preferences of Latin American immigrant communities. In Florida, a grafted sapote plant can cost as much as $45 and the dehydrated pulp of sapote up to $10 a pound (Morera, cited by Muñoz and Fuentes 1995; Gazel Filho et al. 1999).

The Importance of Red Mamey (*Pouteria sapota*) in Home Gardens

In tropical America, where *Pouteria sapota* originated, the demand for sapote is still met by wild or managed trees growing around homesteads. Sapote cannot be considered a fully domesticated species, and there is as yet no intensive commercial production from planted stands. The size and phenology of the tree, particularly the years it takes to bear fruit and the difficulty of harvesting it, have been factors against its being brought under full intensive production. In Cuban conucos, the mamey is a highly valued species; it is considered attractive, a symbol of a healthy and well-established home garden, a provider of fruits for home consumption, fetching good prices when sold. Conucos also contain other sapotacea species (e.g., *Pouteria canpinchiana*), lecheimito (*Chrysophyllum cainiato*), and níspero (*Manilkara sapota*), but these were less frequent and less valued than red mamey.

Anecdotal evidence suggests that the number of sapote trees is declining due, in part, to a decline in small independent farm households making conucos. In addition, given the 12 to 18 years that are needed for a sapote tree to enter into full production, only households with clear intergenerational tenure over their farm holdings will plant and tend a sapote. The size of the tree also means that, from an economic perspective, its optimum environment is in the home garden where other species can flourish under the canopy. The future of the sapote tree, with its growing economic potential, thus remains linked to its diversity and management within Cuban conucos. We will show that, fortunately, there is still time and sufficient sapote diversity for it to be maintained and conserved in conucos by Cuban households (Castiñeiras et al. 2000).

The process of maintaining and selecting variation in sapote can be readily studied in Cuban conucos. Households have been observing the tree, and using the fruit over generations. By analyzing key traits of sapote and preferences among households, it is possible to identify trends in the ongoing process of domestication within home gardens, in particular the identification of sapote cultivars from seed types. Rural households in Cuba have several uses for sapote. The mature fruit, with its pleasant flavor, is widely used in making ice cream. The green fruit is astringent and is therefore effective in treating diarrhea. The nut of the mature seed is used to prepare a cream that is used in the preparation of confectionary. The grated nut is bitter and can be ground into a paste that is used to treat skin discolorations. According to the literature, the seeds can be used for hair-care products or in medicinal applications (Comisión Nacional de Fruticultura 1974). It is customary in Cuba to apply mamey nuts to children's hair, as protection against lice. The seeds of sapote are used for handicrafts and jewelry. The wood is used in the construction of houses and work tools, although in general, mamey trees are seldomcut and can reach ages of over one hundred years; for example, in the east almost all the trees are over forty years old.

Despite the Cubans' great appreciation for the red mamey or sapote, this species has hardly been studied. Traditional Cuban farmers have acquired a vast practical experience in growing tropical fruits, but this knowledge has not been adequately recorded. It was to fill this gap, and to provide information that may be used to promote the continued use of this valuable home garden tree, that we began to use the knowledge that farmers have to characterize the diversity of *Pouteria sapota*. We chose two regions in Cuba where home gardens or conucos are important for the maintenance of agrobiodiversity in tropical farming systems.

The Market

A market study covering the period from September to December 2000 enabled us to evaluate the availability of fruits during the time when they are not in production in the home gardens studied (March to July). From a phenological point of view, the variability in the maturation period of this species has not been well documented. This indicates the need to broaden the spectrum of trees included for in situ conservation efforts for sapote fruit trees. The results of the market study indicated that, in early November, 12.5 percent of the vendors had medium-sized fruits for sale. The price of an individual fruit can vary from 4 to12 pesos, with the higher prices being paid later in the year. When we inquired as to the source of the fruit, we found that they were being brought from distant locations, such as Guantánamo, Santiago, and, in some cases, Camagüey. The quality of fruit was, on average 6.15, meaning that the fruit was of intermediary to good quality and the average price 6.15 pesos. In the current economy of Cuba, the promotion of red sapote represents an indigenous option to increase peasant incomes and to increase the availability of fresh fruits to urban dwellers.

Characterization of Sapote Diversity in Conucos

The key set of characteristics that govern human selection of sapote types is the quality and nature of the fruit. The detailed morphological characterization of *Pouteria sapota* was done on a sample of 42 trees found in home gardens in the central and eastern regions of Cuba (see map, Fig. 14.1). In Pinar del Río Province, in western Cuba, 30 trees were studied in the areas of San Cristobal and Candelaria, and 12 trees in the districts of Yateras and Guantánamo, in the Guantánamo Province. The difference in the sample size of the two regions reflects the frequency with which sapote is found in the home gardens of different regions.

The morphological characterization was carried out directly in the home gardens where the trees are grown. We also included one tree from outside the study region, to serve as a control and a reference point because of the widely renowned quality of its fruits. Eleven descriptors were selected, based on descriptor lists developed by de España (1997). These were modified as necessary and are listed below as variables used in measuring variation within sapote (Table 14.1). The data analyzed consisted of an average of ten measurements per sample on fruits

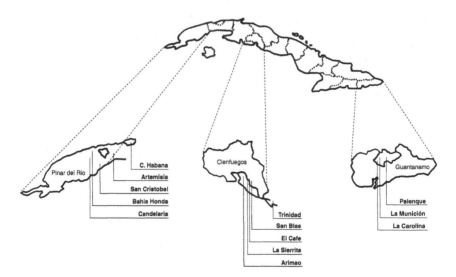

Figure 14.1. Map of the study sites of home gardens in Cuba

Table 14.1

Parameters as descriptors for sapote trees in two regions of eastern and western Cuba

Variables	Length of fruit (cm)	Width of fruit (cm)	Number of seeds per fruit	Length of seed (cm)	Width of seed (cm)	Thickness of seed (cm)	Average weight of fruit (g)
Average	11.6961	7.6454	1.4502	7.12785	3.1438	3.0720	401.8147
Standard deviation	2.2283	1.1087	0.4398	1.0989	0.4547	0.4383	208.3849
Range	10.9	5.62	1.5	4.1	1.88	1.75	1130.1
Minimum	8.04	5.8	1	5.17	2.43	2.32	194
Maximum	18.94	11.42	2.5	9.27	4.31	4.07	1324.1
Coefficient of variation (%)	19.05	14.50	30.33	15.41	14.46	14.26	51.86

that were collected randomly from each tree. The data were grouped into matrices to produce statistical correlations among the 11 variables that farmers and consumers use to define fruit quality. These variables were identified on the basis of an intensive qualitative survey to reveal the values and perceptions that farmers had of different sapote types. This survey included the use of semistructured interviews, direct observation, and group workshops with farmers in the two regions studied. A market survey was also carried out between September and December in three markets of different sizes in order to assess sapote availability during those months. The quality and price of the fruit was also noted.

A standardized data matrix of the 11 variables was used to conduct a principal component analysis (PCA), in order to observe a grouping of morphotypes using the statistical program STAT-ITCF (Foucart 1988). The data on the analysis were used to develop a figure corresponding to size of fruit (component C1) and seeds per fruit (component C3) using EXCEL software. In addition, we took into account the date on which the material was collected in order to observe the frequency of distribution of the seed and fruit characteristics in the two regions studied.

Results

In Table 14.1, we show the general distribution of distinctive characteristics for the 42 trees sampled. We found that the most variable indices for observing variation in fruit type within the species were length and width of the fruit, thickness

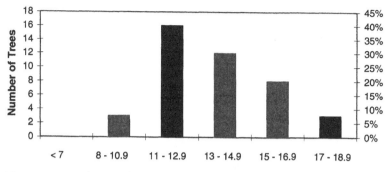

Figure 14.2. Distribution of trees with respect to length of fruit

of the pericarp, and the number of seeds per fruit. The results of the PCA of the three main components revealed a 73.1 percent total variability, with a high percentage of variability in component C1 (Figs. 14.2, 14.3, Table 14.2). Based on the PCA, the characteristics that contributed most to the expression of the component C1 were the width of the fruit, the length of the fruit, the length of the seed, the average weight of the fruit, and the width and thickness of the seed. It is evident that the value of some characteristics is higher due to its correlation with others. For example, length and width are characteristics that are highly correlated. The length of the seed and the length of the fruit are also highly correlated. For the second principal component, C2, the weight of the seed and the average number of seeds per fruit, the thickness of the mesocarp, and, to a lesser extent, the thickness of the pericarp carried the most weight. The third principal component, C3, was determined largely by the thickness of the pericarp and the number of seeds per fruit. The role of these characteristics in distinguishing fruit types

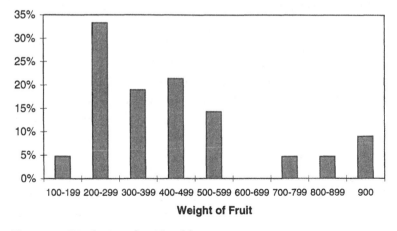

Figure 14.3. Distribution of weight of fruit

Table 14.2

Result of PCA applied to *Pouteria sapota* in two regions

	C1	C2	C3
Contribution	45.2	16.7	11.2
Percent accumulated	45.2	69.9	73.1
Length of fruit (cm)	0.3804	0.1393	−0.1728
Width of fruit 1 (cm)	0.4115	0.0053	−0.0709
Width of fruit 2 (cm)	0.4176	0.0319	−0.0853
Thickness of pericarp (mm)	−0.0769	0.3282	−0.6508
Thickness of mesocarp (mm)	0.2345	0.4682	0.1529
Number of seeds per fruit	0.0618	−0.4777	−0.5325
Length of seed (cm)	0.3494	0.0052	−0.2049
Width of seed (cm)	0.3242	−0.2376	0.2343
Thickness of seed (cm)	0.301	−0.2388	0.3371
Weight of seed (g)	0.1399	−0.4843	−0.1263
Average weight of fruit (g)	0.331	0.276	−0.0321

is similar to their role in Guatemala (Azurdia et al. 1997). If we observe the characteristics of sapote in each region and look at the distribution of trees with respect to length and weight of fruit (see Figs. 14.4, 14.5), we observe a wider distribution of genotypes in Pinar del Río than in those from Guantánamo. The Guantánamo sapotes are located in quadrants 3 and 4, and the populations here tend to have more pronounced traits associated with C3. The variation within sapote populations from Guantánamo, while distinctive, is not as great as the variation observed within sapote populations from the western region of Cuba, where the most significant characteristics in the PCA were the numbers of seeds and the thickness of the pericarp.

In the eastern region, the fruits of one tree exhibited an average pericarp thickness of 3.06 mm, making it very difficult to cut the fruit. A similar type called "mamey sapote" was observed in the western region: it has a thick pericarp and is also characterized by having a smaller fruit weighing less than 295g on average, with a high number of seeds: often up to 4. The name of this cultivar can be attributed to its similarity with the species *Manilkara sapota*, which is also known in the west of Cuba as sapote. In the western part of Cuba, the only cultivar collected outside the area of study was from the town of Puerta del Golpe. This one sample is clearly separate from the other genotypes as can be seen from its position on the right of the graph because of the weight of its fruit, which can at times exceed 2.7 kg. In our survey, the average weight was 1.32 kilos. This and other qualitative traits that were highly appreciated indicate that this genotype was

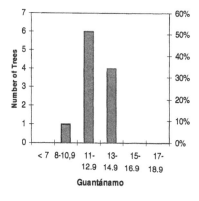

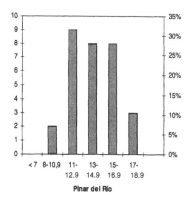

Figure 14.4. Overall distribution of sapote types according to the length of the fruit and as compared across the sites

carefully selected by local farmers as it has a length of 18 cm, a bright red, fiberless pulp with a thick mesocarp, only one seed per fruit, and large numbers of fruit per tree. According to the farmers who grew this tree in their home garden, one tree can produce up to 2,000 fruit per year. This variety was an exceptional cultivar developed and conserved by Cuban small farmers in their conucos. Today, some of these varieties are conserved ex situ in the farm of an agronomist, who has a collection of 18 varieties of high quality that are reproduced vegetatively using different grafting techniques. In most cases, these trees are over 30 year old and constitute a strategy for an ex situ and in situ national collection of sapote trees (González et al. 1996/97).

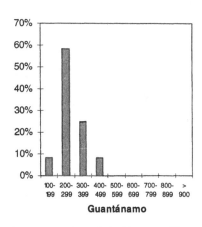

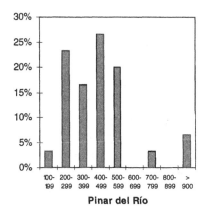

Figure 14.5. Overall distribution of fruit type by weight and as compared across home-garden sites where sapote was evaluated in situ

Table 14.3

Characteristics of sapote fruits from Pinar del Río and Guantánamo

		Pinar del Río			
Descriptor	Average	Descriptor Evaluated	Minimum	Maximum	CV%
Length of fruit (cm)	12.19	2.36	8.23	18.94	19.36
Width of fruit 1 (cm)	8.01	1.25	6.32	11.62	15.67
Width of fruit 2 (cm)	7.89	1.18	6.09	11.42	14.90
Thickness of pericarp (mm)	1.59	0.26	1.18	2.05	16.42
Thickness of mesocarp (mm)	20.25	4.04	13.63	31.80	19.96
Number of seeds per fruit	1.57	0.43	1	2.50	27.26
Length of seed (cm)	7.47	1.04	5.47	9.27	13.91
Width of seed (cm)	3.27	0.47	2.43	4.31	14.34
Thickness of seed (cm)	3.24	0.38	2.49	4.07	11.65
Weight of seed (g)	39.86	13.23	19.23	73.25	33.19
Weight of fruit (g)	445.61	229.46	194	1,324.1	51.56
		Guantánamo			
Length of fruit (cm)	10.46	1.27	8.04	12.44	12.12
Width of fruit 1(cm)	7.23	0.79	5.8	8.76	10.90
Width of fruit 2 (cm)	7.02	0.63	5.8	8.11	8.97
Thickness of pericarp (mm)	1.82	0.58	1.22	3.06	31.86
Thickness of mesocarp (mm)	20.48	4.28	14.5	28.7	20.88
Number of seeds per fruit	1.14	0.33	1	2.1	28.75
Length of seed (cm)	6.33	0.76	5.17	7.86	11.96
Width of seed (cm)	2.82	0.18	2.48	3.15	6.3
Thickness of seed (cm)	2.65	0.24	2.32	3.03	9.18
Weight of seed (g)	24.9	5.45	17	31.93	21.89
Weight of fruit (g)	290.70	71.96	196.4	418.59	24.75

In Table 14.3, the coefficients of variation of the average weight of the fruit, weight of the seed, and the number of seeds per fruit is highly significant for both of the regions surveyed. When the number of seeds was high, the fruit was considered less desirable for consumption. Nonetheless, due to the high number of fruits per plant, in some cases over 3,000 fruits per tree, these types are used as livestock feed when green and still immature. The color of the pulp varies considerably, from a deep red to a reddish orange, which is the most frequently observed color. Some types of mamey can be yellowish, orange, or even brown. Most of the fruits have a sweet and pleasant taste; nonetheless, some are known for their bitterness and disagreeable odor. The presence of fibers in the fruit

Table 14.4

Matrix showing correlation between characteristics of *Pouteria sapota*

	Length of fruit	Width of fruit 1	Width of fruit 2	Pericarp	Mesocarp	Number of seeds per fruit	Length of Seed	Width of seed	Thickness of seed	Weight of seed	Weight of fruit (g)
Length of fruit	1										
Width of fruit 1	0.69695403	1									
Width of fruit 2	0.72325368	0.97940743	1								
Thickness of pericarp	-0.04951911	-0.20080938	-0.16207181	1							
Thickness of mesocarp	0.40197399	0.4867026	0.53829236	-0.02116494	1						
Number of seeds per fruit	-0.01509585	0.16542387	0.13498947	-0.04642412	-0.48962372	1					
Length of seed	0.84990243	0.53149188	0.56085235	0.00080501	0.20701105	0.10687127	1				
Width of seed	0.45042829	0.62220619	0.5979068	-0.3362869	0.04818133	0.0070972	0.53490392	1			
Thickness of seed	0.34282837	0.48054206	0.48441186	-0.49512576	0.12146486	0.07426297	0.47139606	0.6585876	1		
Weight of seed	0.67177062	0.69939598	0.70917692	-0.26813621	0.20851016	0.01661573	0.7423962	0.87182494	0.74820968	1	
Weight of fruit (g)	0.8427238	0.94290279	0.94970369	-0.18465541	0.52968888	0.05173194	0.62419604	0.57390709	0.41051649	0.70234444	1

Branches with sapote fruits

makes them less appetizing to humans. Table 14.4 shows the correlation between *Pouteria sapota* characteristics.

The overall range of dates of maturation of fruit is between March and July, and it is generally believed that mamey should be harvested in the waning phase of the moon. It was observed that farmers prefer varieties that can be harvested ripe between the months of April and May. There are, however, popular types that reach maturity later, in the month of June. A study of mamey in Guatemala (de España 1997) noted that the months with the greatest production of sapote, in decreasing order, were January, February, December, November, and March. Based on a comparison of these data, one notes the complementarity in the timing of sapote production between Guatemala and Cuba: May and June being the most productive months in Cuba, but very unproductive in Guatemala.

The distribution of sapote diversity is compared across two major regions where this tree is a key component of the conucos. Figures 14.4 and 14.5 show the general distribution of sapote types by region, the length of the fruit, and the annual weight of the fruit, respectively. In Figure 14.4, one sees a fairly even distribution of fruit ranging from 11 cm to 12.9 cm in length. This type was the most frequent in both regions studied. The fruits are smaller in Guantánamo than they are in Pinar del Río, where there is, nonetheless, a significant number of cultivars whose length is greater than 17 cm. In Guantánamo, the fruit weight ranged from 200g to 299g, whereas in Pinar, the range it was 400g to 499g. In Pinar, there were fruits weighing over 700–900g. The study noted the frequency with which cultivars bore two, three, or four seeds per fruit. Consumers consider this multiple seed characteristic undesirable. In Guantánamo, as in Pinar del Río. there was a very low frequency of fruits with over four seeds. Nonetheless, we observed a notable number of cultivars with two or three seeds per fruit. In most cases, trees with two seeds per fruit represented the more rare cultivar type; however, most cultivars did contain individuals that produced the occasional two seeds per fruit. Only the cultivars in Puerta del Golpe, and cultivar Number 25 in Pinar del Río, were uniform with respect to a single seed per fruit. In the case of Guantánamo, the multiple-seed characteristic was less frequent, and we noticed six cultivars in which none of the fruits contained multiple seeds.

Based on the characteristics described, we have been able to catalog the sapote trees into five groups. Fruit size is an important characteristic for grouping cultivars. Thus, we have one group of small fruit that includes the so-called mamey sapote type. These fruits are smaller than 10 cm long and weigh up to 300g per fruit. The medium-sized sapotes are those with fruit greater than 10 cm long, with an average weight of between 300 and 500g. The big sapote fruits were over 12 cm

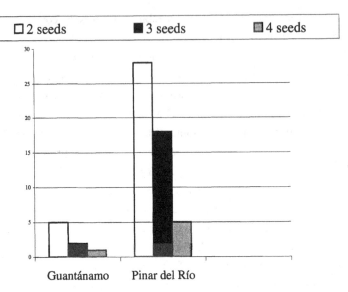

Figure 14.6. Frequency distribution of sapote types based on the number of seeds per fruit

long and the average weight varied between 500 and 900g. There are some very big fruits that measured over 15 cm and weighed over 900g. In the latter case, these cultivars are found in the eastern region. The epicarp of the fruits is darker than those in the west.

Farmers' Perception of Sapote Diversity

The farmers' perceptions, used in the identification of the different varieties, were not always consistent with the formal characterization and evaluation of fruit tree genetic resources as carried out by a genebank. Farmers' classification systems recognize phenological variation, such as date of maturity, and morphological characteristics of the fruit as features that define sapote types. Farmers will also merge characteristics and include their own subjective criteria for determining fruit quality. Farmers' knowledge of the sapotes in their conucos extends to details of productivity and optimal harvesting times in relation to different climatic patterns from year to year. Because propagation of this species is by seed and the trees can reach great age, it is difficult to define the varieties that refer to the farmer's choice of seed. When questioned about variety choice, replies tend to be vague. The most popular varieties are "mamey sapote" and "mamey blanco." In only 5 percent of trees studied did farmers give us a specific cultivar name. More sys-

Sapote trees growing in a Cuban conuco

tematic work is needed on the folk taxonomy of sapote and on ways to use this information in more formal characterization and evaluation of sapote diversity. In the western part of the country, one notes a high variability in sapote types within home gardens; local farmers recognize one to five types based on their own criteria. In many cases, we observed a high density of sapote cultivars per unit area, especially in the mountainous areas where the trees were often one hundred years old or more.

Conclusions

This brief study has allowed us to document the existing variability in *Pouteria sapota* cultivars that are maintained in Cuban home gardens or conucos. The variability in sapote was greater in the western region as opposed to the east, despite the difference in the number of cultivars studied. The characteristics used most frequently to describe sapote variability in situ were: the width of the fruit, the length of the fruit and seed; the average weight of the fruit and the width and thickness of the seed; the weight of the seed and the average number of seeds per fruit; and the thickness of the mesocarp. We proposed a grouping of sapote cultivars into four classes based on the dimensions and weight of the fruit.

We recognize the need to broaden the spectrum of cultivars of these fruits in ex situ collections and in household production systems of the traditional Cuban conucos. It is still necessary to document and rescue some of the sapote types that are most appreciated, either for their high production of fruit or for their taste, and include them in a program of fruit tree propagation while developing a strategy to motivate further their maintenance in a network of conucos. Given their size, breeding system, and phenology, studying sapote trees in situ, and using farmer's intimate knowledge of the trees and the quality of their fruits within their home gardens would be a good starting point for both the conservation and development of this species in Cuba. In some cases, it is possible to begin assisting farmers in the propagation and distribution of types that are clearly highly valued and recognized. Given the presence of greatest diversity in sapotes near the forest and nature reserves in Cuba, conucos within or surrounding those reserves should be good sites for in situ conservation of this species, as well as a breeding ground for developing high-value sapote cultivars.

Acknowledgments

We would like to acknowledge farmers of the two regions who gave freely of their time and knowledge. Deutsche Gesellschaft für Technische Zusammenarbeit (GTZ) provided financial support under the International Plant Genetic Resources Institute Global Project on the Contribution of Home Gardens to in situ Conservation of Agrobiodiversity. At IPGRI we thank Pablo Eyzaguirre and Annie Huie for translation and editorial comments and the technical assistance of David Williams and Michiel Hoogendijk of IPGRI and Helmer Ayala of Guatemala in sampling and characterization.

References

Azurdia, C., E. Martínez, H. Ayala, and B. Nufio. 1997. Colección nuclear, una alternativa para el manejo de colecciones de germoplasma: caso del zapote en Guatemala. *Revista de Ciencia y Tecnología* (Universidad de San Carlos de Guatemala) 2(1): 105–14.

Castiñeiras, Leonor, Z. Fundora Mayor, S. Pico, and E. Salinas. 2000. The use of home gardens as component of the national strategy for the in situ conservation of plant genetic resources in Cuba. *Plant Genetic Resources Newsletter*123: 9–18.

Comisión Nacional de Fruticultura, México (CONAFRU) 1974. *El cultivo del mamey.* Serie de Divulgación. 14. SAG/México.

De España, E. A. 1997. Caracterización morfológica y fenológica *"in situ"* de los cultivares de zapote *Pouteria sapota* (Jacq.) H. Moore & Stearm, en el Departamento de Suchitepequez. Tesis presentada, Universidad de San Carlos de Guatemala. Facultad de Agronomía, Instituto de Investigaciones Agronómicas. Guatemala, noviembre del 1997.

Foucart, T. 1998. Analyse en composantes principales. Service des Etudes, Statistique et Informatique, II 20.1–8.

Gazel Filho, A. B., J. Morera, P. Ferreira, J. León, and J. Pérez. 1999. Diversidad genética de la colección de (*Pouteria sapota* (Jacq.) H. Moore & Stearm) del CATIE. *Plant Genetic Resources Newsletter* 117: 37–42.

González, G., V. R. Fuentes, N. N. Rodríguez, M. Torres, Marisela Capote, J. Cañizares, H. Lima, and P. Orozco. 1996/97. Colecciones y recursos fitogenéticos en la Estación Nacional de Frutales de Cuba. *Jardín Botánico Nacional*,17–18: 123–36.

León, J. 1987. Botánica de los cultivos tropicales. Instituto Interamericano de Cooperación para la Agricultura (IICA), San José, Costa Rica, pp. 210–12.

Muñoz, S., and V. R. Fuentes. 1995. La familia Sapotaceae, un recurso genético de baja explotación al nivel mundial. Monografía (copia Archivo M/N/95/46). Estación Nacional de Frutales, Cuba.

Conclusions

Pablo B. Eyzaguirre and Olga F. Linares

This book brings together several perspectives on home gardens that are important for the conservation of biological diversity in agricultural systems. Based on the empirical analysis of tropical home-garden systems in eight countries, the chapters have amply documented the species and genetic richness contained in tropical home gardens. Methodologies applied at the ecosystems, species, and genetic levels have explored the structure and function of home gardens and their importance for conservation of both cultivated and natural ecosystems. The cultures, ecologies, and methods of cultivation have been varied. So what is it about home gardens that makes them an important conservation system across cultures and environments? The home garden provides a bridge between the social and the biological, linking cultivated spaces and natural ecosystems, combining and conserving species diversity and genetic diversity.

Home gardens as studied in this book are simultaneously biological and cultural spaces, concentrating biological diversity that is imbued with sociocultural and economic value. The concomitant presence of both biological and social values within a single microenvironment presents a unique opportunity for bio-diversity conservation, for it is now commonly accepted that "in the end, the primary challenges of biodiversity conservation are social, economic, and political" (Young 2001: 784). However, despite the recognition that conservation ultimately depends on socioeconomic factors and human decisions, the human impact on ecosystems is still largely regarded as interference, as a source of disruptive pressure on biological resources. While no doubt true at the global scale, the search for better practices in managing and conserving biological diversity obliges one to look more deeply at what people actually do when they depend on biodiversity for their livelihoods. Here is where the home gardens assume their greatest importance. As the chapters in this book demonstrate, people use home gardens as a cultural practice, to concentrate and protect those biological resources such as crop landraces or useful wild species that are important for cultural, nutritional, or economic reasons. These are becoming scarce, as natural ecosystems are eroded and farming systems change in response to market and environmental factors. The case study in Ghana, for example, focused on how millets have moved from being largely a field crop to becoming a home-garden species as the modern agricultural economy continues to marginalize this nutritious and hardy grain. In Guatemala, local food culture places great value on loroco, a flowering forest vine used in tamales. As erosion of forests and demographic movements make access to this forest species more difficult, farmers have moved loroco into their home gardens, where a process of domestication is underway. Similarly, in Nepal forest trees used as fodder and medicine are now increasingly planted in home-garden nurseries, while large tropical fruit trees like sapote that are widely dispersed and threatened in forest ecosystems have become a key species of Cuban and Central American home gardens. The many examples contained in the previous chapters illustrate how home gardens provide a niche where people keep those plants that are precious to the household for religious, cultural, health, and economic reasons. They are the biological heirlooms of these communities, and home gardens are one of the more salient examples of the ways in which farm households perform a conscious conservation function.

Home gardens are often the focal point of a household's social interactions within the family and with visitors. One of the important functions that home gardens perform is to keep knowledge of varieties and uses of diversity alive from generation to generation. In home gardens, children and visitors can learn from the family experts in plant diversity and its uses. These can be nutritional, commercial, aesthetic, and spiritual. Home gardens in all the cases studied served as refuges for the "heirloom crop varieties" that were valued and maintained in the family but had little place in commercial markets. Households were also able to exchange their home-garden varieties as part of the social visits. Sharing and exchanging plant-genetic resources are common features of visits between households.

A second link that home gardens provide is between conservation of natural ecosystems and the ecosystem services required and provided by agriculture. A fundamental distinction made between wild and agricultural ecosystems is the reduced levels of species diversity and functional complexity that is present in farming systems. Measuring the impact of reduced biodiversity within agricultural ecosystems is an important topic that is largely ignored despite the fact that "the relationship between biodiversity and ecosystem functioning has emerged as the central issue in ecological and environmental sciences during the last decade" (Loreau et al. 2001: 804).

Understanding and measuring ecosystem functions in agricultural landscapes under intensive human management is a major new research challenge that emerges from this book. In addressing this challenge, home gardens may provide the most fruitful ground for research. It is now posited that species richness is required to sustain ecosystem functions in landscapes under intensive land use, such as those under crop cultivation (Loreau et al. 2001: 804). What we have seen is that home gardens provide a niche or microenvironment right in the heart of a farming system that is rich in species diversity. Furthermore, while rich in species, this system also maintains the complex interactions at different trophic levels that may be crucial for effective functional substitution of species communities. While this topic calls for further research, this book has affirmed that those traditional and complex (some agriculturalists might say messy) home-garden systems that have evolved within cultures over time are most likely to provide those ecosystem functions that contribute to sustainability, resilience, and buffering in agriculture. They provide a link and a buffer to the surrounding, eroded, threatened, or protected natural ecosystems. For these reasons, some nature conservationists such as those in UNESCO's Man and Biosphere programs are focusing on home gardens as the model of a buffer zone of human managed landscapes around protected biosphere reserves.

The role of home gardens in maintaining geneflow across wild and cultivated ecosystems is also important. Several cases in this book documented how germplasm from the wild was brought under cultivation in home gardens. This complex ecosystem close to the house, where plants can be closely observed and managed, makes it a convenient site for traditional plant experimentation and domestication. For some of the root crops such as taro and yams, ruderal material from the wild is continually being brought under cultivation in home gardens to renew the vigor of the germplasm for planting in larger fields. Some home-garden species that exist in both cultivated and uncultivated forms are also income earners. The study in Guatemala focused attention on loroco (*Fernaldia pandurata*), a wild species that is also cultivated and widely commercialized as a vegetable for use in tamales, the production being almost entirely from home gardens. Similarly varieties of eggplants and peppers appear in both cultivated and uncultivated forms in home gardens.

With all the conservation values and economic benefits that home gardens may provide, is there any role for scientists concerned with biodiversity conservation and rural livelihoods? Yes, there is a clear role to counteract and correct two main trends. One is in the area of agricultural modernization and development that tends to undervalue the contribution of small, diverse, and messy patches such as home gardens. Often what is grown in home gardens is not sold or is consumed only occasionally; it may be medicinal or have spiritual value, but it is still ignored or looked down upon. For these reasons the contribution and importance of the traditional home garden is overlooked. Development efforts are made to transform it into a vegetable patch or an orchard or to simply allow it to disappear as markets, health clinics, and higher yielding crop varieties take the place of the many products and services that the traditional home garden provides. The other trend is to view home gardens from a single viewpoint or objective, be it income, nutrition, gardening, or species conservation. Only by considering the home garden holistically with all its cultural, ecological, spiritual, and economic services, can we provide the basis upon which this crucial system can continue to flourish. In the final analysis, whether we conserve the biological and cultural resources of our world depends on how close to home the issues are felt. Those millions of households throughout the tropics that keep their biodiversity close at hand, that use it daily for multiple purposes, that imbue it with cultural and spiritual value are providing a lesson to all humanity about the importance and value of biodiversity. If only for this reason, home gardens are to be celebrated, supported, and conserved.

References

Loreau, M., et al. 2001. Biodiversity and Ecosystem Functioning: Current Knowledge and Future Challenges. *Science* 294: 804–8.

Young, K. A. 2001. Defining units of conservation for intraspecific diversity: Reply to Dimmick et al. *Conservation Biology* 15(3): 784–87.

Contributors

D. K. Abbiw
Department of Botany
University of Ghana
P.O. Box 55
Legon, Accra
Ghana
Tel: +233 21 501735
Fax: +233 21 500940

V. M. Anchirinah
Crops Research Institute
P.O. Box 3788, Kwadaso-Kumasi
Ghana
Tel: +233 051 60396/60389/60391/60425
051 502221/50222
Fax: +233 051 60308/60396/60425/60142
Telex: C/o 3036 BTH 10GH
E-mail: criggdp@ncs.com.gh

I. K. Asante
Department of Botany
University of Ghana
P.O. Box 55
Legon, Accra
Ghana
Tel: +233 21 501735
Fax: +233 21 500940

Zemede Asfaw
P.O.Box 3434
Department of Biology
Addis Ababa University
Addis Ababa
Ethiopia
Tel: +251 114 323, 55 31 77 Ext. 181/196
Fax: +251 1 552 350 or 552 150
Email: biology.aau@telecom.net.et

G. S. Ayernor
Department of Nutrition, Food and Science
University of Ghana
P.O. Box 55
Legon, Accra
Ghana
Tel: +233 21 501735
Fax: +233 21 500940

César Azurdia
Facultad de Agronomia - FAUSAC
Universidad de San Carlos de Guatemala
Apartado Postal 1545, Zona 12
Ciudad de Guatemala
Edificio T8
Ciudad Universitaria Z1Z
Guatemala
Tel: +502 476 9794
Fax: +502 476 9770
Email: azurdiac@usac.edu.gt

Samuel Odei Bennett-Lartey
Plant Genetic Resource Centre (PGRC)
Bunso, P O Box 7
Eastern Region
Ghana
Tel: +233 81 24138
Fax: +233 81 24124
Email: blartey@homemail.com

S. K. Boateng
Plant Genetic Resource Centre (PGRC)
Bunso, P.O. Box 7
Eastern Region
Ghana
Tel: +233 81 24138
Fax: +233 81 24124

Leonor Castiñeiras
Instituto de Investigaciones Fundamentales
en Agricultura Tropical (INIFAT)
Calle 2 esq. 1, Santiago de las Vegas
Ciudad de la Habana
Cuba
Tel: +53 683 4039, 2323
Fax: +53 7 579014
Email: lcastineiras@inifat.esihabana.cu

Raul Cristóbal Suarez
Instituto de Investigaciones Fundamentales
en Agricultura Tropical (INIFAT)
Calle 2 esq. 1, Santiago de las Vegas
Ciudad de la Habana
Cuba
Tel: +53 683 4039, 2323
Fax: +53 7 579014
Email: inifat@ceniai.inf.cu

P. Ekpe
Department of Botany
University of Ghana
P.O. Box 55
Legon, Accra
Ghana
Tel: +233 21 501735
Fax: +233 21 500940

Pablo B. Eyzaguirre
International Plant Genetic Resources Institute (IPGRI)
Via dei Tre Denari 472/a
00057 Maccarese (Fiumicino)
Italy
Tel: +39 06 611 8267
Fax: +39 06 61979661
Email: p.eyzaguirre@cgiar.org

Victor Fuentes
Instituto de Investigaciones Fundamentales
en Agricultura Tropical (INIFAT)
Calle 2 esq. 1, Santiago de las Vegas
Ciudad de la Habana

Cuba
Tel: +53 683 4039, 2323
Fax: +53 7 579014
Email: inifat@ceniai.inf.cu

Zoila Fundora Mayor
Instituto de Investigaciones Fundamentales
en Agricultura Tropical (INIFAT)
Calle 2 esq. 1, Santiago de las Vegas
Ciudad de la Habana
Cuba
Tel: +53 683 4039, 2323
Fax: +53 7 579014
Email: inifat@ceniai.inf.cu

Resham Gautam
Local Initiatives for Bio-Diversity, Research
and Development (LI-BIRD)
Mahedrapul Kaski, Pokhara
P. O. Box No. 324, Pokhara
Kaski District
Nepal
Tel: +977 61 26834/32912/35357
Fax: +977 61 26834
Email: rglibird@fewanet.com.np
URL: www.panasia.org.sg/nepal

Monika Gessler
Swiss Federal Institute of Technology
Zurich (ETH Zentrum)
HG E 46
CH 8092 Zürich
Switzerland
Tel: +41 1 632 7745
Fax: +41 1 632 11 84
Email: gessler@sl.ethz.ch

Luigi Guarino
Secretariat of the Pacific Community
Private Mail Bag
Suva

Fiji
Tel: 679 3370733
Fax: 679 3370021
Email: LuigiG@spc.int

Margaret Gutiérrez M.
FONAIAP-CENIAP
Apartado 4653
Maracay 2101
Venezuela
Tel: +58 43 47 10 66
Email: recfitog@reacciun.ve
margaretg@cantv.net

Urs Hodel
Swiss Tropical Institute (STI)
Socinstrasse 57
Postfach CH-4002 Basel
Switzerland
Tel: +41 61 284 81 11
Fax: +41 61 271 81 06
Email: Urs.Hodel@unibas.ch

Michiel Hoogendijk
Melis Stokelaan 73
1813 DB Alkmaar
The Netherlands
Tel: +31 72 540 9798
Email: gualanday@yahoo.com

Nguyen Ngoc Hue
Vietnam Agricultural Science Institute
(VASI)
Vandien, Thanhtri, Hanoi
Vietnam
Tel: +84 4 61 4326 or 8434
Fax: +84 4 8613937
Email: ntngochue@hn.vnn.vn
ngia@vasi.ac.vn

José Miguel Leiva
AGROCOMSA
2a. Calle B, 1-05 Zona 2, Colonia Lomas del Sur
San José Villa Nueva
Guatemala
Fax: +502 630-0400
Email: jmleiva@itelgua.com
jmleiva@internetdetelgua.com.gt

Olga F. Linares
Smithsonian Tropical Research Institute
Unit 0948
APO AA 34002-0948
Balboa
Panama
Tel: +507 212-8083
Email: linareso@tivoli.si.edu

Carol M. Markwei
Department of Botany
University of Ghana
P.O. Box 55
Legon, Accra
Ghana
Tel: +233 21 501735
Fax: +233 21 500940

Trinidad Pérez de Fernández
Universidad de los Andes
Av. Medina Angarita, Carmona
Trujillo, Venezuela
Tel / Fax: +58 43 47 10 66
Email: recfitog@reacciun.ve
Trinidad-maria@hotmail.com

Consuelo Quiroz
Universidad de Los Andes
Centro para la Agricultura Tropical Alternativa y el Desarrollo Integral (CATADI)
Apartado Postal # 22,

Trujillo 3102, Estado Trujillo
Venezuela
Tel: +58 272 2360467, 59 272 6721672 (home)
Email: consuelo@cantv.net

Ram Bahadur Rana
LI-BIRD
Mahedrapul Kaski
P.O. Box 324, Pokhara
Nepal
Tel: +977 61 26834 / 32912
Email: rblibird@mos.com.np

Deepak Rijal
Noragric, Agricultural University of Norway
PO Box 5001, N-1432 Aas
Norway
Tel: +47 64 94 99 50
+47 64 94 98 17
Fax: +47 64 94 07 60
Email: deepak.rijal@noragric.nlh.no

Jürg Schneider
International Affairs Division
Swiss Agency for the Environment Forests and Landscape
CH-3003 Berne
Switzerland
Tel: +41 31 322 68 95
Fax: +41 31 323 03 49
Email: juerg.schneider@buwal.admin.ch
juerg.schneider@swissonline

Tomás Shagarodsky
Instituto de Investigaciones Fundamentales en Agricultura Tropical (INIFAT)
Calle 2 esq.1, Santiago de las Vegas
Ciudad de la Habana
Cuba

Tel: +53 683 4039, 2323
Fax: +53 7 579014
Email: inifat@ceniai.inf.cu

Pratap Shrestha
Local Initiatives for Bio-Diversity, Research
and Development (LI-BIRD)
Mahedrapul Kaski
P.O. Box 324 Pokhara
Nepal
Tel: +977 61 26834/32912
Fax: +977 61 26834
Email: pshrestha@libird.org
pratapshrestha@hotmail.com
afp84a@bangor.ac.uk

Bhuwon Sthapit
International Plant Genetic Resources In-
stitute
Regional office for Asia, Pacific and Ocea-
nia (IPGRI-APO)
3/202 Buddha Marg. Nadipur Patan, Kaski
District
Pokhara 3
Nepal
Tel: +977 61 21108
Fax: +977 61 21108
Email: b.sthapit@cgiar.org
sthapit@fewanet.com.np

Luu Ngoc Trinh
Vietnam Agricultural Science Institute
(VASI)
Van Dien, Thanh Tri, Hanoi
Vietnam
Tel: +84 34 845320
Fax: +84 34 845802
Email: lntrinh@hn.vnn.vn

David E. Williams
International Plant Genetic Resources In-
stitute
Regional Office for Americas (IPGRI Amer-
icas)
c/o CIAT
Apartado Aereo 6713
Cali
Colombia
Tel: +57 2 445 0048 / 445 0049
Fax: +57 2 445 0096
Email: d.williams@cgiar.org

Index

Page references in *italics* refer to illustrations.